"Did
You
Read
Feagler
Today?"

Also by Dick Feagler:

Feagler's Cleveland

"Did You Read Feagler Today?"

Dick Feagler

Richard J. Osborne
Edward J. Walsh
Editors

 GRAY & COMPANY, PUBLISHERS
CLEVELAND

To Julie,
for leading me beside the still waters

GRAY & COMPANY, PUBLISHERS
1588 E. 40th Street
Cleveland, Ohio 44103-2302
info@grayco.com

Library of Congress Cataloging-in-Publication Data

Feagler, Dick, 1938-
Did you read Feagler today? / by Dick Feagler.
1. Cleveland (Ohio)—Social life and customs—Anecdotes
2. Feagler, Dick, 1938—Anecdotes. I. Title.
F499.C65 F42 1998
977.1'32–dc21   98-40199

ISBN 1-886228-23-X *hc*
ISBN 1-886228-26-4 *sc*
Printed in the United States of America
10 9 8 7 6 5 4 3 2 1

First edition

Contents

Preface

Last time, we sought to capture a generation. This time, merely a few moments. A simpler task, we thought.

We thought wrong.

This book, it turns out, represents not so much a new chapter of *Feagler's Cleveland*, published two years ago, as it does a new dimension of the columnist himself. The columns, all drawn from the past four years, show a more contemplative, more serious, and—dare we say it?—*wiser* observer of the way things are and the way they ought to be.

This star burns brighter with age.

Which made our task more difficult than we anticipated. How do you choose the best, when the best is all you have to choose from?

Therefore, we left most of the selection up to you.

Here are the columns that jammed the columnist's voice mail, that stuffed his in-box, that got Clevelanders voicing the familiar refrain: "Did you read Feagler today?" These columns, all drawn from Feagler's recent work in *The Plain Dealer*, are the ones that we all talked about the most. And, we think, the ones that will continue to be most worth rereading.

Enjoy.

Richard J. Osborne and Edward J. Walsh, *editors*

Introduction

There is a trick some TV broadcasters know that writers should steal and use for their own purposes. And it has nothing to do with hair spray, either.

The trick is to forget that you are broadcasting to millions of people. And to just think of one or two people sitting on their couch in their living room. And to talk to those people the way you would talk to a friend.

In 27 years of writing newspaper columns, I have always thought of readers as friends. Of course, In that span of time there has been some evidence that argues against this pleasant notion. Some readers hate my column, have always hated it and plan to go on hating it. The mystery is why they read it, though I'm glad they do.

But most readers, over time, have been kind and generous to me. And, for the past couple of years, they have been able to instantly register their feelings. At the bottom of each column is a phone number connected to an answering machine on which, an editor's note reveals, "messages to Feagler can be left."

This phone number is a great stimulus to reader spontaneity. It saves the reader having to write a little note or even bother to find the newspaper's phone number in the telephone book. It is, in its way, a variation of those invitations you used to see scratched into men's room stalls—"for a good time call SKyline 1-1485."

An average column produces a harvest of 50 phone calls. A column that pricks a nerve will yield about 100. The response to some columns is off the charts. When the Monica and Bill mess began to unfold and I began to write about it, the voice mail would be full by the time I got up in the morning. I was forced to bail it out two or three times each day. It was like a flood plain without a levee. Thanks to the voice mail, I spend more time listening to readers each week than they spend listening to me. But I'm not complaining. Any of us who peddle our opinions unsolicited ought to admit that the revenge of the reader is a just revenge.

When I began to write columns for *The Plain Dealer*, an editor asked me what my goal was. I wasn't ready for this question. I had never thought much about it. The first answer that came to mind hardly seemed politic—"my goal is to get the damn thing written and in on deadline."

But then I realized that I actually did have a broader goal. And even though it seemed a bit presumptuous, I revealed it.

"Somewhere in Parma or Seven Hills or Pepper Pike there is a lady I think of as Mrs. Sewinsky," I told the editor. "I want her to read my column at the breakfast table and hand it to her husband and say, 'Look, Joe. This guy is saying exactly what I was trying to tell you last night.'"

This seems to me about as noble a reward as a pundit could want or expect. The columns in this book were really chosen by Mrs. Sewinsky and other readers. They represent the pieces which brought in the most voice mail, either because they touched a hot button or caressed a gentler nerve. Sometimes Mrs. Sewinsky called to tell me I had taken the words right out of her mouth. Sometimes she called to inform me that I was an idiot.

But it's always nice to hear from her. She is always in my thoughts, each time I sit down at the keyboard. We have never been formally introduced, but my notions and her reaction to them have met many times. And they meet again on the pages of the book you are holding.

—Dick Feagler, September 1998

"Did
You
Read
Feagler
Today?"

This Modern World

....

Medew Netcher, anyone?

The cultural diversity movement is still alive and vital at our NASA Lewis Research Center. They are on the cutting edge of multiculturalism out there.

You may remember that the folks at Lewis celebrated Bodhi Day last December. Bodhi Day being the Buddhist celebration of the enlightenment of Shakyamuni Buddha, 596 B.C. You didn't know that? Well, get with it, bubba!

Then a Native American was invited in to do a rain dance. And look what happened. If all the snow this winter had been rain, we would have had to build an ark.

Then, at Christmas, the Lewis brass decided, in the interest of diversity, to ban Christmas carols from the NASA p.a. system. The vice president in charge of diversity wrote a memo arguing that Christmas carols weren't diverse enough. And that banning carols was more in keeping with the true spirit of Christmas than playing them was.

This march toward diversity has created a new subculture at Lewis. The disgruntled. And, since I have adopted the Lewis diversity program as a kind of beat, the disgruntled look to me as a kind of champion.

Which is why my last batch of mail was full of copies of a leaflet the Lewis people put out advertising a special event for Black History Month. Last Friday, NASA employees were invited to take three hours off from work to learn Medew Netcher.

Medew Netcher being . . . do I see any hands? No?

(Ahh, life is so short and there's so much diversity work to do.)

Medew Netcher is the art of hieroglyphics. At least that's what the leaflet said. It said:

"Come learn ancient Egyptian picture writing. Medew Netcher, commonly call (sic) Hieroglyphs. Sponsored by the African Heritage Advisory Council. Two sessions: 8:30 to 11:30 a.m., 1 to 4 p.m.

"Instructor: Mr. Roosevelt Roberts, associate director, professor and lecturer of the Kemetic Institute of Chicago. Learn to write your name in hieroglyphs."

One look at that and the disgruntled at Lewis dashed to the Xerox machine and skimmed off copies to me with anonymous notes attached.

If I were to summarize the main points of their disgruntlement, they would be:

(1) Doing this on company time is cheating the taxpayers.

(2) Mr. Roosevelt Roberts didn't come here for nothing, so who paid him?

(3) What does learning hieroglyphics have to do with the space program?

My pen pals obviously thought I would be on their side. And at first I was. Because I was looking at things the old way. But then I tried looking at things the new way. The way you do that is, you bang your head several times sharply on the edge of a table to rearrange your focus. Looking at things the new way, you never know when hieroglyphics might come in handy in outer space.

Suppose, for instance, that some day we send a space mission out beyond the stars. And suppose it lands amid an alien civilization that does not communicate in language as we know it.

Certainly, it would be helpful to climb out of the spaceship with a pencil and pad and approach the alien leader and draw "Hi, I'm Dick Feagler from the planet Earth. Where's the men's room?" in Medew Netcher. It sounds like a terrific icebreaker to me.

Yes, but I can hear you saying, "Suppose the alien was from a planet that didn't have diversity training. And suppose, therefore, he had no knowledge of Medew Netcher. What then?"

That's a fair question. But the beauty of Medew Netcher is, you don't have to have a doctorate in it to understand it.

Around the edge of the leaflet was some stuff in Medew Netcher, placed there, I suppose, to give the customer a little taste of what was in store for him under the tutelage of Mr. Roosevelt Roberts.

There was, for example, a picture of a mouth, under which was written "mouth." And a picture of a leg, under which was written "leg." And a picture of a lion, under which was written "lion." There was also a picture of a pretzel, under which was written "reed shelter." Just in case anybody thought the course was going to be a snap.

So we all already know a little Medew Netcher. And if we know some, why not learn more. I, for example, have no idea how to write my name in Medew Netcher. Taking my cue from the example on the leaflet, I made a stab at my first name. But I can't believe I got it right.

If Medew Netcher might make the difference between life and death on some alien plain, what's the matter with importing a lecturer to teach it? None of the disgruntled would see anything odd about having a professor from MIT in for a chat. So why not an associate director AND professor AND lecturer from KIC, the Kemetic Institute of Chicago? You say you see a difference? Do what I told you. Bang your head.

Multiculturalism is here. And we ought to try to adjust to it. So I say to you disgruntled out at Lewis. Give up. Relax and enjoy it. Stop writing me these letters.

And in case you've forgotten where to stop writing them . . . it's 18th and Superior.

* * *

Speaking of the mail, Anne Engel in Westlake writes to tell me about a little mystery she thinks she has solved. Some time ago, she sent a letter to the president imploring him to work to reduce the debt and stop government waste. She received, on White House stationery, this reply:

"Dear Anne:

"Thank you for writing. I appreciate hearing your views regarding waste incineration policies. As you probably know, the General Accounting Office is reviewing the process of permitting waste incinerator facilities to operate. The Environmental Protection Agency is thoroughly examining all proposed incinerators and will determine whether or not these incinerators will be safe in the suggested locations.

"I welcome your views and I am confident that we can achieve a responsible solution to this issue.

"Sincerely, Bill Clinton."

Anne figures some kind of scanner saw the word "waste" in her letter and zapped it over to the "garbage" file where a switch was tripped and she got the official "garbage letter."

"This reply leaves me wondering who, or what, is running our country," she writes.

Ah, but if she'd written her letter in Medew Netcher. . . . See?

—February 25, 1994

....

Deadly television

There is trouble in TV freak-show land. A guest on the *Jenny Jones* show was so upset by what happened to him there that he bought a shotgun and murdered another guest.

Police arrested Jonathan T. Schmitz, 24, of Orion, Mich. Schmitz had been invited to appear on a show as part of a panel of people who were there to meet secret admirers. Schmitz assumed his secret admirer would be a woman. Instead, the *Jenny Jones* people brought out Scott Amedure, 32, a man Schmitz knew slightly. Amedure told the nationwide audience he had a crush on Schmitz.

Schmitz told police he didn't know what to do or what his "television rights" were. So he sat through the show. But he said the experience had "eaten away" at him. So, a few days later, he went to Amedure's house and shot him twice in the chest.

The *Jenny Jones* people, according to interview-seekers, can't come to the phone right now. An unprecedented abashment has settled over Jonestown. The *Jones* people find themselves in the position of children who prankishly start a fire in which somebody is burned to death. It is time to nervously hunker down and plot a way to evade responsibility.

Gay watchdog groups and journalism professors are, for different reasons, spouting concern about the implications of this bloodshed. But little is said about the two groups most involved in the incident: morons and panderers.

Never before in media history have so many mercenary panderers achieved national audiences as talk-show hosts. And never before have the nation's morons, weirdos and imbeciles been so sought-after as guests and so eagerly encouraged to pollute the culture with their idiotic blatherings.

I returned to the scene of the crime yesterday morning to watch an episode of *Jenny Jones*. Then I staggered over to view the human condition as it is exhibited on *The Jerry Springer Show*. Then I bought a cake of Fels Naptha soap and tried to scrub the effects away in a hot shower. But the water turned cold before I could finish, so I'll scrape what's left on this page.

The topic in Jonestown was moms whose teenage daughters are sexually promiscuous.

The moms and nymphets were arranged in pairs across the wide Jonestown stage, facing a hooting, screaming audience that appeared to be left over from *Wide World of Wrestling*. The little girls, some dressed like child prostitutes in the windows of an Amsterdam bawdy street, ranged in age from 13 to about 15. They testified that they had had numerous sexual partners—85, one young lady said.

Their mothers squirmed in agony at these revelations. The agony seemed odd when you considered that the revelations were no surprise. These were all sleaze volunteers. To donate your humiliation and dysfunction to Jonestown, you call a toll-free number and if they gag at the sound of you, they fly you in.

At one point in the show, a little strumpet angrily said that it was her mother's extramarital affair that had driven her to a life of statutory fornication. Mom dabbed at her nose with Kleenex—presumably purchased by the bale in Jonestown for guests who might otherwise use their sleeves.

Then, rushing in from the wings came an "expert"—an intense woman dressed in black, with silver hoop earrings fiercely bouncing from her lobes. She counseled the errant mom to apologize to her horrible offspring. Absolutely not, said the mom. "No, no!" yelled the audience. "Listen to yourselves!" wailed the counselor. But I had heard enough, so I turned to Jerry Springer, which was like going from the lying pan into the mire.

The *Springer* show, which has no murder in its wake, seemed more carefree. The day's subject was "People Who Are Here to Tell Their Parents, 'Mom, Your Man Is a Loser!'" All the people who were there to do that seemed to have come from the same Appalachian hollow. They possessed a level of sophistication and articulation that would make L'il Abner, in comparison, seem like the Prince of Wales.

Ray, who was there to tell his 49-year-old mother that her 27-year-old man was a loser, got right to the point. "He's a son of a [bleep] and if murder was legal, I'd kill him tomorrow," Ray said. Ray added that while he was in jail for a year (he wouldn't say why—just "somepin' real bad") his mom hardly visited him. Whereas she had faithfully visited her man, Dave, when he was in for drunken driving.

It was next revealed that Dave slaps Mom around a lot. And that, on first meeting Mom's daughter, Dave "French-kissed her." Mom, who professed love for Dave, leaped to his defense. He had only done that, she said, because he was under the influence of fumes he inhaled while "puffing paint." Then Mom dabbed at her mouth with the house Kleenex, inadvertently revealing that on top of her current woes, she suffered from a pre-existing medical condition. No teeth.

Now, all of that is just a tiny part of one morning's commercial television emissions. The panderers in charge of this effluvium blame the public for it. "The *Springer* show is not the best moment of my day," said NBC President Robert Wright, "but it's obvious the audience is out there."

In other words, the freak-show hucksters—executives in paneled offices with flunkies all around—have no responsibility for their toxic emissions. It is up to us to hold our breaths. Jenny

Jones will beat the rap in the shotgun slaying. But what about all those dry brain cells snapping throughout America like Rice Krispies?

Calculated terminal dumbness is doing more damage than the Russians ever did. This is no time to stop funding Public Television. If money is short, we ought to borrow from the defense budget.

—March 15, 1995

Friends, Romans, taxpayers . . .

It happened in ancient Rome, too.

One day in ancient Rome, a man who some (perhaps unjustly) called Ominous Cantankerous announced he would have to move the Roman Lions out of town unless enough money was raised to fix up the Coliseum.

So the big-shot Roman politicians held an emergency meeting. Devious was there and so was Ambitious. Righteous showed up, along with Hilarious and Preposterous. Serious chaired the meeting. Cautious called in sick.

"Let's just put the Coliseum issue on the ballot and see if people want to pay for it," Hilarious said.

Naturally, this brought down the house. When they all got through laughing and wiping their eyes, Ambitious spoke up.

"We better be careful here," Ambitious said. "If we back a ballot issue and lose, we can kiss our careers goodbye. Why do you think Cautious isn't here? This is the third time he's gone to his grandmother's funeral. She dies every time we build a new stadium."

Preposterous took the floor.

"How about a tax on standing?" he said.

They all looked at him blankly. "What do you mean, 'A tax on standing?'" Serious wanted to know.

"Well," said Preposterous, "we're running out of things to tax, and I was thinking that a lot of peasants come downtown and just stand around looking at things. So when we see them standing there, we go up to them and charge them an extra 15 percent."

"An extra 15 percent of what?" Serious asked.

"Uh . . . uh . . . an extra 15 percent of what we're already taxing them for, I guess," said Preposterous.

"I say let the peasants vote on that," Hilarious said. And it was several minutes before mirth subsided and decorum returned. Then Righteous spoke.

"Is there money anywhere in the empire to pay for this project?" he asked. "Maybe we could get it out of Gaul."

"That's preposterous!" said Ludicrous.

"That's ludicrous!" cried Preposterous.

"The less said about Gaul, the better," said Ambitious. "Remember that all Gaul is divided into three parts. Speaking as a county commissioner, I don't want to remind anybody of my part."

Then they all looked to Devious. As they always did.

"Friends, Romans, countymen," Devious began. "This is an hour for leadership. If the Lions move out of Rome, some of Rome will go with them."

"Do you mean the people they ate?" asked Ludicrous.

"No," said Serious. "He means the tourists who flock here to see men broken and torn apart. He means jobs. All the people outside the Coliseum who sell airsick bags and big Styrofoam thumbs for fans to turn up or down. But more than that, he means the image of Rome as a major atrocity town. Don't you, Devious?"

"To be candid," said Devious, "I was thinking more of us. If we don't find a way to save the Lions, people may blame us for it and throw us out of office. It's kind of a 'thumbs down if we do, thumbs down if we don't' situation for us. We can't go to the voters and ask for money. So we'll just have to get more from the sinners. Are there any sins we aren't taxing?"

"There are plenty of them," said Righteous. "There's prostitution and cock fighting and . . ."

"Those are illegal sins," said Devious. "We can't tax illegal sins unless we make them legal. Are there any more legal sins to tax?"

"How about meetings like this one," Hilarious said. But this time, nobody laughed and he hung his head and sulked.

"Hearing none," said Devious, "I move we extend, without a vote, the tax on drinking and smoking. It was scheduled to expire in 10 years. I propose we extend it an additional 2,410 years. Does that seem reasonable?"

They all enthusiastically said that it did. Except for Serious, who pointed out that smoking hadn't been invented yet.

"Then we'll start by taxing drinking and lepers," Devious said. "In 1995, smokers will be the lepers of their time. When's the last time you saw a leper swing an election?"

So that's what they did. And the Lions stayed in Rome, which flourished until it lost its moral center, taxed itself to death, grew soft and purposeless and fell victim to invasion from other countries that demonstrated firmer and more focused resolve.

But right up to the very end, when the barbarians were at the gates, the people of Rome were still able to say:

"How 'bout them Lions!"

—May 26, 1995

....

Real reality beats the virtual kind

It's Splitsville for a Wisconsin couple 'cause hubby charges wife with adultery on the Internet. He says he read her e-mail and discovered she was linked in virtual reality passion with a subscriber named "Weasel." Lawyers have begun dismantling the union. . . . Next:

In California, a homeless man named Neal Berry, forced to choose between renting a room or buying a computer, pitched a tent and bought a laptop. Gendarmes came through his flap and arrested him for powering his program with batteries stolen from a state warehouse. He was logged off to jail for five days, then released without bail. . . . Next:

Dateline Willowick—They're still buzzing about the city councilman and two constituents whose names were pasted on an Internet porno board. Fifty perverts a day placed help-wanted calls to the trio of innocents. There's more than one "Weasel" in the Web. . . . Next:

Never mind. That's enough. The Internet has replaced O. J. as a media obsession from which there is no escape. First they tell us about the raunchy, filthy, bawdiness of the global computer network. Then they tell us that it is the great shining hope for our future.

Whatever it is, I'm part of it.

I ain't proud of it. Years ago, they made me trade my Royal typewriter for a computer. I fought, but they won. That Royal was part of me. Sometimes I can still feel it tingling under my fingers, like an amputated memory. I'd had it since my days on rewrite. Those dear old "slug it 'slay' and write it tight" days, forsaken for the muzzy paragraphs of punditry.

My little household of two is a microcosm of America. Fifty percent of us (that's me) hate computers. The other 50 percent of us (that's she-who-is-my-destiny's-pilot) adore them. One night, she told me my equipment needed upgrading, a remark that wounded me deeply until she explained herself.

She called in a wizard and the two of them happily monkeyed around with my equipment while I sat glowering at them from the couch. When the wizard departed, I had a lighter checkbook and a computer with a built-in encyclopedia and e-mail capability.

She dashed upstairs to her own computer and sent me an e-mail message. "Hi," it said. Then she galloped back down and demanded that I admit this was wonderful.

"I would say it was wonderful if I had never heard of a telephone," I said. She said I was being purposefully negative and suggested we surf the Net.

"Should I put on some Polynesian music?" I asked. She told me to shut up and grabbed my mouse. We entered the surf and eventually beached ourselves in a "chat room." That's a place on the Internet where people from all over the world can talk to each other. The night we dropped in, here's what they were saying:

"You stink."

"You stink too."

"You smell bad."

"So do you."

My surfing companion turned to me eagerly and asked if I'd like to contribute to this discourse. I told her I'd rather go to the food court at Great Northern and chat with the kids in baggy pants with their hats on backward and earrings in their noses.

"Let's try the encyclopedia," she said grimly.

At that point I did something I shouldn't have done.

"I'll make you a bet," I said. "You pick any topic and you look it up in the computer's encyclopedia and I'll look it up in the *Britannica* over there on the shelf and we'll see who finds it faster." We picked Shakespeare and the race began. I threw myself into it with unusual gusto. I felt like John Henry in the ballad, racing with the steam drill. I envisioned the contest as the spirit of man pitted against the encroaching threat of the machine.

She was equally motivated. But she was limited to the computer's speed and its habit of pausing in mid-search to display pretty pictures and play tinny, computerized harp music. I beat her to Shakespeare by 30 seconds. She did not take the loss well.

They tell us that computers will make better students of our children. But they don't know that. It's just something comforting and unprovable to throw in the face of educational blight. My experience with technology is that it doesn't make things better. It just makes things different. Different is not better.

Beneath virtual reality lurks real reality. And the tug of real reality is inescapable. Ask Shakespeare. Ask Splitsville in Wisconsin and his wanton wife. Ask her weasel.

—February 5, 1996

Nobody answers any more

If you call me, I won't answer my phone. If I call you, you won't answer your phone. What the hell are we paying phone bills for? Nobody knows.

The other day, a woman called me, but, naturally, she didn't get me. She got my voice mail instead. That was all right, though, because she didn't really want me anyway.

"I didn't really want you anyway," she said, her voice full of a deep and weary sadness. "I was trying to get somebody else at the paper." And she named an old pal of mine whose byline is a household word, especially in households with servants' quarters.

"I couldn't get a human voice," she wailed. "I keep getting machines. It made me feel so depressed, I called your number just to hear the sound of a live voice. But you're not alive, either. You're a machine, too."

Stung by this rebuke, I zapped her with a double-punch on the "7" button. But I couldn't get her out of the memory bank of my mind. For I, too, have felt her pain.

It used to be that, when phones rang, people answered them. The words "Let it ring" were only used in the movies, in moments of deadly menace or erotic passion.

"Let it ring," the burglar would say to the man he held at gun-point. And then the camera would show a close-up of the phone ringing until it finally stopped, ending all hope of rescue.

"Let it ring," the amorous leading man would say to the will-ing leading lady. And again we would see a close-up of the phone while we guessed what the blissful couple were up to off-camera. For that was before such guesswork was replaced by lit-tle classes in clinical anatomy.

The whole purpose of voice mail was supposed to be to answer the phone if you weren't around to answer it yourself. But, in the last year or so, that has changed. Now, in offices all over America, voice mail provides an excuse for people never to answer their phones, period.

A couple of times a week, I have to call a fellow whose real name and organization I will not reveal, lest the revelation subject him to corporate wrath. Every time I do this, I repeat the same scenario.

I know better than to call him on his direct line. This he has ignored since about August. So I call the switchboard instead.

My call is answered by a receptionist who sits 15 feet from the guy I want.

"Is Joe Coma there?" I ask. "He sure is," she says, brightly. "I'll switch you."

"No!" I holler. "Stop! Don't!"

But it is too late. She switches the call to his desk. I hear four rings, then a quick fifth ring. And his hollow recorded voice comes on, lying through its mechanical teeth, claiming that he is off the premises.

So I hang up and call back. I get the receptionist again.

"Joe Coma didn't pick up his phone," I say.

"I'll sw . . . "

"FREEZE!" I bark like a TV cop. "Can't you just yell over and tell him to answer?"

But such an archaic idea seems outlandish to her. What? Yell 15 feet across a room in this, the age of communication miracles?

"I'll page him," she says. "I'll put you on hold."

So I sit there, listening to crummy electronic music produced in a cave in Texas by a machine that is struggling to be a piano. Will Joe Coma answer his page? Or will five minutes go by until the music stops, the phone rings again and the receptionist returns to ask, in tones of astonishment:

"Are you still there?"

The telephone has ceased to be a reliable means of communication. And yet, there are more phones than ever before. So many people are unsuccessfully calling other people who are unsuccessfully calling them back that more area codes are needed to handle the chatter of machines apologizing to other machines.

I am a culprit, too, and I have taught my machine to tell lies. But at least I have enough humanity left to feel sorry for the lady who didn't really want me but just wanted to hear a real live voice. Would a parrot do, Madame?

—April 22, 1996

....

A *sales pitch to die for*

On the Sunday before Memorial Day, Gerry Laube of Rocky River paid a visit to the cemetery where most of her family is buried.

Ms. Laube has a sister living in Michigan. But the rest of her family is in Sunset Memorial Park. Her parents lie in the mausoleum there. Her brother, Richard, is beneath a blanket of grass. When Ms. Laube visits her brother's grave, she brings flowers and a pair of grass shears to keep his plot nice and neat.

Her stop at her brother's grave is always an especially sad one. Richard Laube died at 28, in a plane crash near Boulder, Colo. When Ms. Laube visits him, she remembers the shock of the long-distance call that reported his accident and the months of grief that followed.

So, as she clipped the grass around her brother's headstone and arranged the flowers in the cone-shaped pop-up vase, she sighed a little and, if you had been watching her, you might have noticed that she looked sad and a bit lonesome.

And someone was watching her. For Ms. Laube looked up from her chore to see that a young woman was standing next to her. This young woman was in her 30s. She wore a black hat and a black coat and there was something in her look and manner that made Ms. Laube think she might be a minister of some sort.

"Oh, my dear," the young woman said. "How are you doing? Are you all right?"

Touched by this concern, Ms. Laube said that, yes, she was all right. It was just that memories of her brother made her feel depressed. It was just that the visit to the cemetery reminded her that most of her family was gone.

The young woman listened to all this, nodding sympathetically several times. Then she spoke.

"I'll tell you what," she said brightly. "How would you like me to help you plan your funeral?"

"Huh?" said Ms. Laube, who had taught school all her life but whose standards of articulation were undermined by this astonishing question.

"It's never too soon to think about these things, you know," the young woman in the black hat scolded merrily. And she began to speak to Ms. Laube of vaults, caskets and the everlasting satisfaction of perpetual care.

But Ms. Laube shooed her off. This sales pitch, presented as a tonic to relieve depression, was having quite the opposite effect. The last Ms. Laube saw of the young woman in black, she was drifting toward an elderly couple gazing down, somber and unsuspecting, at a nearby grave.

"I didn't know who else to call about this, so I called you," Ms. Laube told me on the phone. I took that to mean that she realized this was not a case for the I-Team but felt it contained elements worthy of a modest sermon.

"It's just that you can't get away from salesmen no matter where you go," she said. "I don't have an answering machine in my house, just an old-fashioned dial phone. So I have to answer it myself, and I'm constantly getting calls from people who start off posing as something and end up being something else."

Bryn Baracskai, president of Sunset Memorial Park, assured me that her organization does not promote or condone grave-to-grave salesmanship.

"We apologize for what happened to her," she said. "It is true that we had thousands of people visit over Memorial Day. We do like to keep people abreast of what is happening in the park, and we publish a newsletter to that end. But we don't go over the line."

It was a gracious apology and explanation. And with it, Ms. Laube and I are willing to allow her little adventure to lie in repose, relinquishing the rights to all further coverage to the newsletter staff of the *Sunset Memorial Sun*, or whatchamacallit.

We have voiced our concern about the intrusion of unfettered, dog-eat-dog, capitalism. Telemarketers already pursue us

into the shower and interrupt our dinners. Now they have begun
to follow us to the grave. And tomorrow, who knows? Perhaps
beyond. Only a sucker would bet against it.

—June 5, 1996

Good deed, bum rap

Sometimes you hear people say that no good deed goes
unpunished. But that's pretty cold and cynical. It's warmer and
fuzzier to say that good deeds are like old cars. They often back-
fire when you least expect it.

The good folks at the First Congregational Church of Akron
found that out. As this newspaper has related, the kind flock
down there permitted James Dunn and his dog Kaye to live on
the front steps of the church. Dunn informed them that God
had told him to live there. What could they say in the face of
such divine flattery?

Thirteen months later, they wished God had touted Dunn on
the Methodists. His cardboard lean-to attracted rats and other
vermin. With enviable regularity, Kaye was a bad girl on the
church lawn. Finally, the church members voted to evict Dunn
and dog from the premises. But it was a narrow vote.

That's because nice people refuse to believe that somebody
who looks like a bum, acts like a bum and lives like a bum
might, in fact, be a bum. Nice people are convinced bumanship
is a phase. And sometimes it is. But often it is a career.

The plight of the Akron folks reminded me of what happened
some years ago to a friend of mine named Bob. Bob is one of the
nicest fellows you would ever want to meet. Some days he is too
nice to roam the planet without a keeper.

Bob noticed that, every morning when he walked to work, the
same old panhandler was waiting, shivering in the cold near his
building.

Old panhandlers make Bob feel guilty. And this old panhandler sent tidal waves of guilt in Bob's direction. Because this old panhandler was a woman.

This was back in the days when panhandlers had started demanding exact sums of money. Instead of saying, "Say, mister, can you spare a dollar?" they had started saying, "Gimme a dollar and 47 cents!" My hunch is that this was a technique taught at panhandler school to lend the extortion an air of organized credibility.

So the female bum asked Bob if he could spare a dollar seventy-five. But Bob is no sucker. He is more of a gumdrop. Fearing she might squander the money on drink or nicotine, Bob weighed in with a counteroffer.

"I'll tell you what I'll do," he said, addressing the woman in a hearty man-to-bum tone. "If you'll come with me, I'll buy you a sandwich."

When interfacing with bums, nice people often assume they can control the agenda. That's the mistake the people in Akron made. But it is a strong desire to set their own agendas that usually inspires bums to take up bumming. Eventually, nice people learn this the hard way. That's the way Bob learned it.

Bob's act of generosity got off to a deceptively good start. The female bum accompanied him to a nearby restaurant, where Bob requested a table for two.

"Smoking!" the female bum said, firmly. Bob, a nonsmoker, decided not to make an issue of it.

And then it developed that the female bum was out of cigarettes. So Bob bought her a pack. Bob hates smoke. But unlike Bob-the-presidential-candidate, Bob-the-gumdrop regards nicotine as an addiction. When he returned from the cigarette machine, the waitress was there to take the order.

"Let's see," Bob's companion said, "I'd like three hamburger sandwiches, one to eat here and two to go. And what kind of soup do you got?"

Then Bob's protege turned to Bob. She shook a finger under his nose.

"Remember," she said. "You still owe me a dollar seventy-five." After peering at Bob to make sure her point was made, she turned back to the waitress.

"And I'll take a couple of pieces of pie," she said.

With that, Bob told me later, something snapped.

"No pie," he said firmly.

"I WANT PIE!!!" the female bum wailed at the top of her voice.

Everybody in the restaurant stopped eating and looked over at what seemed to be a young man abusing an old woman. Frowns and scowls were directed at Bob. Muttered comments on his lack of sensitivity rustled around him. He lurched to his feet. He threw too much money on the table and ran from the restaurant. As he left, the object of his pity was speaking to the waitress.

"A dollar seventy-five of that is mine," she was saying.

Bob is still a gumdrop. But now he is sometimes heard to say that God helps those who help themselves. That's not a bad piece of philosophy. Though, when you think about it, that's what Bob's bum and Jim Dunn were doing.

—July 8, 1996

··

Please hang up and dial again

When I was a kid, the cheapest kind of phone system you could buy was a party line. That's what we had. The drawback was, you couldn't always make a call when you wanted to.

Sometimes you would pick up your phone and somebody else on the party line circuit would be chatting away. The other parties on your party line were anonymous. Only the phone company knew who they were. But, if you weren't a heavy breather, you could eavesdrop and find out a lot about them:

". . . so I told her, Mildred, I said, 'Listen here, that dog of yours did his business in my begonias again,' I said. And she said, 'What makes you think it was my Spot?' And I told her, I said, 'Your Spot has ruined so many of my begonias that by now I can recognize what your Spot leaves me to clean up, just as sure as if he'd written his name in you-know-what,' I said . . ."

After a little of this, you would put the receiver down with a little clunk. You hoped maybe the clunk would signal the dog business seminar that somebody else on the party line was waiting to make a call. But five minutes later, when you picked up the receiver again, it hadn't necessarily worked:

"'. . . pull down my shades so your little Tommy doesn't get an eyeful? Your little Tommy sits over there with a telescope looking at bedroom windows on the moon,' I said. And then I . . . MILDRED, I THINK SOME VERY RUDE PERSON IS LISTENING IN ON OUR CONVERSATION. IF HE HAD ANY MANNERS, HE'D WAIT UNTIL WE WERE THROUGH TALKING TO . . .'"

Clunk.

Party lines were a problem. Maybe one out of every six times you wanted to use your telephone, somebody else was on the line. But then progress struck.

Party lines disappeared. Touch-tone arrived. Automobile phones were ushered in. Then pagers. Then pocket cellular phones. Then voice mail. And then the opportunity to access the Internet and enter the world of cyberspace and feast on misinformation and unregulated pornography.

We were surfing on a wave of communications euphoria. Not for nothing was it called a communications revolution. We could do things without telephones we had never dreamed of doing. We could, for instance, call somebody from our car and say:

"Hi, I'm calling you from my car."

Phone power made us drunk with self-esteem. Arrogant TV commercials showed bratty little punks razzing rich men in limousines because, in the new phonocracy, punks, too, could enjoy mobile-phone entitlement.

We could fire up the computer in the living room and whisk across the phone line to a chat room to pass the time of day with satanists and button collectors and members of the Montana Militia. Faxes replaced letters. Machines gave us a ring at mealtime to offer us deals on aluminum siding. Politicians preached that if struggling schoolchildren could only get a bite of an Apple computer, they would shinny up the Tree of Knowledge and, their brain cells expanded like balloons, float away to middle-management jobs and homes in the suburbs.

The telephone line became an umbilical leading to a parallel cyberworld of free association. Freaks and weirdos could find out about each other without consulting the 11 o'clock news. A Maryland housewife met a man on the Internet who offered to sexually torture and kill her if she went to North Carolina. She went, and police say he did. She died of the information explosion, though a coroner ruled it strangulation.

All these marvels I have witnessed in my lifetime. So much has happened through the years that I had almost forgotten the little black telephone that sat in its niche in my dining room. And the party line that linked Mildred and me to the lady who wouldn't let us get a word in edgewise.

And then, this week, news came from California that there is trouble on the line. The phone lines out there are so clogged with beeper signals and fax messages and car-phone chatter and voice-mail quizzes and computer calls and Web site chats and Internet messages from Married Perverted Female Seeks Man of Similar Tastes, Non-Smoker, that . . . guess what?

If you try to use your telephone to make an old-fashioned phone call, there's a one-in-six chance that you can't because the line is already in use.

The great law of unintended consequences has put us all on a great big party line again. And our pirouetting planet, tumbling through space, has once more twirled us back to where we started from. Except we're a little worse off. That's my party line, anyway.

—November 1, 1996

Vulgar verses

You tell me.

I was in the supermarket buying another gross of fat-free cookies when I remembered my sister's birthday was coming up and I needed a birthday card. Fast.

Fortunately there was a card rack over near the vegetables. So I wheeled the cart over there and found the section that said: "Birthday, female, relative." I plucked a card from the display.

The cover of this card had the following sentiment:

"Here's a beauty secret for your birthday. To increase the size of your breasts, try rubbing toilet paper on them."

Inside it said:

"It made your butt bigger, didn't it?"

I stared at this awhile, wooden-faced. Then I slowly put it back and picked another one. The cover of this one said:

"Another year older and you can still touch your toes. . ."

Inside it said:

". . . with your boobs."

A drawing accompanying this sentiment showed a bent-over woman with her bosoms dangling to the floor like a pair of twin Slinkies.

I returned this congratulatory missive to its proper place in "Birthday, female, relative." Then, with some nervousness, I sneaked a peek over my shoulder to make sure a time warp hadn't snatched me out of the supermarket and deposited me in the Adults-Only section of the *Twilight Zone*.

But no, the venue hadn't changed. I was in a swanky food store in a West Side suburb that thinks rather well of itself. All about me, upscale hunter-gatherers were celebrating their position in the food chain. Crab pate was available at the deli counter. Live lobsters sulked in the bottom of a water tank nearby. The shoppers were attired in fashionable chore clothing from L.L. Bean and Polo Sport. The parking lot was haughty with imported German cars and those expensive safari vehicles the wealthy drive lest they encounter a lion or wart hog on their way to the country club.

I dipped my hand gingerly back in the card rack. This time I skipped "Birthday, female, relative" and took a chance on "Birthday, general." The first card I withdrew had this on its cover:

"Birthdays are like B.M.'s."

Inside it said . . .

Never mind what it said. If you want to know, get a baby-sitter for the kid, put on a raincoat and go lurk around the avocado counter.

Eventually I found a card I wouldn't be embarrassed to have my sister read aloud in the presence of my parents. But the whole experience dismayed me and I've been asking myself why. And I've answered myself. I know why.

It isn't because I'm a choir boy. My language, while talking to friends, lapses all too often into crudity that would make a sailor flinch. People used to say that the use of profanity was a sign of a limited vocabulary. Nobody says that much anymore, a shrinking vocabulary having become the norm except among psychobabblers and internet addicts.

But the language on these cards wasn't just dirty. It was dumb-dirty. It was fourth-grade, sniggering dirty. It was the kind of stuff that most people used to grow out of. You got to a certain age and you left it behind you along with "moron" jokes and belching contests.

The culture expected that maturity would teach taste. And that taste would substitute toilet humor with wit. Wit relies on intelligence and finesse to achieve humor. And the humor produced through wit used to be mainstream humor. You heard it in the lyrics of songwriters and in the dialogue of movies. You read it in the essays of Thurber and Benchley. The kind of thing we laughed at spoke of the kind of people we were and the kind of culture we valued.

It still does. Except now our mainstream culture is bumper-sticker, Howard Stern, drive-time-radio, Comedy Club, barn-yard, bathroom, class clown, narcissistic, ain't-I-cute?, tee-hee-hee, "Teacher! Billy said butt!" kind of culture. That's the mainstream. It must be. Because, if it weren't, it wouldn't be on display in the "Birthday, female, relative" card section of a suburban supermarket. If it's there, it's everywhere.

So what do you think? Am I overstating it? Is it an ominous sign when a nation is peopled by citizens who grow old without growing up? Another year older and you can still touch the floor with your knuckles? Are the dummies winning?

You tell me. You have to live here, too.

—December 4, 1996

You can't kill a squirrel

It is hard to even say hello any more without fear of offending somebody. In Kentucky, bus drivers were ordered not to insult their passengers by saying "Merry Christmas." They were instructed to use the nonoffensive seasonal greeting, "Ho-Ho-Ho," instead.

This, too, has its pitfalls. Suppose the boarding passenger is bald or tubby or has punky purple hair and a diamond chip in her tongue. Greeting such a person with a hearty "Ho-Ho-Ho" might be construed as an offensive act of look-ism. So maybe the safest thing to do is just stay home and mind your own business.

But don't tell that to Selma Lubinsky. She won't buy it.

According to news accounts, Selma Lubinsky was minding her own business in her New Jersey home when two squirrels broke into her attic and started eating her house.

Ms. Lubinsky, a grandmother, did not know how to cope with this situation. So she telephoned an exterminator. Or rather, she telephoned what, in her youth, was called an exterminator. In these days of heightened sensitivity, exterminators have become pest control persons. And soon, a pest control person arrived at Ms. Lubinsky's door.

The pest control person set a couple of traps on Ms. Lubinsky's roof. The traps worked. And a short time later, the squirrels had passed away.

But Ms. Lubinsky's problems were not over. A neighbor, shocked by this act of squirrelicide, reported Ms. Lubinsky to authorities. There are, it seems, authorities who police such wanton abuse of rodent rights. And now, Ms. Lubinsky and the pest control person each face a $250 fine. Ho-ho-HO!

This small event in New Jersey has sent waves of consciousness-raising rippling across the country. The reason I know is, I got a call on my message machine from a lady who had heard about the case *Squirrels of New Jersey v. Lubinsky*. The lady who called me sounded very worried.

"I, too, have squirrels in my attic," she said. "They're up there now. I don't want to do the wrong thing. Please call me and tell me the right way to handle this."

I haven't called her back yet. I'm still mulling it over. She is wise to have thought of me. For I happen to be fond of squirrels. Some people think of squirrels as merely rats with a bustle. But I get a kick out of them.

I share my life with a self-professed animal lover. We run a kind of 24-hour animal smorgasbord. Anything that can crawl or creep into our yard will find a plate of stale bread or gourmet seeds awaiting it. Word of our generosity has spread throughout the animal kingdom. We often draw raccoons with Indiana license plates.

Yet my friend of the forest can't stand squirrels. She has spent a fortune on so-called squirrel-proof bird feeders—devices that belong in the Scam Hall of Fame along with diet cookies and painless dentistry.

Every time a squirrel hangs by its tail and picks the lock on a squirrel-proof bird feeder, my woodland nymph is out of the house with a broom, screaming at the top of her lungs. "No, no, NO!" she yells. "Get outta there!" And this from a woman who can't take her eyes off the Discovery Channel and complains when I switch to A&E to watch Hitler lose.

But I blush to admit that, broad-minded though I am on the subject of squirrels, even I harbor a Lubinsky-like prejudice at the thought of them moving into my attic and eating my house.

This comes from growing up in an era before multi-species-ism, when the unenlightened went around thinking that people rights were more important than animal rights.

To the lady with squirrels in her attic, I suggest the following: Knock on the attic door. If invited in, take a little house-harming gift. A can of cashews from Harry and David's, perhaps. A pecan pie. A CD of the *Nutcracker Suite*.

Drug the dog. Tranquilize the cat. Greet the squirrels with peace and good will in keeping with the spirit of this blessed though nonspecified season. Let them flourish and multiply.

Then, when they've flourished and multiplied enough, a man from the Board of Health will come out to remove you from your house as the neighbors cheer. And if anybody calls you a nut, walk tall. Just tell 'em this is America.

—December 16, 1996

Hollywood *Flynt* a hustle

When I heard they were making a movie called *The People vs. Larry Flynt,* I drew the only logical conclusion.

I figured it must be about some other Larry Flynt.

The only Larry Flynt I had ever heard of was a pornographer who published a magazine called *Hustler* down in Columbus, Ohio. *Hustler* was a kind of low-rent version of *Playboy*. In the society of skin magazine entrepreneurs, Flynt was to Hugh Hefner what Billy Carter was to Jimmy. A little blob of fungus on the family tree.

Flynt's magazine was so raunchy, idiotic and tasteless that it was rarely taken seriously, even by the righteous crusaders of the anti-porn squad. It was considered so dumb it was beneath contempt. Stories about occasional attempts to ban it from magazine racks were treated as second-class news. Little tempests in a chamber pot.

As I recall it, the thinking was that *Hustler* was so repulsive in content and moronic in tone that its toxic effect on society was self-limiting. After all, in order to read *Hustler*, one must be bright enough to have acquired rudimentary reading skills. And how many people smart enough to read *Hustler* would want to? The odds were it would have trouble making the best-seller list at a truck stop.

For those unable to read, *Hustler* did furnish cartoons. But these were inferior in quality and wit to the drawings, available free, on the walls of broken flush toilets in greasy-towel filling stations.

Flynt and his magazine did achieve one noxious splash of page-one notoriety. That happened when *Hustler* printed a "parody" that alleged the Rev. Jerry Falwell had slept with his mother. Falwell sued and Flynt won on the grounds that Falwell was a public figure and thus constitutionally fair game for any slime ball who wanted to defame him.

The stir this case created was Flynt's most public hour. Until now. Now, he is the hero of a major motion picture, opening soon in a theater near you—and a thousand miles away is quite near enough.

I had pretty much forgotten all about Larry Flynt until Hollywood's publicity machinery cranked up and began to do its thing. Then, suddenly, everywhere you looked, feature stories about Flynt and the actor who plays him appeared like a blotchy rash all over the hype immunity-deficient epidermis of newspapers and news magazines. And by gosh, it was true. Hollywood was making a movie about THAT Larry Flynt. So the only question left was, why?

That question is answered in the movie's credits, which list Oliver Stone as the producer. Ollie has had another vision. Having distorted the history of the Kennedy assassination and invented his own Richard Nixon, Stone has decided to shine his bright, hallucinogenic light on the tawdry career of this porn jester and revise him into Mr. First Amendment or, as the studio publicity puts it, "the era's last crusader." A crusader more into raincoats than capes.

I am mildly nauseated about this, but Gloria Steinem has

gone ballistic. Ms. Steinem and I have much on which to disagree, but I share her astonishment at Hollywood's canonization of Larry Flynt as a force for social progress, when others more deserving—Tiny Tim, say, or the Chippendale dancers—await recognition in the wings.

In an op-ed piece in the *New York Times*, Ms. Steinem reminds us that Flynt's magazine specialized in images of "women being beaten, tortured and raped and subject to degradations from bestiality to sexual slavery."

"Filmgoers don't see such *Hustler* features as 'Dirty Pool,' which depicted a woman being gang-raped on a pool table . . . A few months [later] a woman was gang-raped on a pool table in New Bedford, Mass. Flynt's response . . . was to publish a postcard of another nude woman on a pool table, this time with the inscription 'Greetings from New Bedford, Mass., The Portuguese Gang-Rape Capital of America.'"

Ms. Steinem goes on at some length to document what we already knew. That *Hustler* was slime and Flynt was the hustler who hustled it. What we didn't know and couldn't have suspected was that some day, Oliver Stone would turn such pollution into a great crusade.

From what I've read, the movie's theme is an old one. Let them suppress the oozings of Larry Flynt, the message goes, and next they'll come for Dr. Seuss and *Rebecca of Sunnybrook Farm*. This has always been stirring stuff, whether anybody believes it for a minute or not.

Larry Flynt is still the same old Larry Flynt. It is Hollywood's view that he was ahead of his time and that society is finally ready for him. Hollywood thinks that, these days, we can't tell an oaf from an oracle or a smut hustler from a freedom fighter. Thank God, Hollywood is wrong. But just barely.

—January 8, 1997

Cleveland fountains disappoint

The superb artist Maya Lin has been hired to redesign the main library's Eastman Reading Garden. She plans to put a fountain in it. I wish her well. I hope she knows a good plumber.

Our town is not friendly to fountains. There is more water in the average Lakewood basement than you can find oozing from the spout of a typical Cleveland fountain. I don't know why this is so, but it is. Our track record with fountains is a civic embarrassment.

Last summer in Chicago, I took some friends over to see *Buckingham Fountain*, which has been faithfully spritzing on the lakefront for years. It has survived Capone, riots and other ominous events, such as the arrival of Albert Belle. It is a revered tourist attraction that has enchanted me since I was 7.

Cleveland, of course, has the *War Memorial Fountain*, which miraculously works some of the time. But we have buried more fountains here than Rome ever heard of. The ones we don't bury fill up with dry leaves and squashed cigarette packs. The annual liquid output of the fountains in our town could be absorbed by a package of Pampers.

Beneath the concrete plaza next to Public Hall are the interred remains of the *Hanna Fountains*, which were set aspew in the '60s with a great deal of fanfare. Lyndon Johnson himself turned them on by flicking a switch in the White House. Sort of. The switch he flicked sent a signal to the Hall, where somebody whispered, "Now!"

I remember the event well because it's as close as I ever came to being a presidential speech writer. Word was sent to my newspaper that it would be nice if somebody on the staff prepared some appropriate words for the president to utter. Several of us were given a crack at it. But one of the managing editors rejected our efforts and nominated himself for the task. He wrote:

"Today, Cleveland experiences the rebirth of a bright, new future."

"A future can't have a rebirth," I muttered sourly. But this was chalked up to sour grapes. I was accused of splitting hairs and invited to take my morose and nitpicking attitude over to the copy desk, where people were paid to reduce the burning fever of creativity with sobering doses of grammar. Johnson never used the line. Which was good, because our born-again future was heading for a date with default.

For a while, the *Hanna Fountains* were a foaming centerpiece downtown. Then, as happens to fountains here, they spent more and more time A.W.O.L. (Annoyingly Without Liquid.) Finally, they sputtered and died.

The cops euphemistically dubbed the pathway around them "the racetrack." It became a popular trysting place for those who, in these enlightened times, can buy personal ads in the columns headed "Men seeking men." Now the fountains have vanished and the plaza is as dry as the Sahara.

Beneath the Galleria are the remains of absolutely the ugliest fountains anybody never saw. Every time the *Erieview Fountain* was turned on, it leaked into the parking garage beneath them. Our local engineers have always had trouble constructing a dry garage or a wet fountain. So *Erieview Fountain* use was limited to short spurts, the way you use a drinking fountain.

In winter, however, when the temperature dropped below freezing, the fountain basin was turned into an ice rink. Canned music was piped across the arctic plaza to mingle with the howling wind blowing down from Canada. Two or three masochists each winter risked frostbite to skate around the squat, pod-shaped fountain bases. The scene was as cheery as an exercise yard in a Siberian gulag.

Now those fountains, too, are history, gone without a trace. A flood of publicity, a trickle of use, a mildewed decline, then oblivion. That's the story of the typical Cleveland fountain. Clevelanders, drawn to the sound of running water, find greater rewards in their own bathrooms. If they don't jiggle the handle.

Here's hoping Maya Lin's fountain will reverse this trend. I am a fountain fan and I don't care who knows it, and if there's anything Freudian in it, I don't want to hear about it. It's tough to be a fountain fan in a town where the Fountain of Youth would have died in its infancy.

—January 13, 1997

Shame and fame

I am old enough to remember shame. But people my age won't be around forever.

Therefore I feel a duty to leave some written record of what shame used to be like and how the shamed used to deal with it. Though I don't expect anybody under 40 to believe me.

Here's an example of the way shame used to work:

Imagine a man who is a high-level adviser to the White House. A confidant of the president. A man privy to state secrets. We'll call this man Dick Morris.

Now let's suppose that, during the convention in which his boss was being renominated, this Dick Morris was discovered to have been a sort of prostitute's ambassador to the White House. A man who, in his spare time, sucked the toes of a hooker while gymnastically holding a telephone to her ear so she could eavesdrop on conversations with the president of the United States.

Suppose that this news was so embarrassing that Dick Morris was put on a plane in the middle of the night and spirited away from the convention city. Suppose he arrived home to confront a pack of reporters full of questions about his dereliction. And suppose the pressure of this episode ended his marriage.

Such a man, sitting in an empty house, his career down the drain, his name an inspiration for ribald national ridicule, his family shattered, would very likely have put his head in his hands and said:

"I feel ashamed of myself."

And if he hadn't said it, just about everybody else would have said it for him. "That Dick Morris ought to be ashamed of himself," the public would have muttered, with hardly a dissenting voice.

That's the way it would have been back when there was such a thing as shame.

But then, after a period of wretched agony, the shamed man might have consulted some kind of spiritual adviser. And he might have found the inner strength to pick up the pieces of his life and make a fresh start.

"I'll move to another town," he might have said. "Someplace where the media doesn't know me. Maybe I'll even change my name. I'll go into another line of work, selling open-toed shoes, for instance. No. Maybe not that. Maybe I'll find a job working with my hands instead of my . . . Yes! I'll get my respect back and my credibility and someday . . . someday . . . I won't be ashamed anymore."

Some people actually thought that way, back in the age of shame. Today we have a word to describe such people. We call them dopes.

That's because the age of shame was replaced by the age of fame. And in came a whole new set of rules.

Let's take the same Dick Morris and put him in the age of fame and see if we notice a difference. Do we? Yes, we do.

Now our Dick Morris doesn't put his head in his hands and murmur that he's ashamed of himself. He simply toasts himself with a slug of Scotch and says:

"Well, you win some, and some you lose."

Instead of calling a spiritual adviser, he calls an agent.

"Dickie, baby," the agent says, "You read my mind. I was just gonna phone ya. I've already got a book contract and a *Larry King* appearance scheduled for you."

"What's the statute of limitations on national disgrace and public humiliation in America today?" our new-age Morris asks him.

"Figure five months at the outside," the agent says. "After that you'll be back on murderer's row. I can have the media fawning all over you by mid-January. I got you great billing. You play the media circuit right after they get through fawning all over Larry Flynt, the famous pornographer."

"Wow! Listen, you don't think I should move to another town and change my name or anything like that, do you?"

"What are you, nuts?" the agent says. "All you got going for you is your bad name. Whaddaya want to call yourself, Albert Schweitzer? I'd be lucky to get you on *Charlie Rose*. Whoever heard of you before you got caught with that hooker? Toe-suckers are a dime a dozen, but you are the only official toe-sucker of the president."

"And you don't think the media will be, uh, what's the word, ashamed to give me the publicity, huh?"

"Ashamed? What's that? Never heard of it," the agent says. "Look, I gotta go. I got Dennis Rodman on the other line."

There you are. That's a little example of how the disappearance of shame changed America. Nobody seems to miss shame. Nobody can remember any advantage to it. I can hardly remember any myself.

Well, it did help us separate the good guys from the bad guys. But outside of that, nothing.

—January 20, 1997

Tubonics

There is a brisk debate in linguistic circles about so-called tubonics—the unique dialect spoken only by people who work in television.

But no one denies that tubonics differs sharply from standard spoken English. This can be easily demonstrated.

Suppose you board a bus and the bus driver ignores you and stares straight ahead with a grumpy look on his puss? You will instantly recognize this as the standard English greeting from bus drivers.

But suppose the bus driver turns to you, smiles and says:

"Hi. I'm Joe Smith sitting in for the vacationing Bill Jones. Thanks for joining us."

This is a tubonic welcome. You won't go wrong inferring that this bus driver once made his living on the television tube. Perhaps as one of the thousands of anchormen fired each year because of hair loss, the onset of puberty or the inability to look properly terrorized while warning viewers of a January snowfall.

Whatever our race, creed, ethnic background, blood type, SAT score or taste in pizza topping, we all hear tubonics spoken every day. But to hear it is not necessarily to understand it. Let's look at another typical, tubonic anchorman greeting:

"Good evening. I'm Harry Hopeful sitting in for Lance Lavish, who is on special assignment tonight."

Translated into standard English, this sentence takes on an entirely different meaning, to wit:

"Good evening. I'm Harry Hopeful. Lance Lavish isn't here because he got free tickets to *Damn Yankees*. But he sulks if we don't mention his name.'

Like almost all television persons, I am bilingual. When in the humdrum world of three-dimensional people with untidy hair, I speak standard English. But then, at night, I enter the exotic world of television people and make the effortless linguistic switch to tubonics. If I didn't, I might lose my job.

Let's face it. Television employers expect their employees to speak clear and proper tubonics. The presence of standard English in a television newscast is jarring and gives a bad impression. Here, for instance, is a common and perfectly acceptable tubonic sentence:

"Now, for an up-to-date report on today's tragedy, we go LIVE to our Patty Perk, who joins us from the scene. Patty, what's the latest?"

Translated into standard English, the very same thought would be expressed this way:

"To be honest, there are no new developments in this story. But we've asked Patty Perk to go out in the middle of the night and stand shivering in the very same empty lot where an awful lot was happening a mere eight hours ago. She will introduce some tape we shot this afternoon. Patty, your nose is running."

Which newscaster would you hire? The one proficient in tubonics or the one burdened by standard English?

Here are some more vivid examples of the differences between the two forms of expression:

Tubonic English: "There's a lot more news still to come, so stay with us."

Non-tubonic English: "Actually, that's about it. But if you can stay awake for another five minutes, we've got some tape of a water-skiing squirrel the producer thinks is cute."

Tubonic English: "The police are doing a good job, the mayor told Channel Two today in an exclusive, Two-For-The-Road, Mobilcam Two, Two-on-One interview."

Non-tubonic English: "He fed the same Cream of Wheat to Channel Nine yesterday. But he's not talking to Channel Eleven until tomorrow."

Tubonic English: "That's all the news for tonight. Thanks for joining us."

Non-tubonic English: "A lot more happened today, but nobody sent us any pictures of it. There was some talk of a comet hurtling toward Earth, but the astronomer who said so was as dull as Jell-O. Join us tomorrow morning on *Wake Up, Cleveland, Or You'll Be Late For Work,* when we'll pretend that the killer drizzle Sam predicted has paralyzed rush-hour traffic. Plus a hilarious live report from Bob, who interviews residents in North Olmsted who scientists say may be in that Earth-destroying comet's path. Plus our absurd telepoll question, 'If a comet struck your home, forcing you to evacuate, which would you want to take with you, wedding photographs or credit cards?' If you don't want to watch, at least turn the TV on. We're in ratings month."

As you can see, there is a great difference between tubonic English and the other kind. The question is, should tubonic speakers be paid large sums of money to speak tubonics over the nation's airwaves?

The answer, obviously, is yes. Damned if we tubonicists know why. But we thank you.

—January 27, 1997

Can Tiger improve America's handicap?

Airwaves and news columns have warbled a weeklong rhapsody to Tiger Woods and all that his triumph is said to mean.

The ethnicity of his person was examined, subdivided and charted like a meat diagram in a butcher shop. There is a cut of him for everybody's taste—a brown exterior, a black and Asian

interior, a small flavor of white and American Indian. The media served him to us as a one-man band capable of playing a whole symphony of diversity.

The words we heard most were "social implications." "Tiger Woods' record-breaking round of golf (the announcers instructed us) was significant not just as an athletic feat, but for its social implications as well."

We were expected to vaguely infer that the civil rights odyssey, begun on the back of a bus in Montgomery, had navigated itself with high purpose and profound result to the front seat of a golf cart in Augusta. Things were on the right track. Bigotry had been bonked with a putter and knocked momentarily senseless.

Tiger was on everybody's front page and front porch. *Time* magazine named him one of the most influential people in America (in a list that included Rosie O'Donnell and omitted the president and everybody who ran for president.) *Newsweek* extended Tiger's range by naming him as a person who will shape the next millennium. Deodorant companies and sportswear manufacturers were quick to wave money and shout amen.

But if you left this lawn party and wandered inside the newspapers, you came upon a sobering sight in the little news columns that are used as mortar to fill the space between the underwear ads.

While Tiger Woods was breaking records in Augusta, the town of Philadelphia was busy producing social implications, too—though nobody from ESPN showed up to behold them and whisper, "Gee whiz!"

The scorecard from the City of Brotherly Myth read like this:

Seven white men have been charged with attacking a black woman and her family who trespassed in a white neighborhood.

Two black men were subsequently arrested for gunning down a white teenager during a robbery in the same neighborhood.

A civil rights march through the neighborhood was greeted by white residents who jeered or turned their backs.

Louis Farrakhan, scenting blood, arrived to participate in the march. Philadelphia's mayor persuaded him to stay out of it by agreeing to appear with Farrakhan at a rally.

Representatives from Jewish and Catholic organizations refused to attend the rally, charging Farrakhan with anti-Semitism and bigotry.

None of this made front-page news because it wasn't front-page news. It is the kind of tired old saga that plays itself out again and again in this town or that one. An ugly little fever of bigotry and fear and power and politics.

The elements of diversity that combined so enviably in Tiger Woods—blended in him by an act of love—are still an unstable and volatile mixture in the neighborhoods of America. What happened in Philadelphia does not tarnish the achievement of the young golfer. But it rubs some of the frosting of symbolism away. Sports is not always a good metaphor for life. The great 50-year journey from Jackie Robinson to Tiger Woods—from baseball justice to golf excellence—was a righteous crusade in a parallel universe.

As Woods crossed the threshold of sports immortality this week, elsewhere in the land, away from the greens and floundering in the hazards, America continued to struggle with its old, chronic handicap.

—April 18, 1997

Star quality

"I remember you. You used to be big," a visitor tells an aging actress in the movie *Sunset Boulevard*.

"I am big," she says. "It's the pictures that got small."

Jimmy Stewart was big. His obit led the national newscasts the day he died, and the next day the papers observed his departure with spacious stories on page one. The size of our fondness for him is testimony that it's the pictures that have gotten small—shrinking with the narrowing vision of the people who make them.

What would they have Stewart do on the screen today? Dress in a Batman suit and play a cartoon? Spend 90 minutes battling with plastic, computerized dinosaurs? Shuck his clothes and hop into a revolving bed for the mandatory, voyeuristic sex scene?

It's impossible to imagine Stewart finding a place in the current special-effects Hollywood that force-feeds us the superhuman, the inhuman and the subhuman. For it was his humanity that was Stewart's own special effect. He may have been up on that screen, 30 feet tall, but he came from our world—a world where most of us shoot and miss; try and fail; love and lose and make the best of it.

"He was a propagandist of the American self-image," one obit said. There is a tiny tinge of disdain in that sentence, and it isn't quite right. Stewart didn't show us what we were, he showed us what we might hope to be. The message he sent was that decency was within everybody's grasp but that, often, it was a strain to reach it.

It is probably beyond the ken of a TV generation to understand the impact Stewart and his generation of actors had on a lot of us kids sitting out there in the dark. For one thing, they taught us manners. Grant, Gable, Holden, Stewart and the rest gave little boys lessons in how to react appropriately to a variety of situations both stressful and embarrassing. They were our role models, and they were safe ones.

There was such a thing, we learned, as class. Not class in the economic sense, but class in the behavioral sense—an attribute that transcended economic boundaries. Class, it seemed, had something to do with courtesy and something to do with character. So we absorbed instruction on these characteristics, too. All of this for a tuition that ranged in price from a dime to a dollar.

Decency, character, class and manners. It's hard to believe we actually built movies out of such subtle stuff. Where's the karate kick to the groin? The automobile that explodes in a gout of oily smoke and orange flame? The automatic weapons spitting bullets by the hundreds? The little flowers of blood forming a bouquet on a shirt front?

"Of course, today's movies have a realism that Stewart's didn't have," said a slick movie critic from one of the nation's biggest papers.

By this remark, one presumes she meant all of the above. Plus a liberal sprinkling of f-words, nose-picking, flatulence and the opportunity to watch actors pretending to copulate. Swell. But does the realism of the slaughterhouse enhance the flavor of the steak?

Most of us get through life by walking a narrow but eventful path. We don't battle dinosaurs or shoot Uzis or chase drug smugglers in helicopters. Our personal dramas are less flashy but no less intense.

Sometimes we feel like failures and wonder if it really matters that we were ever born. We struggle with physical handicaps that threaten to limit our dreams. We try to hang on to our beliefs while others mock and humiliate us. We know we ought to be brave, but we are too scared to try. We do our best while plagued with doubts that our best is not worth very much.

We had company in Jimmy Stewart. These were the demons—our demons—that he grappled with up there on the screen. Somehow he managed to make virtue seem attractive and nobility seem attainable.

No wonder his passing was big news. He left us an awful lot to miss.

—July 4, 1997

....

Why Wahoo ought to go

A couple of years ago I had to go into the hospital for an operation. It wasn't a very serious operation, but you never know.

So I decided to make my last column before the knife an exercise in devil-may-care recklessness. And I wrote that it was time the Indians got rid of the Chief Wahoo logo—a little minstrel show kind of caricature that would certainly have been banned long ago if it depicted any other ethnic group.

My reasoning was this: If I died during the operation, I wouldn't have to listen to the several hundred furious calls the column was bound to attract. If I lived, I would be in such a state of relief and euphoria that it wouldn't bother me much to hear a chorus of Indians fans vote me an All-Star idiot.

I lived. They called. They swore. They were still calling when the euphoria started to wear off and I began feeling an occasional twinge from the steady onslaught of wrath.

Many callers identified themselves as Irish. They pointed out that they were not offended by the logo of the Notre Dame "Fighting Irish" football team, which is, apparently, some sort of leprechaunish figure. If the Irish could live with that, they said, Native Americans ought to be able to live with Wahoo.

But this reasoning contradicted the modern rules of offense. According to these rules, people who aren't offended don't get to vote. The issue of offense is a one-sided issue. The non-offended don't have a side. Nobody has to pay any attention to them.

I have a pal named Jerry, who is an American Indian and proud of it. His heritage brings him great joy. He manages to take it seriously and get a big kick out of it at the same time.

When the Indian movement picked up momentum, Jerry announced that he was going to take an Indian name. He had seen the movie *Dances With Wolves*, he said, and it had inspired him. The name he had selected for himself was Dances With Women. This name, he said, captured much of his personal essence and aspirations.

Once, I quizzed Jerry about the Chief Wahoo logo. I said I judged it offensive, demeaning and embarrassing. He replied that, as far as he was concerned, there was nothing embarrassing about the Indians that some decent starting pitching wouldn't cure.

This put me in an awkward position. How could I, a non-Indian, lecture Jerry about what he ought to be offended by? Was I supposed to say, "What kind of an Indian ARE you?" Suppose he responded, "What kind of an Indian are YOU?" Where would we be then?

A while back, I had to attend a mandatory daylong seminar at work so I could learn how not to offend women and minorities. The thrust of the lecture seemed to be that if a woman or a minority claimed to be offended, I better pay attention or they might take me to court—a circumstance that could prove corporately expensive.

So I began to monitor myself carefully. I attacked unintentional offenses of thought or deed at the root, weeding them out like crabgrass. I was making progress, too, until the other day, when I was startled by an offense communique from the National Federation of the Blind.

The federation voted 3,000 to 0 to protest a remake by the Disney Co. of the cartoon character Mr. Magoo. Mr. Magoo, the federation said, was as offensive to the blind as Little Black Sambo and *Amos 'n' Andy* are to blacks.

Now, my recollection of Mr. Magoo is that he was nearsighted. I believe, in fact, he was called "the nearsighted Mr. Magoo." His misadventures seemed to stem from the fact that he resisted wearing glasses—like a couple of teenage daughters I raised.

Even back in the callous days before sensitivity seminars, I doubt if many people would have laughed at the plight of a character billed as "the blind Mr. Magoo." We had some sensitivity even before sensitivity was cool.

But according to the modern rules of offense, Mr. Magoo is offensive if an organization of the blind says he is. And any blind person who isn't offended by him doesn't count.

Since the idea of offending blind people is appalling to me, I may have to change my opinion of Mr. Magoo. Or pretend to, anyway. If I encounter a blind person who thinks Mr. Magoo isn't offensive, I guess it's OK if I agree with him. Provided that, if I encounter a blind person who thinks he is offensive, I agree with him, too.

The business of being nonoffensive is getting more complicated all the time. And the harder we work at nonoffense, the greater the numbers of offended people who seem to pop into view.

Sometimes I have a subversive thought. I think things were better in the old days, when we chuckled at each other's group stereotypes but worked to respect each other as individuals.

Except for Wahoo. I still think he ought to go. And I'll tell you why I say so.

I'm leaving town for a couple of days.

—July 7, 1997

....

Diana and electronic excess

Obviously we didn't know how much she meant to us until she was gone.

In fact, many of us were in the dark as recently as last Saturday morning. It would have been hard, five days ago, to start a coffee-shop conversation by saying, "Let's talk about Princess Diana and how she's touched the lives of all of us."

In retrospect, after hours of CNN, my own previous lack of Diana awareness seems astonishing. A glimpse of her face on a tabloid (unpurchased) in the checkout line. The sight of her on the cover of a *People* magazine (unread) in the dentist's office. Twenty seconds' worth of her high-fashion presence on TV, reading a speech in honor of some worthy cause.

She was one of maybe 20 people, living and dead, whom the media use like flash cards. Elvis, Cher, Arnold, Marilyn, Liz, or the two Michaels, Jordan and Jackson. Pop them in front of the customers under a provocative headline and you get instant recognition and maybe a quick newsstand sale. To the media, they are commodities, and Diana was one of them.

But her niche was something special. She didn't sing or moonwalk or bench press her way to international stardom. She and her hapless husband took a thousand-year-old English fairy tale and wrote the make-believe out of it and made it less Arthurian and more Jenny Jones.

What would we have said about her last week? That she was a new kind of princess for a new kind of age? The old idea of the princess who marries and lives happily ever after (or pretends to) is out of sync with the divorce statistics. Diana was a new version. An *Oprah* kind of princess. A marriage-busted, single-mom, true-confessions, shared-parenting symbol of an age where Selfhood is in Flower.

She wanted to be, she said, the Queen of Hearts. This is not the kind of thing you say if you wish everybody would just go away and leave you alone. In order to accomplish her wish, she had to marry the media. So she married on the rebound and traded one destructive, authoritarian kind of wedlock for another.

The media made her life larger than life. And for the last 72 hours, it has made her death larger than death. I, who am a sensation junkie, have watched almost all of it. It is a terrible and riveting thing to watch—this last, great electronic excess, the grand finale of Diana-as-commodity.

First, there was the righteous condemnation of the paparazzi from the likes of *People* magazine and the *National Enquirer,* whose editors showed up in studios to say, "Me good journalist, them bad journalists." But nobody was quite certain where the foul line was. Nobody ever is. The consensus was that, when somebody dies, things have gone too far.

Then came news that the limo driver was drunk and driving at an insane speed. This took some of the heat off the paparazzi, though not much. The anti-paparazzi interviews were already on tape, and repeating them was useful. So we entered a period of dueling villains that seems destined to last for a while.

A representative from Mercedes-Benz appeared to proclaim that, given such a crash, the car was innocent. A seat-belt advocate gave his solemn words that seat belts could possibly have prevented Diana's death—a statement that casual analysis revealed to be empty of significance. A professional driver shared his insight that it is unwise to drive 100 mph through an underpass.

Child psychiatrists showed up with free pointers on how Prince Charles should employ his parenting skills to meet the challenge of the tragedy. We saw lines of grieving people arriving places with flowers. Such scenes inspired more grieving people to arrive with more flowers. And one endlessly repeated clip showed us a woman lying face down in front of the British embassy, sobbing uncontrollably. Was it sorrow or was it mania? To the camera, it didn't matter. As long as it played.

The secretary of labor appeared to praise Diana's work for "all the children lost in land mines." You wondered if she had been hastily briefed and thought a land mine, like a coal mine, had an entrance to it. In California, a model showed up with her lawyer and announced that, out of respect, she was dropping her breach of promise suit against Diana's companion, Dodi Al Fayed—a moving gesture in a litigious America. And so the story grew and grew.

It is the tragic story of a rich and famous young woman who went into a tunnel and never came out. Where would her journey have led if it had continued? Would she have become Mrs. Dodi Fayed? And, if so, would she have lost her luster—another Jackie turned Mrs. Onassis?

Would she have always been what we wanted her to be? Or would we have grown tired of her and dropped her? Would she have missed the publicity she claimed to despise? Or clung to it like an aging ingenue with face-lifts and cleverly cut fashion?

For her two sons and a few others, the grief is sharp and real. But the rest of us are only voyeurs. We didn't know the woman. We knew the myth. We weep for the fairy tale. And for her death, which gave us the ending.

—September 3, 1997

Saving souls for Arbitron

If I were Catholic, I might move across town to get into Father Ray's parish. He's not really a priest, but he plays one on television. And, in the broad-minded universe of television, there is no "right" or "wrong." There are just lively differences of opinion, like on *Crossfire*.

In last night's much-publicized opening episode of *Nothing*

Sacred, Father Ray is approached by a woman who says she is planning to have an abortion. What does he think about that?

"You're an adult with your own conscience," Father Ray tells her. "I can't tell you what to do."

This is the kind of advice the woman could have gotten from a stranger sitting next to her on the No. 55 bus. But, coming from Father Ray, it packs more punch. It was worth the trip to the confessional to get the official word that God has no authoritarian opinion in these matters. Go and do your thing and come back next week for forgiveness if you feel an annoying loss of self-esteem.

Of course, the abortion issue is a hot potato. Father Ray could hardly be expected to start right off violating the teachings of the Book of Arbitron by offending the demography of a significant number of pro-choice viewers.

So maybe he is saving his firm judgments for the easy ones. Critic Florence King wondered what Father Ray would have said if, instead of abortion, the woman had come to him to confess that she was thinking about taking up smoking. Maybe, like a drill sergeant, he would have ordered her to her knees as penance for considering one of the few sins everybody loves to hate.

Unfortunately, I have to work on the nights that Father Ray brings guidance and comfort to his television flock. It would be fun to watch him bob and weave his way through the entire Ten Commandments, which, under his stewardship, presumably are merely the Ten Opinions.

Episode Two: Sally and Jim, distraught parents, tell Father Ray that their son, Rodney, is playing rap records that take the name of the Lord their God in vain. Father Ray points out that such music is merely a mirror of the reality of life in the streets and, as such, is not overtly wrong. Much relieved, they thank him and go out to buy ear plugs.

Episode Five: Heather, a distraught child, pours out her heart to Father Ray. She would like to honor her father and her mother. But when she came home from the mall with a rhinestone stud embedded in her tongue, her mother called her a hurtful name and locked her in her bedroom. Father Ray puts her in touch with a Verbal Abuse Hotline.

Episode 10: Sam confesses the sin of coveting. He covets not only his neighbor's wife and his neighbor's house, but half a dozen other wives, entire housing developments in Westlake, and Michael Jordan's annual salary. Father Ray advises him to vote for those political candidates who favor a more equal distribution of the nation's wealth.

A favorable review in the *New York Times* praised *Nothing Sacred* for its "ambiguity" and its "refusal to preach. Though the series offers a complex study of faith in the real world, its great strength is that it works as engaging human drama apart from its religious concerns."

The key word there is ambiguity. In the new age, there is a great market for a religion that is ambiguous, which, the Book of Webster tells us, means not clear, indefinite, uncertain, vague. If the rules get squishy enough, it is actually possible to pass through them without breaking them. That way, maybe heaven can't get enough evidence to convict you.

Once, Hollywood turned out human dramas that didn't need to stand apart from religious concerns to be engaging. Take a look at *The Bishop's Wife* the next time it shows up on the American Movie Classics channel. And of course there's the old war horse *It's A Wonderful Life,* which is trotted out every Christmas.

Both of these movies feature angels who come to earth to show people the error of their ways. The presumption is that the people are in error, there's no two ways about it and Somebody Up There knows it.

These days, Anybody Up There so cocksure would be considered a fascist. An old priest in *Nothing Sacred* says, "God is just like me. A wise old man."

If that's true, any wise old man will do. Or even a so-so wise young man, if he's a little ambiguous and refuses to preach. The annoying strictures of religious doctrine only clutter things up. Which may be the real sermon coming from the pulpit of *Nothing Sacred.*

—September 19, 1997

Cleveland, city of unavoidable pain

"Look at it this way," my friend Marc said. "Whoever said winning builds character?"

"That's right," I said. "What does winning really teach you? Nothing. So you won, so what? Speaking for myself, I can honestly say that the most valuable lessons I've learned in life, I've learned from losing."

"And, putting it that way, losing is preferable to winning," Marc said.

"In the great scheme of things, it certainly is," I said.

Then we paused for a while to sob and to swear. Marc recovered first.

"Mine were tears of joy and oaths of thanksgiving," he said.

"So were mine," I said.

"I couldn't help thinking how glad I am not to be living in Miami, where they think winning is such a big deal," Marc said.

"Or New York or Atlanta," I said. "They won last year and the year before. But what did it mean to them this year? Absolutely nothing. That shows you how fast the thrill of winning can come and go. A junk-food high, that's what winning is."

"But take losing, on the other hand," Marc said. "Losing stays with you, like garlic. Long after the joy of winning has faded in those other cities, the terrible shock and pain of losing will be as fresh as ever in our town."

We stopped to kick a few desks and filing cabinets.

"Only one thing bothers me," Marc said. "How can I explain to my kids that they ought to be grateful that we lost? They don't understand the advantages of losing like we do."

"How have you handled it so far?" I asked.

"Well," Marc said, "I called Grief-Counselors-R-Us and talked to a woman named Heather, who advised me to encourage them to vent."

"Are they venting?" I asked.

"It's hard to tell," Marc said. "They pretty much vent all the time without encouragement. One of them broke the aquarium, and we had fish flopping all over the basement floor. But I don't know if that was World Series-related, despite the obvious piscitological connection."

"So you want to know what to say to them that will make them feel better?" I said. "If you don't mind a little advice from an older man, I'll tell you what I would say."

"Please do," Marc said.

"Well," I said, "I would begin by reminding them of the things they've always heard. That the best man usually wins. That the team with the most heart prevails in the end. That it isn't whether you win or lose, it's how you play the game. And that everybody roots for the underdog. Then I would tell them that all that stuff is bunk. And they are lucky to be living in the one city in America that knows that."

"That's pretty inspirational so far," Marc said.

"I would tell them that, on their journey through life, they will find that the worst man often wins. That the biggest heart has room for the most heartbreak. That no matter how you play the game, losing hurts and winning doesn't. And that, if everybody roots for the underdog, somebody forgot to tell the announcers on NBC. They dissed us for the whole Series."

"When does the cheering up part come in?" Marc said.

"I'm getting to that," I said. "I would point out that living is painful. And that the mistake most people make is to try to avoid the pain. Or to numb their hearts so they can't feel it. But in avoiding the pain, they avoid its lessons. In numbing their hearts to pain, they deaden their hearts to joy."

"My kids are just kids, you know," Marc said. "They aren't little Dr. Laura What's-her-names. When's the happy part?"

"The happy part is that they live in Cleveland. The one city in the universe where pain is unavoidable. Where, after 50 years of various kinds of suffering, we finally suffered what is unquestionably the most painful World Series loss in the modern history of baseball!"

"You're right," Marc said. "We weren't supposed to get past the Yankees, but we did. We weren't supposed to get past the Orioles, but we did. Then we got to the Marlins and we thought, 'Finally, a team we might be able to beat.'"

"And we WERE beating them," I said. "Until we got to the ninth inning of the seventh game. And we knew, all along, that in the ninth inning, Jose Mesa would come in to pitch. We knew he shouldn't. We knew it was a mistake. But we knew there was nothing we could do to stop it. And we knew that, if he came in . . ."

"We'd lose," Marc said. "And he did and we did."

"So that's it," I said. "That's as bad as it gets. You can tell your kids to cheer up. The worst is over. No matter how many years they have ahead of them as Cleveland sports fans, they will never again witness a moment of such pure, unadulterated, character-building agony."

"Do you really believe that?" Marc said.

"Frankly, in our town you can never be sure," I said. "But they're only kids. Somebody has to show a little mercy."

—October 29, 1997

Bizarre is best

Lock up the kids; it's ratings month on TV again. Is that why Barbara Walters was talking to Marv Albert on ABC the other night? Yesss!

Ms. Walters, as always, was compassionate, caring and crafty. Crafty in the sense that she understands the double-think that is a requirement of her craft.

"How did it feel to have the whole nation discussing the private details of your sex life?" she asked.

Albert replied that it felt awful. And then, a few moments later, Ms. Walters did her duty and sacrificed privacy on the altar of viewer edification:

"Do you wike wuff sex?" she asked, in that disarming way of hers.

"No," Albert said.

Was biting a staple of Albert's sexual repertoire?

He said no to that one, too. Tersely, as if the query left a bad taste in his mouth.

At this point, I was hoping for one of Ms. Walters' passionate twick questions, which leave the elusive interviewee no place to hide. Such as:

"If you were a sex organ, which sex organ would you like to be?"

If he had said a bicuspid, she could have said, "Gotcha!" But the moment passed. And my mind began to wander. And I began to think about celebrity shame and forgiveness, celebrity sin and absolution.

Barely three weeks had passed since Marv Albert was going through the dark night of the soul. His teething problems, which would have confounded Dr. Spock, had been disclosed to a snickering public. He had, apparently, fibbed to his NBC bosses, who fired him for it, relieving him of a dream job and the millions that went with it.

Then there was the worst humiliation of all. A woman testified that, in her struggle to avoid becoming a midnight snack, she found herself holding Albert's toupee in her hand. Most TV anchormen realize that, like Samson, their strength is in their hair. If they can't grow their own, they buy some. Or have it landscaped into their scalps like creeping-bent grass.

And now this indignant Delilah had publicly and mercilessly scalped him. The last illusion was gone. In the future, people he encountered would fail to meet his eye, but would gaze, instead, a few degrees scalpward, covertly seeking some evidence of a seam or a smear of Elmer's glue. All his secrets were out. He was totally exposed—from head to mouth.

Rehabilitation was vital. But how long would it take? To find out, Albert used his sportscaster training. He went to the stats.

The previous record for whirlwind recovery from abject humiliation belonged to Dick Morris, adviser to presidents and toe-nuzzler to strumpets, who allowed a hooker to listen in on private presidential phone conversations. For telephone service to his country, which included call-girl-waiting, Morris was branded as a man of kinky habits, bad judgment and little sense.

It was assumed he was through forever. Forever lasted three months.

Now he is persona most grata on all the political blab shows. You see him everywhere. His public infamy made him a sought-after commodity. He is possessed of the trait the media value above all others. He has become bizarre.

Count the number of times you hear the word "bizarre" uttered in TV promos during this ratings period. "Tragic" is good, "brutal" is good, "heroic" is so-so. But "bizarre" is best. I used to try to get it into every news promo. A traffic accident is just a traffic accident, but a "bizarre traffic accident" may keep you awake until 11:20 p.m.

Marv Albert has attained bizarredom. In exchange for this valuable attribute, the media that made him, then broke him, is ready to embrace him again. He has begun the rehabilitation process—first Barbara, then Oprah, then Larry and then the book. Then Oprah again, then Larry again and then who knows: the Fox network? Too soon to say "Yessss!" But who can rule out maybe?

We try to explain shame to our children, but it's harder than it used to be. Shame is an affliction reserved for us nobodys. For public figures, it has become merely a branch office subsidiary of fame.

In limo land, if an agent calls and says, "You ought to be ashamed of yourself," there's only one appropriate answer. "Great! When do I start?"

—November 10, 1997

....

Thanksgiving dinner with Jerry Springer

Last night I had a horrible dream. I dreamed I was invited to Thanksgiving dinner at Jerry Springer's house. All the recent guests from his talk show were there.

Sitting near me was the woman from the episode "My Pimp Won't Let Me Go." Naturally, her pimp was there, too.

Across the table was a woman in maternity clothes. I recognized her as the star of the show titled "I'm Pregnant by a Transsexual." She was telling everybody that she was hoping for a boy. "We're going to call him Scott-Heather," she said.

Suddenly, two women pushed their chairs over backward and began writhing on the floor and clawing each other. Nobody paid much attention.

"Who are they?" I asked an attractive woman sitting nearby.

"Oh, they're nobody," she said with a sniff. "They were on the program called 'I'm Pregnant by Your Man.'"

"There certainly are a lot of pregnant people around," I said. "Are you pregnant too?"

"Certainly not!" she said icily. "Perhaps you don't know who I am. I appeared on the show called 'Honey, I'm Really a Guy.'"

"Who's the woman over there near the cranberry sauce?" I asked. "There's something familiar about her, but I can't place what it is."

"You mean the one without any clothes on?" said Ms. Really-a-Guy. "She was on last Friday's show. The one called 'I Refuse to Wear Clothes.'"

"Oh, yeah," I said. I had seen that one. Ms. I-Refuse-To-Wear-Clothes had been sitting on the set, merrily in the nude, with her intimate zones covered up by those shimmery little squares TV uses to mask the faces of juveniles and rape victims.

"I Refuse to Wear Clothes" had an especially poignant moment. The nude young woman's mother was brought from the wings. She sank into a chair next to her daughter and began to sob.

"How can you do this to us?" she wailed. "You are ruining our family. You have driven a wedge between your father and I."

The nude looked honestly flabbergasted.

"There are problems between you and Dad because I'm naked?" she asked in amazement.

All of these shows really happened just the way I've described them. But, in my dream, Jerry Springer walked into the dining room carrying a huge turkey. Or was it the turkey that carried

Springer? I can't remember. It's beginning to fade.

I do remember that, in my dream, Springer made a little speech.

"I want to thank all of you dear and fascinating fruitcakes for giving me a Thanksgiving with something to be thankful for," he said.

"As you know, television is a tough business. My show is in a bitter ratings war against Oprah. For years, she has been the queen of daytime TV talk."

He was interrupted by a fit of giggling. It came from three young women who had appeared on the *Springer* show titled "Pregnant Bad Girls." He waited until it stopped.

"Oprah has been fighting a conventional ratings war," he said. "She has been using trite old topics like 'Movie Star Makeovers' and *People* magazine's 'Sexiest Man Alive.'"

A woman named Kristen abruptly pushed back her chair and stood up.

"I HAVE A SECRET LOVER!" she yelled at us. I remembered that she had spoken those same words to her fiance, Mark, on a recent *Springer* show. Then she introduced her secret lover, a woman named Shelly.

"I knew I could never beat Oprah with conventional ratings warfare," Springer continued. "So I turned to the only answer — biological ratings warfare. All of you have the biological makeup of sickos, wackos and weirdos. So I unleashed you on the TV audience. Think of it this way: I'm like Saddam, and all of you are like anthrax."

They all cheered at that.

"And it worked," Springer said. "I beat Oprah in the ratings. I have you to thank for it. I learned a lesson back when I was on Cincinnati's City Council and the press found out I had paid a hooker with a check. 'Jerry,' I said to myself, 'if you want to dabble in prostitution, next time make sure you're the one who gets the check.'"

Suddenly, a bunch of new people raced into the dining room and began yelling at each other and pelting each other with bread sticks.

"Look out!" the nude yelled. "Those are the people from the show 'Past Guests Do Battle!' Duck!!'"

I ducked so hard I woke up. And then I realized it was Wednesday and everything was all right.

The November ratings period ends tonight.

—November 26, 1997

....

A *nation off-key*

"I hear America singing, the varied carols I hear." So rejoiced poet Walt Whitman in *Leaves of Grass,* the book President Clinton handed out to Monica Lewinsky and others as a party favor.

Of course, Walt Whitman never heard the Grammys.

There was a time when I used to like to hear America singing, too. But not anymore. These days, when America starts to sing, I clap my hands over my ears and chant "rhubarb-rhubarb-rhubarb" to drown America out.

That's why I skipped the Grammy Awards on TV the other night. The Grammy Awards are like a toxic waste spill. Why wallow in it? It's frightening enough to read about it in the paper the next day.

And, sure enough, the next day's *USA Today* published an account of the show that contained this paragraph:

"Grammy's double whammy started when rapper Ol' Dirty Bastard commandeered a microphone and rambled about his Wu-Tang Clan group as Shawn Colvin arrived on stage to accept the trophy for song of the year."

I absorbed this information with only mild interest. I had no idea who the people involved were or what a Wu-Tang Clan is. It was like reading about unrest in some obscure and backward nation nobody would want to visit.

Except it wasn't some obscure and backward nation. Well, not an obscure one, anyway. It was America I was reading about. America singing.

Now it so happens that, at the same time the Grammys were broadcast, there was a superb show called "America in the '40s" on PBS. It was great television, so, naturally, comparatively few Americans bothered with it. The Grammy show outdrew "America in the '40s" in ratings by about 8 to 1.

The show was full of wonderful old songs. Popular tunes are the poetry of the unlettered. Listen to them and you are listening to the soul of an era.

"The '40s began with bad news and good music," said host Charles Durning. And who can quarrel with that? No age group in this century has faced such a steady onslaught of bad news as the kids who came of age in that decade.

From 10 years of Depression, starvation, poverty or the immediate threat of it, lynchings and Jim Crow, Americans had been plunged into war, death, uncertainty, fear and the Holocaust. And the more bitter their fate became, the sweeter grew their music.

I called a young friend of mine the next day and asked him if he had happened to see the show. He said he hadn't. He said he had watched the Grammys instead.

"Did any of the songs on the Grammys have lyrics like this?" I asked him. And then I recited:
"I'll be seeing you,
In all the old familiar places,
That this heart of mine embraces,
All day through.
In that small cafe,
The park across the way,
The children's carousel,
The chestnut tree,
The wishing well . . ."
"That's kind of nice," he said.
Thus encouraged, there was no stopping me.
"I'll be seeing you,
In every lovely summer's day,
And everything that's bright and gay,
I'll always think of you that way.
I'll find you in the morning sun,
And when the night is new,
I'll be looking at the moon,

But I'll be seeing you."

"Gee," he said. "What group made that?"

"A whole generation made it," I said. "I guess now you'd call them Ol' Sentimental Bastards."

"Oh yeah, right," he said. "I think I've heard of them."

The newspaper story about the Grammys contained a mention of this incident:

"A perplexed but unflappable Bob Dylan continued to sing 'Love Sick' while a man with 'Soy Bomb' painted across his bare chest gyrated beside him for 30 seconds . . .

"Organizers ejected the crasher. Outside, he identified himself . . . as a 'multigenre mastermind artist and budding superstar.'

"'Soy' is protein and life and energy, and 'bomb' is explosive and propulsive," he told the *New York Daily News.* "All art should be soy bombs."

What do you make of it, Walt, this poetry sung by the VISA and MasterCard generation? For them, war has shrunk to the size of a video game. The poverty of the Welfare State is a faint shadow of the grinding, killing poverty of the Depression. Racism, once a lethal poison without antidote, has lost much of its power to kill and maim.

So is it boredom that has spawned this narcissistic vulgarity? This make-believe Halloween "rage"? This short attention span? This class-clown, spoiled-brat ambition to shock and then snicker about it?

I hear America trying to sing, tin-eared, off-key and with no range. Without the vocabulary of beauty and the subtleties of romance. Even the '40s, which robbed so many of so much, couldn't do that kind of damage.

—March 2, 1998

Security has changed

In the early '60s, when the Federal Office Building went up at the foot of E. 9th Street, it soon became obvious that there were grave security problems.

The building was an aluminum finger sticking up into the winds that blew off Lake Erie. Its bulk changed the direction of these winds, which swirled around and dive-bombed pedestrians trying to cross the plaza.

At the time, the *Cleveland Press* had a marvelous Golden Age writer named Marie Daerr. Marie took good care of her geriatric readers, many of whom had to cross the Federal Office Building plaza to visit the Social Security office.

So she vigorously campaigned for a handrail to save them from the malevolent and capricious forces of nature. The rail was installed, and those of us who were Marie's admiring friends promptly christened it the "Marie Daerr Gale Rail."

That's an example of the kind of security problems public buildings faced in 1965. And an example of the kind of remedial measure that could solve them.

The other day, I had to visit the Federal Office Building. I hadn't been in it for a couple of years. Right inside the door, I encountered a metal detector, an X-ray machine, a conveyor belt for my car keys and Zippo and a cop.

"How long has this been going on?" I asked him.

"Since Oklahoma City," he said.

The winds have changed in 30 years.

The malevolent and capricious forces of nature now include crazed humans like Russell Eugene Weston, Jr., whose mad agenda claimed the lives of two brave policemen at the U.S. Capitol Building on Friday.

Weston detected the metal detector before it could detect him. So he stepped around it, drew his gun and opened fire. The question on the Sunday talk shows was whether security around the Capitol needs to be increased.

The answer, in cold, actuarial terms, depends on how many

Russell Eugene Weston Jr.'s are walking around out there. If, as I suspect, our nation has for years been going slowly crazy, it is likely there are more Westons on the fringe than there used to be.

If so, we don't need more metal detectors. We need more Weston detectors.

Weston's meandering journey toward Capitol murder did not exactly pass unnoticed. It is too early for much of his biography to have emerged. But the highlights that have been harvested are chilling.

In 1996, according to a *New York Times* report, Weston was diagnosed as a paranoid schizophrenic and involuntarily placed in a mental hospital. This commitment must have worked wonders for him. Five weeks later, psychiatrists released him, saying he was "no longer a threat to himself or others."

He was supposed to visit a mental health center. Nobody is sure if he did. But the people he came in contact with, as he shuttled back and forth between Montana and Illinois, could hardly have been impressed with his emotional stability.

In Montana, he thought a neighbor's satellite dish was bombarding his mind with manipulative messages from the government. In Illinois, his father threw him out of the house about a week ago after he shot 16 cats with a .22-caliber rifle.

Weston was a man who attracted notice. His rantings brought him to the attention of the Secret Service, which two years ago, put him in the presidential protective file. But if the Secret Service had to follow every nut case in America around, it would have to swell its ranks to the size of the Chinese army.

When children began shooting their classmates on playgrounds, students were begged to immediately report any strange behavior of their fellow students to authorities. Killing and torturing small animals, we were told, was a dead giveaway to impending violence.

But the people who encountered Weston—psychiatrists, neighbors, his father—seemed inclined just to wash their hands of him. Maybe that's a normal response. And maybe it's a response America can't afford anymore.

It would be hard to convince a person of 30 that once there

were no metal detectors in federal buildings. Or in high schools. And that there was a time when you could buy a ticket and board an airplane without an electronic body frisk and an X-ray of Grandma's pocketbook.

Now, metal detectors are a way of life. They are getting more sophisticated and efficient and common all the time.

But they couldn't stop Weston from murdering two cops. Only a Weston detector could have done that. He arrived at the door of the Capitol with his pistol concealed. But for two years, his madness had been an open book.

And nobody hit the buzzer.

—July 27, 1998

....

Trojan offers concertgoers a nightcap

I needed a lift. And the woman on the telephone supplied one. Apparently you don't have to be as old as I am to be startled by the Shock of the New.

"I'm younger than you," she said. "And I'm no prude. The other night I took my kids to a rock concert at Blossom Music Center.

"We went to see the Dave Matthews Band. It's not extreme or hard rock. It's kind of middle-of-the-road, in case you didn't know."

(That was thoughtful of her. Of course I didn't know. To me, it's all been noise since Elvis.)

"Anyway," she said, "my kids and I were leaving the concert when all of a sudden this guy comes up to me with something in his hand. He offered it to me and I reached out and took it. It was a condom. A Trojan.

"I looked around and saw other people doing the same thing. I couldn't believe my eyes. They are passing out condoms at Blossom like after-dinner mints. Doesn't that shock you?"

No.

But only because nothing does anymore. My shocks are worn out. Too many bumps on the rutted road of cultural life leading to that bridge to the 21st century. No place to make a U-turn, either.

There was one glimmer of hope. Maybe the lady was putting me on. So I called David Carlucci, the general manager of Blossom. And the glimmer went out.

"We have a sponsorship relationship with the Trojan Co.," Carlucci said.

"For some concerts, they come in and set up little tents. Nothing too extreme. I mean, they don't have inflated condoms flapping around like balloons or anything like that."

Carlucci said some discretion is used in the selection of condom nights.

"We wouldn't have them at a Spice Girls concert, for instance," he said.

"Why?" I asked.

"The audience is too young," he said. "We pick concerts when the audience is older. The next condom night is, let me see, Pearl Jam."

"How about when the Cleveland Orchestra is playing?" I asked. "Would you have a condom night if the orchestra was playing Ravel's *Daphnis et Chloe Suite*? That always gets my juices going.'

But Carlucci explained that classical-music audiences don't get condom nights. Which certainly seems like a form of sexual discrimination to me. Not to mention reverse-snobbism and lack of libido diversity.

My mind wandered to a wonderful summer night shortly after Blossom opened. I pictured George Szell, his lip thrust out in a scowl, leading the orchestra through a soaring performance of "Prelude and Love-Death" from *Tristan and Isolde*. And there, in the background, gently wafting in the breeze, I tried to imagine the filmy tent flaps of the company that makes Trojans, waiting to supply each euphoric customer with a nightcap.

"Isn't it a little . . . tacky?" I asked Carlucci.

He explained that, as a parent himself, he felt that condom

night was an expression of concern for the well-being of concertgoers.

Then I asked him if Blossom would express such concern if it wasn't getting a big hunk of dough from the Trojan people. And how much dough was Blossom getting, by the way? He said that he was not at liberty to say.

We parted civilly. And I guess, within the madness of our culture, it all makes sense. After all, sporting-goods companies spend hefty sums to be the "official shoe" of the Olympics or beverage companies the "official drink" of some golf tournament.

Considering the kind of sporting activities encouraged by the music of the MTV generation, it's probably good marketing to be the "official condom" of Blossom Music Center.

But I share the feelings of the woman who phoned me. Once, we thought we had some idea of the fitness of things. Do's and don'ts. The appropriate and the obscene.

Now, the outrageous is gradually becoming the norm. The previously unthinkable regularly arrives in our midst. It broaches our flimsy defense with stealth and cunning. Like a . . . like a . . .

Trojan horse, huh?

—August 14, 1998

Generations

....

Nixon took us where we are

At a funeral, you cry for yourself. You cry because all life is mortal and the proof is there in front of you.

You cry because the man going into the ground is taking a span of time with him. And the time he's taking belongs to you, too. And you won't get it back, either.

There is an America, dim in my memory, that is gone now. It was an America handed to me at 21 like an heirloom. The way you might be handed your grandfather's watch. At the time, it seemed a thing of substance like a watch. It seemed like a thing that would last. But it didn't last. It disappeared almost as soon as I got it.

If you didn't live it, it's hard to imagine how fast it went. The speed of its departure was especially startling to those of us who graduated from high school between, say, 1950 and 1963. We were the generation that America had ripened for. We were supposed to live the great third act.

Our fathers and older brothers survived the Depression and won the war. Then they came back and claimed the fruits of victory. They sold the old houses and moved to the suburbs and discovered charcoal briquettes and power lawn mowers. They read Dr. Spock and passed school levies and eased their children through mild adolescent rebellions involving Elvis and James Dean.

They took us down to Richman's or Sherman's or Bartunek's and bought us blue blazers and striped ties. And sent us off to state schools to be the first college graduates in the family. And on Graduation Day, we were handed the keys to America. We married girls who were English majors or had education degrees. And we set out to keep the whole thing going.

It was supposed to be a caretaker job. Water the patriotism

and the liberty. Honor the flag and the sacred traditions. Say your prayers and save your money and America will provide for you. That's what they told us and that's what we believed.

Well, it vanished like Pompeii. Ten years and it was gone, that America they said would last us a lifetime. Kennedy was assassinated and we said it wasn't possible. Martin Luther King and Bobby were assassinated and then we knew it was possible and always would be. Fifty thousand of us, raised on John Wayne movies, died in a war so dirty not even Hollywood would touch it. The ones lucky enough to get back were welcomed with spit. We were now a nation that shot our leaders and spat at our soldiers.

In the South, we were blowing up black children in church because their parents claimed they were Americans, too. Out in the new, white suburbs, our idea of black America had been Nat King Cole and Louie Armstrong. Now H. Rap Brown was in our living room, yelling "Kill the pigs." Everywhere we looked, there was killing or talk of it.

At college, the kid brother trashed the blazer and bought a field jacket at the surplus store. He copulated on a blanket under the old campus elms. He smoked dope and tripped on acid. He burned down the ROTC building, wearing a second-hand uniform with stripes on the sleeve that had belonged to a sergeant who waded ashore at Inchon.

Johnson got out while the getting was good. Somebody shot Bobby in the head and Humphrey's slap-happy Rotarian good humor was preposterous against a backdrop of burning cities and television pictures of napalmed children. We were killing kids who looked like the children in "The King and I." But by now our nerves were numb and we were in a trance.

Nixon came back through a crack in the world and walked past the chaos into the White House. He bombed Cambodia. The National Guard opened fire at Kent State. Dr. Spock had followed his children from their playpens to their protest rallies. But there was no chapter in his book about making the baby bulletproof. Four of his children died. Blood was trickling in from everywhere and collecting in pools.

Harry Truman died. But by now he seemed a relic from a civilization so long vanished he might have been a pharaoh.

Nixon's shady and sour vice president resigned after cutting a deal to evade charges of taking illegal kickbacks. And finally, Nixon himself became the first president in the history of the country to leave office in disgrace. For covering up a bungled burglary inspired by paranoia and dirty politics.

All of this in 10 years.

Nixon is the last of them to go into the ground. Speaking personally, I can say that they sure showed me something—the men at the helm of America in my formative young-adult years.

When I was 25, JFK was murdered. When I was 29, I found myself passing a pipe between a Hell's Angel and a hippie in Haight-Ashbury. At 30, I rode a chopper up to Dong Ha and prayed the weather would stay lousy so I wouldn't have to land at Con Thien, where it was raining mortar rounds on Spock's children.

The next summer, I ran from Daley's cops in Chicago, who were hitting anybody with a press pass. In May of '70, I walked through the battlefield at Kent State the night of the shootings and felt the chilly presence of ghosts who had been kids hours before. A helicopter with a searchlight chased me away. The sound of choppers was the sound of death then.

In '72, I smoked dope (and inhaled) with a tent full of Vietnam Vets Against the War. That was in Miami, where they were handing Nixon his second term. By then, I had no idea who I was or what America was. And neither, it turned out, did Nixon.

It's been 20 years since he was driven from office. And we have not been able to invent a new America to replace the old one. He is the last of the men who took us from there to here, wherever here is. A lot of us will pause today to ask how we got so far from where we were. We have no answers. Soon we won't even be able to see our footprints. That's when you cry.

April 27, 1994

The stink of greed

My mother remembers a kid in the old neighborhood named Steve Sundra. He grew up to pitch for the Yankees. If you look him up in the Baseball Encyclopedia, you will see that he was no Cy Young. But he was fast enough to earn the nickname "Smokey." On the block, though, he was called Mrs. Sundra's kid.

In the off-season, he pumped gas at the corner filling station to make a little extra money. If he had an investment portfolio, he never mentioned it. This was around E. 93rd St. and Union Ave., where an investment portfolio, like the Grand Canyon, was something many had heard of but few had seen.

Mrs. Sundra's kid was an idol to what would now be called the inner-city youth. They could go over to the gas station and watch him change oil. They could say "Hi" to him, and he would say "Hi" back. He was not insulated behind walls of capitalism like the millionaire players of today. He was real, and he brought back change with grease on his hands.

When I was a kid, Early Wynn lived in a shabby apartment at the corner of Scottsdale Blvd. and Lee Rd. It was the kind of building today's Yuppie couple would think uninhabitable. The apartment was next to a vacant lot where we played ball. Wynn would lean through his window in an undershirt and throw us scuffed baseballs and cracked bats.

This dismayed Mrs. Pressman, who lived next to the ball field. We tried to mollify her by making it an automatic out if you hit her bedroom window. We thought this gesture magnanimous. It wasn't our fault she lived in left field. But if she appreciated it, she thoroughly hid her feelings. "I'll call the cops," she would yell.

It was to escape the cops that we built the ball field. It was a diamond in the rough, with a backstop made of tree trunks and chicken wire. Before we built it, we used the street. A sewer opening was first base. Second was a flattened garbage can lid and third was a fireplug. The plate was a real plate—a 1946 license plate from somebody's father's Ford.

But some neighbor was always calling the cops. The police

car was 422. It kept breaking into the game like a beer commercial. You'd have two strikes on you and a man on second in the third game of a triple-header. "Heads-up," somebody would yell. That meant a car was coming. "Oh-oh," somebody else would yell. "It's 422."

Slowly, 422 would coast up to us. "Gowan, you kids. Get outta the street," the cops inside would yell. We would retreat to a driveway and wait. We knew 422's habits by heart. We knew 422 would circle around the block and come back to make sure we hadn't started playing again. Then it would leave for good and we could get back to the game. That's the way it always happened. It drove the neighbors nuts.

Tris Speaker lived in a fancy house way up the street. A fancy house was a house where you didn't eat supper in the kitchen. Sometimes we would go up and stare at Speaker's house. If you wanted to get a look at him, you stepped on his grass. If he was home, he would fly out and yell at you. "That's Tris Speaker screaming at us," you would tell a new kid as you ran away. "He's in the Hall of Fame."

One year, Jim Hegan lived in a little house on Glendale Ave. a couple of streets away. It was the kind of house where you did eat in the kitchen. Once, I took a brand-new baseball, still smelling of the paddock, over to Hegan's house. He was in his little front yard raking leaves. This amazed me. Jim Hegan, raking leaves! Just like a human being!

All I had brought was the stub of a pencil. He put down his rake and signed the ball. He gave me a pitying look. "It will fade," he said. "Yes sir," I said. I knew it would, but so what. He was writing on my heart.

Some year, when I wasn't paying any attention, kids stopped playing baseball in the street. Little League was formed and something called T-ball. In the old days, if you couldn't hit, you couldn't hit. If you were too little, you were too little. You waited. When you were big enough, you played, but they chose you last. You sweated it out while the big boys chose up sides, hand over hand, on a bat. Whoever got stuck with you put you in right field where, if things went well, you could just stand there.

Now it's all slick. Playgrounds and leagues and coaches. Real bases. Home plates without license numbers on them. Uniforms and aluminum bats. No cruelty. No sexism. No yelling "Hey, kid, you throw like a girl!" Everybody has rights. It is all as smooth and well-run as General Electric. Corporate and capitalistic. A business.

We like to pretend we are a partner in this business, but we're not. We like to imagine that we've bought in with our money and with our memories. Maybe we can't hit, and maybe we can't field, but we furnish all the magic of baseball's yesterdays—all the sweet nostalgia that makes the game mythological. We bring love and all we ask is to be loved back. Or at least respected. Or, at the very least, not humiliated.

But now that's asking too much. We may be dumb, and we may be sentimental, but we've got a sense of smell. They can spray perfume on greed and call it a virtue, but we know the stink of greed because we've smelled it before. We used to smell it in the old working-class neighborhood, coming off the millionaire capitalists who held us in contempt. Now baseball smells that way. It smells the way America always smells when it starts to go bad. Greed and contempt. You can't deodorize them.

It's still our game, though. Better men in better days autographed our hearts. As far as I'm concerned, the guys who walked out today couldn't carry Steve Sundra's glove.

August 12, 1994

Shut out

The day I retired from organized baseball was a soft day in the month of June. The precise year does not come back to me, but I remember the exact sky of my retirement day. It was a sky the color of June Allyson's eyes, which, as some of you well know, were a very deep blue.

Clouds as white as clean soapsuds floated in the blue bowl of that sky. Everything was pure that day—even the dirt on the ball diamond was clean dirt. So were the brand-new T-shirts we were handed to wear. Yellow shirts with the words "Fisher Food—News" across the chest in navy blue.

When my friends and I pulled these shirts over our heads, we were, for the first time in our lives, in baseball uniforms. Abbreviated though they were, we felt as snazzily and completely dressed as tuxedo-clad ushers at a society wedding.

The writing on the T-shirts did not interest us. Fisher Foods was only a grocery store and the News was only a newspaper. The sandlot league name of our team was the Dale Mitchells. That was the relevant and exciting fact. For Mitchell was a hero, described by Jimmy Dudley as the "fleet-footed, left-fielder lead-off man" of the Cleveland Indians.

Until this day we had been mere street players. Our bases were sewer entrances and garbage can lids. Now we stood on a real baseball diamond off Miles Avenue near Lee Road. The Erie tracks ran along the edge of this diamond, and passengers on their way to Hoboken could be seen eating in the dining car as the trains made their scheduled journeys through the timeless landscape of our youth.

Word had spread among us that the Dale Mitchells were holding tryouts, so we slipped our gloves over the handlebars of our bicycles and nervously joined the pilgrimage that other kids from other neighborhoods were making. We were met by a full-grown man who displayed an enviable, cocksure, slightly exasperated adult nonchalance. He said his name was Duke. Thinking back on him, he was probably about 19.

Duke waved the crowd of us into the bristling crabgrass of the outfield. Then he picked up a bat and hit us pop flies. We had never seen balls gain such altitude anywhere but at the Stadium. We staggered beneath them, peering into the June Allyson sky, stumbling over our own feet like drunks in a back yard looking at an airplane. We made last-minute lunges as the balls dropped in front of us. Some of us were successful. The rest of us felt shame.

Then Duke pitched to us. We had never been close to a well-thrown ball. At Indians games, we had heard a baseball slap into

Jim Hegan's mitt. But we had never before heard one sizzle and sing as it approached us. Some of us hit Duke's pitches. Some of us could merely wave our bats frantically while scrambling out of their path.

At the end of the morning, Duke pointed at a few of us. They were now Dale Mitchells. The rest of us were excused. We were out of organized baseball. One ego-shattering morning was our whole career. Never again would baseball be a dream we owned. It belonged to other people and we could only watch them. It was necessary for us to pick something else to do with our lives. Some second-class dream to dream.

Now I know that, bitter as that moment seemed, it was a lucky one for me. My obvious ineptitude had saved me from one of life's great sadnesses. I was blessed by being lousy. I had escaped the chronic agony of being pretty good but not good enough. I was saved from the curse of having sufficient skill to hope, but not enough to succeed.

This week, that curse laid a rough hand on hundreds of replacement baseball players. Baseball used these men as pawns in a Monopoly game, then said goodbye to them. Some will wander back to the lesser kingdoms of the minors. Others will go back to selling shoes or fighting fires. Men who were good enough to hit one-for-four will again change oil for a living, replaced by men who can hit one-for-three-and-a-half.

The baseball they played looked pretty good in the televised spring training games. They were playing for their hearts, not their wallets, and that lent magic to the enterprise. There were pitchers among them who could have got the bases-loaded strikeout. There were batters who could have slapped the tie-breaking hit in the ninth.

They came as close as possible to making reality out of yearning, on clean dirt beneath soapsud skies. And it would have been nice if they could have played in one real game that went into the record books. It might have been the purest game in a season that will begin still fouled by the stale stench of last year's greed.

Reality arrives for everybody sooner or later. The last time I saw Dale Mitchell at bat was during a World Series when Don

Larson needed one more out for a perfect game. The Dodgers sent up Mitchell and Larson overwhelmed him with reality. Mitchell always swore that third strike was a ball, and it probably was. When things start to go, they really go.

But for my sentimental soul, reality came too soon for the replacement players—the boys of spring who were forbidden to enter summer. The people who own the game will say that baseball was too good for them. Just as Duke, with a sneer, once indicated that baseball was too good for me.

Strange that now, all these years later, it doesn't seem good enough.

—April 5, 1995

Hiroshima revisited

Twenty years ago, I was traveling through Japan with the Cleveland Orchestra. Pushed by an irresistible impulse, I left the tour, flew alone to Hiroshima and checked into the Hiroshima Grand Hotel.

It is hard to convey to a fresh generation the impact the word "Hiroshima" had on people my age—people too young to have fought in World War II, but old enough to have experienced the spin-off effect it had on our lives.

Mr. Maver, the affable man next door, became an air-raid warden and patrolled the block in a hard hat at night, looking for slivers of light treasonously escaping beneath carelessly pulled window shades. Fathers, uncles and cousins were missing from family gatherings. Telegrams came. People wept with grief or with joy. Santa Claus left bugles, wooden rifles, and little B-29s under the tree at Christmas. He, like Mr. Maver, had joined the war effort.

When our working mothers tried to get steak or butter, store merchants would cock an eyebrow and say, "What's the matter, lady? Don't you know there's a war on?" It was the perfect squelch. It shut you up on the spot. There was a war on and we all knew it. We would do whatever it took to win it, and if silk stockings were a fighting tool, then silk stockings would be employed.

We had few doubts that we would win the war. The question was when, and at what cost. In the dark of the Shaker Theater, or the Fairmount, we could see newsreels of our dead Marines rolling in the surf and hear an announcer speak in tones of astonished disgust about Japanese who launched suicide charges or killed themselves in caves rather than give up.

Then one night on the movie screen we got our first look at the giant mushroom from the ultimate victory garden in Los Alamos. The mushroom grew and grew on the screen, but the music that went with it was not a victory march. The newsreel people had chosen music usually reserved for horrible inhuman disasters—hurricanes, floods, volcanic eruptions. For this was a Frankenstein mushroom. Men had concocted a formula and uttered an incantation and brought this Thing into the world, and we knew from the first that the Thing was more powerful than the men who had created it. That it was the Thing that was to be feared now.

The Thing had a name. It was called Hiroshima.

The waiter in the rooftop restaurant in the Hiroshima Grand Hotel was friendly and eager to please. In the kitchen, the chef made a valiant attempt to create a hamburger from my description, for I had grown tired of weeks of curry and prawns. But it was a terrible hamburger. The Japanese talent for mimicry was channeled in the direction of automobiles and television sets. Sandwiches were unimportant. There was a trade war on.

The next morning, I walked through a city where nothing was old except the broken eggshell dome of a single pre-Bomb building. I was the only Westerner in the crowds of people touring the museum built to capture glimpses of the nightmare of the bombing. It was quiet in there. With scores of uniformed Japanese schoolchildren, I pressed my nose to the glass case behind which dimly lighted mannequins shuffled with skin hanging from their arms and backs. There was the slab of stone with the silhouette of a woman etched in it at the moment of her vaporization. And there was the half-melted wristwatch, its hands forever stopped at the moment the Bomb exploded.

If you want to know whether, in that place and in that company, I felt guilty, the answer is yes. That is my honest answer, but it's only half an answer. It is the half that history revisionists have seized in order to peddle their arguments that the Bomb never should have been dropped.

The history revisionists have stolen the watch from the glass case and set its hands forward 50 years. With the smugness of hindsight, and banking on the current dogma that America is always the villain, they have selectively picked snippets of interviews and used them to buttress flimsy theories. To sell books. Or advance an agenda.

Their indictments of America have rained down on us all year. And all of them are flawed. When the watch in that glass case stopped, the Japanese had not surrendered. The war cabinet was still arguing over terms. The emperor had not intervened. Generals were still preparing for a suicidal defense of the home islands. Anything that might have happened to change any of that had not happened.

And there was a war on. The second-guessers don't know there was a war on. There wasn't a seminar on. Not a doctoral examination where interesting theories get patient and friendly evaluation. There was a war on, and we were out to win it, just like Japan was. With whatever it took. We had the Bomb, they had kamikazes. Advantage us.

My guilt in the Hiroshima chamber of horrors was not American guilt. It was the shame I felt as a human being that we haven't learned that modern wars, once begun, obey no niceties, spare no innocents, stop for no theories, shrink from no prejudices. Wars are born in the minds of men, but wars are beasts that turn on their creators.

Old soldiers know this. Those who pretend otherwise are the warmongers. There are old men alive today who might have died in their youth of a half-baked theory. They know what time it was.

—August 7, 1995

The old men's war

And now the old men have had their final parade. Grandpa is just Grandpa again, not the turret gunner who spent the summer of his nineteenth year searching the sun for fighters over Germany. Or lying on the sand of a beach with no lifeguards.

World War II has taken its curtain call. Now the historians can claim the living truth of it, to bend and shape according to their will and whim.

America is no longer a country where the young listen to the old. The old of our land are segregated now. They are gently steered into a culture of Medicare and mall-walking and square dances at the senior center and package tours of Amish country.

Once, the young sat on front porches and heard the old tell of how things were. We listened to Grandpa talking through the twilight and learned history from his story. And a chain of remembrance grew, with each new generation a link.

"Poor Cousin Dave came back from the war with an arm off," my grandmother told me one day. The war she meant was the Civil War.

"The South used poisoned bullets, you know," she said sternly. She was repeating something that the old man had told her when she was a little girl. He could not or would not describe the red-aproned field surgeons and the instant amputations and the piles of limbs outside the tent. Better to blame the loss of an arm on the notion of an enemy's treachery than the split-second decision of a doctor in a hurry.

As an old woman, she handed me the story of Cousin Dave, and when I handed it to my children (adding the surgical footnote), a chain of 130 years was complete.

It is sad to see an old man with a story to tell and no one to listen. Thirty years ago, I was sent to the Old Soldiers Home in Sandusky to interview its last surviving veteran of the Spanish-American War. "The damn fools put the horses on a different boat," he told me. "All the horses was drowned and we had to fight on foot in them hot uniforms."

I took it down. To my shame, I think I portrayed him as quaint and faintly amusing. That is how the young so often treat the old and their stories. The young look into the old faces—wrinkled, toothless, hairless. And the young make a colossal mistake. "That's not me," they say. But it is.

On his deathbed, his voice a sandpaper whisper, my uncle's father urgently wanted to tell me about his life in the German army in World War I. He talked of predawn breakfast fires and black bread and coffee. But then he stopped. His eyes had found an icicle growing outside the hospice window. A nun went out and climbed up and broke it off and brought it to him to cool his burning throat. He spoke no more that day, and no more to me ever.

In the past year, our lives have been enriched by the stories of the old men of World War II. "These are the boys of Pointe du Hoc," a president told us on the beach in Normandy. As the camera scanned their faces, we saw that it was true. They were boys forced to wear the masquerade of age. As someday we would be.

They took our hands and we passed through a half-century of time as easily as ghosts pass through a wall, and we were with them in the landing craft and on the decks of the destroyers and in the mud of France, the mountains of Italy, the skies over Japan. They paused often and beckoned to graves beneath white crosses and made the dead come forth. And the dead wore the faces of boys and laughed at the old men and said, "Why, look what's happened to you."

Today brings us to the final page of their story's final chapter. Fifty years ago today, every horn and whistle in this city blew wildly. People rushed from their houses and went downtown just to be with as many other people as they could find. Church bells rang and churches opened for prayers of thanksgiving. And some people said, "Don't you think somebody ought to go over and be with Mrs. Smith? This must be very hard on her."

I was only 7, but I remember these things. It took 50 more years for me to understand that fifty years is nothing. Now my mirror tells me that age is an illusion and I know that Cousin Dave and my uncle's father and the men at Normandy were all just boys, and when we think of them, we should think "That is me." And we should listen.

—August 14, 1995

Underwear creep

Our mothers were right. They warned us never to leave the house without wearing clean underwear. That way, if we got hit by a streetcar, our underwear would not embarrass us in the emergency room:

"How is he, doctor?"

"I'm afraid it's going to be nip and tuck, Mrs. Feagler. The one hopeful sign is the condition of his underwear, which is immaculate. You have a lot to be thankful for there."

Underwear counts, as the Shaw High School track team discovered last week. The team was temporarily disqualified from a regional meet when some of the runners allowed their underwear to slip below the bottom of their shorts.

An eagle-eyed referee spotted it. "I see England, I see France, I see Shaw High's underpants," the referee shouted. Or words to that effect.

But worse than the fact that the underwear showed was that what showed didn't match. Two of the runners were wearing white underwear while a third was wearing gray underwear. This undermined an ironclad rule of sartorial uniformity.

It looked as if athletes might have to start telephoning each other before a meet to synchronize their crotches.

"Hi, Bill. I just wanted to let you know I'm planning to wear my Calvin Klein, midnight blue 'Nuit d' Amour' briefs to the track meet today. What are you wearing?"

"Gee, Bob, I'm glad you called. I was going to wear my pink boxers with the little smiley faces on them. But I better change or we'll clash in the dash."

Having chronicled America's youth during the era of streaking and the era of mooning, it is my opinion that too much underwear is better than too little or none. And these days, when youthful fashion encourages the poking of diamond studs through tongues and the stapling of metal rings through noses, a little glimpse of underwear hardly seems mentionable.

Common Pleas Judge Patricia Cleary agreed. She had to sort

out the controversy after lawyers for both sides filed their briefs. She gave the matter short shrift and decreed that the Shaw High team would be allowed to compete in the regional meet after all. This made the athletes feel better. Put yourself in their . . . shoes.

Perhaps the referees feared that lax vigilance would lead to an outbreak of undesirable underwear-flaunting. They might have some cause for concern.

For some reason, the makers of men's underwear have started printing their names in big letters around the waistband of their product. Climb into a pair of such underwear and the brand name repeats itself as it circumnavigates your middle like a beer ad stuttering its way around the Goodyear Blimp.

Why this fad caught on, I can't imagine. Men in locker rooms do not, as a rule, stand around perusing other men's underwear. In my circles, even mild curiosity is considered inappropriate. Men do not pad across the lockerroom floor to say:

"Excuse me, but I see you bought some Ralph Laurens. What kind of mileage are you getting out of them?"

I have room around my middle for Ralph Lauren's signature plus the genealogy of the entire Lauren family. But I always feel funny wearing clothes with somebody else's name on them. It puts me in an uneasy mental state somewhere between a derelict and a fetishist.

In the world of sports, however, athletes have become walking billboards for the manufacturers of various apparel. They endorse shoes, gloves, socks and warm-up suits. Former pitching great Jim Palmer once signed a lucrative contract to appear in a series of underwear ads. He posed off the field, but it is only a few short steps from there to the diamond.

So maybe the Shaw High referees feared that underwear creep might open the barn door to commercialism. Or maybe they just got carried away.

But let's not be too hard on them. They would probably do a fine job refereeing the Akron Zips.

—May 27, 1996

A *horse named Trigger*

Summer has stage fright. On Memorial Day, the kids in my old neighborhood wove crepe paper in their bicycle spokes and the high school band played summer's theme song. But summer hid in the wings, planning her miracles, and left us to celebrate with yesterday's warmed-over memories.

One summer day years ago—so long ago that Bob Lemon was pitching for the Indians and there were eight teams in each league and one of them was Brooklyn—a dusty truck pulling a horse trailer rattled down our street and turned in at the vacant lot where we played ball.

It was the sleepy part of the afternoon. Nobody was near the ball diamond. But, on our street, there was a kid telepathy that alerted us. So that soon after the truck pulled in, a half-dozen of us had come to investigate it.

We could only see the back end of the horse sticking out of the van. Occasionally, its tail would wave at us. But, as its head was aimed away from us, this seemed unreliable evidence of a greeting. The man in the truck ignored us, too. He took a small brown bottle from beneath the seat of his truck. He drank from the bottle and put it back. He opened the door and got out of the truck and stretched. He reached around and pulled the damp shirt away from his back. He walked around his battered rig and opened the gate of the horse van.

"Are you gonna take your horse out, mister?" one of us asked.

The man looked thoughtfully at the boy who had asked this. Then he spoke.

"One of you cowboys go get me a bucket of water," he said.

Four of us ran to get him a bucket of water.

When we came back with it, the horse was standing behind first base, staring somberly at the ground as if waiting for the grass to grow long enough to eat. The man was hunkered down on the shady side of the truck.

"Put the bucket down near the horse," he commanded. We did. The horse ignored it.

"Is it your horse, mister?" one of us asked. "Where are you

going with it?"

The man peered up at us. His red, sweaty face modeled a number of expressions. First he looked crafty, then amused. Then he displayed a look of astonishment and left it there.

"Do you mean to tell me," he said, "that none of you recognize that horse?"

We looked at the horse. We shook our heads no.

The man clapped his hand to his damp forehead.

"I don't believe this," he said. "Don't ya go to the movies?"

We nodded. We went to the movies just about every Saturday afternoon.

"Didn't ya ever hear of Trigger?" the man said. "Roy Rogers' horse, Trigger?"

Of course we had heard of Trigger.

"Well," said the man. He jerked his head in the direction of the horse, who was still staring wistfully at the ground. "That's him."

We regarded the horse with renewed interest. The horse was the right color to be Trigger. It was tan, with a mane and tail the color of twine. None of us knew much about horses. Half of us had never been this close to a horse before. All of us had a strong desire for this horse in our vacant lot to be Trigger. But there was something about the horse that undermined this desire.

"He looks skinnier'n Trigger," one of us said at last.

"That's the camera," the man said. "It's a well-known fact that the camera puts weight on you."

"He doesn't seem very smart," said another of us, speaking softly so the horse wouldn't hear. But the man heard and looked offended.

"He's tired, is all," the man said. "He's on vacation."

Then the man motioned us forward. We all took about two steps in his direction.

"I'm gonna take a chance on you boys," he said. "You brought me this water and all, so I'm going to tell you a show business secret. There's two Triggers, see? There's this one and another one. When one gets tired, they send it on a little vacation. They send a cowboy along to make sure nuttin' happens to it."

The horse and we listened to this with interest.

"You mean you're a real cowboy?" one of us asked.

"You ever hear of da Sons of da Pioneers?" the man asked. "Them guys who sing with Roy when he sings around the camp-fire?"

"You mean you're one of the Sons of the Pioneers?" another of us asked.

The man shook his head. "I'm an uncle," he said. Then he looked at us severely.

"Now listen good," he said. "Never tell nobody I told you this. We don't want the word getting around that there's more than one Trigger."

He took a final drink from his bottle and slowly got to his feet. He jerked the horse's head up and pushed the animal back in his van. He waved at us and pulled his truck away from first base and over the curb, and he drove off into the summer day.

That was nearly 50 years ago. Roy Rogers retired. The Dodgers left Brooklyn. They built a Hot Sauce Williams on the old ball field. Time changes things. It took me about 20 years to figure out that the Uncle of the Pioneers had probably just stopped for a snort on the way to Randall Race Track. And that's gone, too. But I don't know for sure. Some things you don't want to know for sure.

Wonderful things do happen on summer afternoons. We just have to be patient and wait.

—May 29, 1996

....

Thou shalt turn off the lights

In our house, we believed the Ten Commandments were OK as far as they went. But my father supplemented them by adding a couple of commandments of his own that he figured God had overlooked.

Thou Shalt Turn Off the Lights When Thou Leavest the Room was one of his big ones. The Book of Genesis tells us that God said, "Let there be light." Had my father collaborated in this event, he would have added, "But shut it off when you're through with it."

Dripping faucets were another thing that got his goat. If my father had been in charge of punishing the earth by sending a flood, he would have sent it a drip at a time through the faucets of sinners who neglected to promptly change their worn-out faucet washers.

It is my father's duty, when he comes to visit, to patrol the rooms of my house looking for signs of improper and wasteful maintenance. We will all be sitting around in the living room when suddenly someone will remark on his absence.

"Where's Dad?" my sister will say.

"Off on a reconnaissance mission," I will reply glumly.

And soon he will come wandering back.

"Your upstairs bathroom faucet is leaking," he will say. "Do you know how much water comes out of a dripping faucet in just one hour?" And he will regard me sternly as a Noah in a flannel shirt who tries to warn the unrighteous of impending watery doom.

If you were a Depression baby, some of this will have a familiar ring to you. A lot of kids were raised under the motto "waste not, want not." But those of us with Depression parents were taught that even "waste not" barely keeps you a half step ahead of pursuing calamity.

So it was with great glee that I tried to imagine a conversation between my father and Todd M. Schneider. Such a conversation will never take place. But if it could take place, I would love to be a fly on the wall, even if both men were armed with fly swatters.

Todd M. Schneider is the Cleveland Electric Illuminating Co. spokesman who is trying to persuade customers to use more electricity in order, he says, to save money on their electric bills. Schneider is paid to explain this idea to reporters. They couldn't pay him enough to get him to explain it to my father. I envision the following conversation in Todd M. Schneider's office:

T.M.S: "Mr. Feagler, might I have a moment of your time to acquaint you with the advantages of our new program, which we call '2002 Energy and Beyond'?"

"And beyond what?"

T.M.S.: "Well, er, and beyond energy. This program is about more than just energy, Mr. Feagler. This program is about getting points for the energy you use. The more you use, the more points you get."

"In other words, you want to bribe me to waste electricity?"

"Oh, no. You wouldn't be wasting it, Mr. Feagler. In a way, you'd be investing it. The more electricity you use, the more points you get toward the purchase of items for your home."

"In other words, you want to bribe me with my own money to waste electricity. You must think I'm a pretty dim bulb, Sparky."

"This isn't bribery, Mr. Feagler. It's an incentive to help you wisely select the new items we recommend."

"What kind of items?"

"Electrical items, Mr. Feagler."

"In other words, if I waste electricity, I get points. If I get enough points, you'll sell me an appliance I don't need. That way, I'll be wasting more electricity, which will give me more points. Then you'll sell me another appliance I don't need. This keeps up until I can't pay the bill anymore and you turn off the juice, right?"

"No, Mr. Feagler. You're missing a major point. The electrical appliances we'd be selling you would be energy efficient. So, you see, you'd be saving both energy and money by using them."

"In other words, if I burn electricity I don't need, you'll reward me by selling me an item I don't want. But I'll get the item I don't want at a discount. Then, if I plug in the item I don't want, I'll be wasting even more electricity, but now I'll be wasting it in an energy-efficient way."

"Well, that's not quite the way we put it in '2002 Energy and Beyond.'"

"Now I know what the 'Beyond' stands for. It stands for Beyond Belief. Say, are we through in here now?"

"I suppose so, Mr. Feagler."

"THEN TURN OFF THE LIGHTS!"

—July 1, 1996

Ghosts of Grant Park

Last night, in the pretty twilight, I took a walk on haunted ground.

The sun was sliding slowly out of the day like a guest reluctant to leave a party. Lake Michigan, bluer than our lake, was the color of bright ink. I waited until exactly 7 p.m., Chicago time. Then I stepped off into the summer evening and crossed into the misty, distant time zone of memory.

Twenty-eight years ago—almost to the day, almost to the hour—America cracked at the seams in this city. You've seen it in all the old film clips. Taunting kids running from grim, blue-helmeted Chicago cops. Clubs swinging, tear gas, bloody faces.

I'm in that movie somewhere. I appear, in a bit part, as a young man just turned 30. A cocky kid with a press pass dangling around his neck who, when the day faded to darkness, had lost his cockiness and thrown away the pass. For by then, the press had become the enemy, and press cards were bull's-eyes for billy clubs.

Last night, I walked in that kid's footsteps. But this time, I was cunningly disguised as a portly 58-year-old man with a bad back, limping along in his Rockports. Such people are invisible, especially to the young.

And Grant Park was full of the new breed of young in their baggy pants, with their hats turned around backward, looking harmless and cute in a grotesque sort of way.

These '90s young had set up booths that advertised tie-dyed shirts for sale. "Size XXXXLG," a sign proclaimed, aimed at a market of nostalgic, middle-aged pilgrims. A rock band thumped away on the stage of the band shell. A spritz of marijuana floated past.

Grant Park was where it all began 28 years ago. A war protester hauled down an American flag and tried to attach a Viet Cong flag to the park's flagpole. The cops—angry, hot, tired, outraged—waded into the thousands of us.

They threw tear gas first, but the demonstrators threw it back.

Then they charged. That was when the clubbing started, and it continued the rest of the day.

History indelibly records that these demonstrators were all long-haired hippies. Draft dodgers. Dope smokers. History lies. There were prim clergymen among them and professors and housewives from places like Rocky River and Cleveland Heights who had ridden in on buses to protest a war they believed was destroying America.

As they marched through the streets, they yelled, "Join us! Join us!" And many of Chicago's citizens stepped off the sidewalks and did just that. So when, in the gathering dusk, the crowd was blocked in front of the Conrad Hilton Hotel, it was no one particular kind of American.

Then the police charged again, and this time we could tell that their anger had crazed them. There were no tactics in this charge. The demonstrators and others were caught in a kind of corral in front of the hotel with no avenue of retreat. The cops tore into this corral, clubbing people to the ground—protesters, tourists, hotel guests, anybody who had the misfortune to be there.

There was a bar in the hotel called the Haymarket Saloon. Its plate-glass windows looked out onto the street. The agile young man I was playing at the time twisted like a matador and jumped aside just as the cops forced a wall of people through these windows, then followed them in, crunching across the broken glass and beating them still.

That's when a television truck pushed down the street like a tank, its flood lamps lighting the scene for the cameras. "The whole world is watching!" the hysterical demonstrators cried. And the cops hauled their prisoners away, and people came out and dragged off the wounded, and Michigan Avenue was littered with glass and eyeglasses and, here and there, a shoe or a purse. And I escaped without a scratch to think about it all.

* * *

It's called the Chicago Hilton & Tower now. The concierge had never heard of the Haymarket Saloon, but the guy next to him on the desk remembered. He pointed me toward a new bar called Lakeside Green, where the drinks come in pastel colors with names like you find on the sundaes at Baskin-Robbins.

I took a window table about 10 feet from the spot where I had frantically given the cops the slip all those years ago. I had taken my little walk back in time from Grant Park across Balbo Avenue and up to the spot where my idea of democracy changed and stayed changed.

I formed an opinion about our government back then that I have carried with me ever since. I carried it to San Diego two weeks ago, and I carry it into this week of platitudes and promises.

A lot of people think government is the cause of our problems. And some people think government is the answer to our problems. But I think government is the result of our problems. It only reflects them. If we are good, government is good. If we are lost, government mirrors our chaos.

We were lost in Chicago 28 years ago. In their frustration, Americans clubbed other Americans, and we are clubbing each other still. There were no great answers in San Diego, and there are none here, either. The answers are back home in our small and noble struggles toward an individual salvation. The rest is all pomp and show biz.

The young man who decided that 28 years ago hasn't changed his mind. In the park and on Michigan Avenue and then in the mirror over the bar, I looked for him. For one fraction of a second, I thought I saw him grinning at me. Then I headed back to the hotel, and where he went I'm not sure. But I think he's gone for good.

—August 26, 1996

Junior G-men

Oh, to be young again. The Clinton administration wants to use 12- to 15-year-old kids in sting operations to nab store owners who sell cigarettes to minors.

According to the plan, a junior G-man would belly up to the grocery counter and say, "Gimme a packa butts." Then, if the clerk complied, the kid would say, "OK, Lefty. The jig is up." Or, "Freeze!" Or whatever hip nab-ism is currently in vogue.

If I were still a kid, this would be right up my alley. Back in the days of Dole, I belonged to every kid law-enforcement agency that existed.

I was a member of the Captain Midnight Secret Squadron, the Tom Mix Rangers and the Sky King whatchamacallits. My dresser top was an arsenal of decoding whistles, periscopes with built-in magnifying glasses and glow-in-the-dark arrowheads with confused compasses set in them.

You could get into these organizations with no questions asked and no background checks required. It was as easy as becoming an Olympic security guard. All you had to do was drink lots of Ovaltine and save lots of cereal box tops.

You mailed these in and, an agonizing number of weeks later, a little brown package would arrive from Battle Creek, Mich., breakfast-food capital of the universe. Battle Creek supplied paramilitary hardware to kids on the same massive scale that the United States provides missiles to people like Saddam Hussein.

Every night you could dash home from school, run up to your bedroom and turn on the Philco. From 5 to 6 o'clock you could listen to the thrilling 15-minute adventures of your favorite crime-stopping hero. Then, at the end of the broadcast, an announcer would say:

"Now here's a special secret message in code, just for all you boys and girls who are members of Captain Midnight's Secret Squadron. Get out your decoding whistles and take this down. Here goes: 12-14-4-9-11-5 . . ."

You twisted the red decoding dial on the blue plastic whistle.

If you did it right, each number would translate to a letter of the alphabet, and the special secret message would begin to reveal itself:

"A-L-W-A-Y-S H-E-L-P M-O-M."

This was pretty tame stuff, even back then. The kids on the radio programs got messages instructing them to blow up bridges or run and get the sheriff. Captain Midnight never relied on us out in radioland for such things. In the war against evil, he left us on the home front, helping mom. Of course, back at headquarters in Battle Creek, that was vital work. It was mom who bought the breakfast cereal.

The problem back then was that there wasn't enough crime to go around. I know that seems preposterous now, but that's the way it was. What crime existed was handled by adults. There was no room for a kid, however eager, to get his hand in.

So I am envious of today's kids, who have been invited by the government to run entrapment operations against their neighborhood grocers. If a president had thought of such a thing back when I was a kid, there would have been something useful and patriotic for me to do.

At least twice a week, my mother would send me with a note over to Shultz's Grocery a block and a half away. There, Mrs. Shultz would give me a Tootsie Roll to chew while Mr. Shultz walked around his store with a big stick with a kind of claw on it that could reach canned goods down from the high shelves.

"Oh," I would say. "I almost forgot. My mom said to get her a pack of Chesterfields."

"Right," Mr. Shultz would say. "One pack of Chesterfields, coming up."

(Ah, but little do the Shultzes know that, only minutes before, I received a special coded message from the president of the United States, broadcast by Beavis and Butt-head. Translated on my plastic presidential decoding device shaped like a Big Mac, it said: "B-U-S-T S-H-U-L-T-Z-S G-R-O-C-E-R-Y.")

"OK, Shultz," I bark. "The jig is up! Put down that reaching stick and freeze!"

What a triumph. Mrs. Shultz dissolves in tears. Mr. Shultz quakes with fear. I spit my Tootsie Roll on the floor in contempt.

An American youth turned rat fink. Betraying his elders.

In the long march toward political correctness, kids can be useful in many ways. All they have to do is keep their little eyes and ears open and report back to authority. And occasionally set somebody up.

Back in my Secret Squadron days, we heard about governments that used kids like that. Except then, they were the bad guys.

—September 20, 1996

Smooch patrol

I tried to resist. I can't stop myself. I gotta add my two cents to the saga of Johnathan (Hot Lips) Prevette, the 6-year-old boy charged with sexual harassment for kissing a little girl on the cheek.

This travesty has been all over the talk shows. It's a talk-show host's dream. The front page of USA Today carried a three-column picture of Johnathan. Yeltsin got one column, astronaut Shannon Lucid got a half. "The Kiss That Shook the Nation," the "nation's newspaper" headlined. And they're right.

Enlisting in the furor embarrasses me. Why stop for this when we are trying to elect a president in six weeks? There is no sport in engaging in this goofiness. It is too easy. It is like shooting fish in a barrel. It is like taking candy from a baby. It is like taking ice cream from a little boy.

The P.C.-brainwashed zombies who run Johnathan's North Carolina school barred him from an ice-cream social for his act of smooch terrorism. Yesterday, a guy in Florida sent Johnathan a check for $100 for ice-cream reparations. Most of the country is rallying to the little boy's defense. But not all of it.

Somebody stuck a microphone under Patricia Ireland's nose. She's the president of the National Organization for Women. A reporter asked her how bad it was for a 6-year-old boy to kiss a lit-tle girl on the cheek. Perhaps uninvited, for at this writing, that part isn't clear.

Well, what do you think she said? Why, she said it's very bad, of course. "Boys who aren't taught to respect girls grow up to be workers at the Mitsubishi plant," she said.

This is a grim and terrible curse, but you have to have a fem-inist code book to understand it. Female workers at the Normal, Ill., Mitsubishi auto plant are suing the company for sexual harassment. NOW is in the vanguard of the action.

So I guess if you want to strike terror into a New Age kid's heart, you invoke the specter of Mitsubishi assembly lines. You don't say, "Stop doing that, Timmy, or your face will freeze that way!" You say, "Stop doing that, Timmy, or you'll end up in a Japanese auto plant!" And then you yell "Banzai!"

Can we say this issue has touched a chord? Ha! It has bruised more chords than a Jimi Hendrix solo. And you don't need me to tell you why, either. You're way ahead of me. That's why this musing is irrelevant.

Beneath the passionate posturing over little Johnathan's problematic pucker, there lies a deeper issue. The issue is this: Has America, in its zeal for agenda-groveling, gone too far?

And the answer to that is yes. Yes is the answer. Yes, yes, yes. I think that's clear enough. But yes, just in case.

To the agenda fascists, common sense is heresy. Anybody who uses it is a subversive. We are becoming a silly nation because the agenda manifestoes have replaced the old-fash-ioned sense of right and wrong.

Back in the horrible old days when common sense ruled, the matter of Johnathan's smooch would have been quietly handled by a teacher. Or by Johnathan's mother. Or by the little girl's mother and Johnathan's mother. It might have even been ignored. (Quick, somebody revive that female activist.)

But now it is an act of national significance, part of a history of sweatshops and chauvinism and tight corsets and wolf whis-tles and soul-withering Tupperware parties and worse. Without common sense, we have no compass. We don't know what's out-rageous and what isn't.

A couple of weeks ago in our town, TV news was aroused by the story of a male teacher at Waverly Elementary School who reportedly began wearing a dress to class.

He was, we heard, halfway en route to a sex change operation. But rather than waiting until his journey was concluded, he chose to model his trousseau early. And he requested that his students start addressing him as Ms. Vanessa Ward.

How long this continued was unclear. But children who daily beheld this metamorphosis told their parents, some of whom complained to school officials. But school officials, the reports told us, weren't sure what to do. How heavy-handed could they be about a teacher engaging in his right of sexual preference or two?

What bailed them out was the discovery that Ms. Vanessa Ward had neglected to renew his teaching certificate. So she was pedagoguely unfrocked, so to speak, and suspended.

We heard little more of this. The agenda fascists considered it far less egregious than a kiss on the cheek from a 6-year-old child. America is addlebrained and America knows it.

No wonder our kids are confused. Now somebody is going to have to explain to Johnathan just what he did wrong. And tell him that if, instead of stealing a kiss, he had demonstrated a condom, he might have made the honor role.

—September 27, 1996

....

How can I get SEX into this headline?

My copy of Newsweek came in the mail and the big headline on the cover said: "ADULTERY." Under that, a smaller headline said: "A new debate about the oldest sin."

I didn't go back and check the Bible, but the way I recall it, the oldest sin is disobedience to God. The second oldest is murder. There wasn't much opportunity for adultery in the Garden

of Eden, due to a shortage of third parties with which to trian-
gulate. Unless you count Eve's fooling around with the serpent
as adultery. But, since Adam was in on it, that was more of a
menage a trois.

There's nothing like a copy of *Newsweek* to set you to rumi-
nating about spiritual matters. This, however, was probably not
the magazine's intention. Having served a short stint in the magazine biz, I figure that *Newsweek* was looking for an eye-catch-
ing-but-printable word to put on the cover to help sell
magazines.

The absolutely favorite word is "SEX." Magazine editors sit
around in meetings and breathe oxygen to expand their brain
cells so they can figure out ways to get "SEX" on the cover of
their magazines.

The word "SEX," standing alone, is a hook without bait. A
trick of the trade is to put the word "new" in front of it. As in,
"The New Sexuality, Is It Changing America?" Then all you
have to do is find a reporter willing to go out and invent a new
sexuality. When he comes back with it, you decide whether you
want to claim it's changing America. If you don't, that's OK.
Questions posed in headlines are rarely answered in stories.

Newsweek promised a "new debate" about adultery. But what
the magazine really wanted to do was concoct a reason to run an
interview with Eileen McGann. She is the wife of Dick Morris.
Dick Morris is the Clinton campaign strategist who was fired
last month for sharing state secrets with a $200 hooker.

The "new debate" about adultery featured a Q and A with
McGann, the wronged wife, who (another headline said)
"speaks out about her pain and anger." Here is a little sample:

Newsweek: "What would you like to see happen now—for
your sake?"

McGann: "I would just like to have my privacy, which I'm
entitled to. I don't make my decisions in public and I don't feel
I owe anyone an explanation of what I do and why I do it."

A woman who makes an appointment to sit down with a
reporter from a national magazine and talk about her husband's
philandering is looking for privacy in all the wrong places. But
this is the way things are done now. Sin and shame are disposed

of by exposing them on talk shows where they are supposed to evaporate under the television lights like mud puddles in the sunshine.

So why am I telling you all this? I'm coming to that. See, I knew you were going to ask.

The same mail that brought *Newsweek* brought a copy of *Vanity Fair*. That magazine contains a long profile of Pamela Harriman, the U.S. ambassador to France. And let me tell you that Pamela Harriman is, and was, something else!

According to the profile, back in the late '30s and early '40s, Pamela Harriman committed adultery with the following list of personages:

The seventh Earl of Warwick. A steel manufacturer named Philip Dunn. Averell Harriman (whom she later married). Jock Whitney (who was married at the time to a former daughter-in-law of President Franklin D. Roosevelt). Edward R. Murrow. Maj. Gen. Fred Anderson (an American bomber commander). William Paley (head of CBS). And Henry Luce (head of *Time* Inc.).

This is a pretty full dance card. The names on it were household names 50 years ago, and some of them still are. In terms of box-office appeal, they leave Dick Morris and his $200 hooker in the shade.

But Pamela and her friends were operating under the rules of the old adultery. Under the old rules, you didn't polish off an adulterous affair with a press conference and a book contract.

The code for sinners back then was simple. If you did it, you didn't talk about it. If you talked about it, you probably weren't doing it. This didn't diminish the sin. But the sinner had the wisdom and propriety not to flaunt it.

Every new generation thinks it invented sex in all its forms. To older generations, this presumption is ridiculous. There is very little new about the games men and women play. What's new is all the blabbing about it. A magazine cover would call that The New Hypocrisy. Forced to choose, I'll take the old.

—September 30, 1996

Recast gender roles—this is the army today

Those of us who grew up on war movies remember the Hollywood infantry squad that was supposed to be a little mirror of America.

There was always the sweet-natured hillbilly private who played the harmonica all the time. War, to him, was just an opossum hunt. He even loved the taste of C rations.

"Ah don' know whut you fellas is complainin' about," he would say. "This is goo-ood."

Then there was always the street-smart wise guy from Brooklyn who palled around with the egghead college professor nicknamed Doc. They enjoyed chatting on landing barges while shells exploded in the ocean around them, spattering them with spray.

"Whassa name of dat book yer readin', Doc?"

"It's called *War and Peace*, Brooklyn."

"Brudder! Dat was close! . . . Hey, any dames in da book, Doc?"

"As a matter of fact, there are."

"Den it must not be about dis war, huh, Doc?"

The Army integrated and went off to Korea. This added some fresh faces to the all-American Hollywood squad. Now there was the black guy who saved the life of the Southerner who didn't like black guys—a new plot twist that used to drive my black friend Stanley nuts.

"Every time I see a black guy hook up with a white guy, I know the black guy is going to get killed saving the white guy's butt," Stanley complained. "That's so everybody can stand around and say what a great guy the black guy was after he's dead. Whenever one of those movies comes on TV, I'm in bed before the funeral."

Time marched on and so did the Army, to new wars large and small. Transistor radios replaced the harmonica as sources of foxhole music. Eggheads got deferments and stayed out of the all-volunteer Army. Many street-smart Brooklyn kids followed the Dodgers to Los Angeles. They don't make many movies about the all-American squad anymore. If they did, they would have to add a couple of newcomers to the roll call.

Now there would be a gay guy who, if you didn't ask, wouldn't tell. And there would be a woman, too. Her part is a little uncertain yet. It is still being written each day in the news headlines.

Sexual equality in the workplace is now one of the diversity ideals worth fighting for, like expansion baseball, Marysville-made Hondas and dad's apple pie. But the Army is not an ordinary workplace. The Army's workplace is a co-educational barracks full of healthy young people far from home. In such a setting, it is inevitable that Yankee Doodle will encounter hanky-panky and much, much worse.

If you ask any Army veteran my age or older, he will tell you, if he's honest, that he can't imagine a mixed-sex Army without mind-boggling problems and headaches. But the odds are, he won't be honest. Why run the risk of arrest by the political correctness police?

My Army days are behind me. I have no plans to go back, and the Army isn't desperate enough to want me. Sitting in the alumni section, I hope the Army works itself through its challenge of female inclusion. But it's shaping up to be one of the toughest campaigns ever fought in peacetime.

First came the allegation that female soldiers in alarming numbers are being raped by their drill instructors. Then, while the Army was investigating that outrage, a group of women came forward to say that they hadn't been raped at all and that their GI sex, if any, had been consensual. Love with the improper sergeant.

But even consensual sex is prohibited in the Army. It destroys discipline and morale. The Army can't run the risk of a sergeant saying, "I want three volunteers. You, you—not you, dear—and you!"

American women have already proved themselves heroes on the battlefield. All they want, they say, is to be treated like anybody else. How do you argue with that request? I don't know how, except to lamely say that it's easier said than done.

All through its history, each time the Army has dropped a barrier to integration, there have been those who predicted it just wouldn't work. And it always has. But the battle for integration of the sexes promises to be the most complex and messiest battle of all. This time, the Army is facing biological warfare.

In the meantime, the new squad is a mirror of the new America. An America where institutions and roles are changing, and nobody is quite sure who's what anymore.

—March 17, 1997

Who says pregnancy is only for the young?

The other day we learned that a 63-year-old woman had lied about her age and fooled a doctor into helping her have a baby. Her husband helped too, of course. It was one of those conceptions in a blender.

This raised the biggest rumpus since sheep-cloning. For 24 hours, the talk shows were predicting a dire outbreak of geriatric pregnancies. Then the fuss died down. This gave us time for sober reflection.

So I have reflected. And I concluded that 63 years old may be a little old to have a baby. The perfect age is probably 60.

It has always been wise to postpone a pregnancy until you are ready. And in today's society, it takes many women longer to get ready than it used to.

Consider the lifestyle of a not-atypical young woman of today. She graduates from high school and college, and then it's off to spend four years as a Marine fighter pilot. After that, it may be time to decide on a starter-career or a starter-marriage or both. These days, probably both.

Suppose the starter-marriage lasts a reasonably long time. Let's say seven years. After that, friends will begin to talk. "What on earth is keeping Heather and Scott together so long?" they will say. "Don't they know it's time for one of them to demand his or her own space in which to grow?"

So Heather and Scott, now in their early 30s, carefully divide the household goods and the vacation photos and seek fresh identities and new fulfillment.

This is a good time for Heather to work on her career and her rock-hard abs. A trip to Pier 1 Imports will furnish her new apartment in a spare but tasteful manner. She will learn the secrets of making nice bookshelves from planks and cement blocks. She will turn her attention to her executive life.

Time to jettison that starter-career and look for something more challenging. The life of a consultant, perhaps. That way she can work out of her home. Over to OfficeMax, where she learns that while she was mired in her old job, the word "office" has become a verb. "We have everything you'll need to success-fully office," a sales representative tells her. And home she goes with enough electronic equipment to furnish the space station Mir.

It's also time to explore new relationships. But here the ground seems barren. She meets Kevin and Shawn and Joshua. Each of them has left his own starter-marriage. They sit on the rattan futon from Pier 1 and show her old vacation photos from their previous incarnations.

"Whose nose is that in the corner of this picture?" Heather says.

"That's my ex-wife, Dawn," says Kevin. "That's my ex-wife, Abigail," says Shawn. "That's my ex-wife, Amanda," says Joshua. "The picture was so good I wanted it even though she was in it," they say apologetically. And sometimes they start to sniffle.

None of them, however, shows any inclination to enter into another permanent, legal relationship. Their aspirations are vague and, one by one, they drift away like balloons. Heather has used up her 30s while they have entertained her wanly, like a dull nightclub act.

Now she is worried about her biological clock. Things are booming in the consulting business. She networks constantly like CNN and mentors younger women who also yearn to office. But what about motherhood?

She fears it will be soon or never. Then one day, she awakens with the feeling it will be never. She throws her energies into her company, Creativity Unlimited. She has a condo, a Miata, a diversified stock portfolio, frequent-flier mileage and a time-share at Myrtle Beach. But there are days when she feels an emptiness.

Through the mail comes an AARP card. She enters the Golden Age of senior citizenry. Reluctantly she attends some singles nights. She finds she enjoys them. And then one night, across the room, she spies a man who looks familiar. He is balding and plump, but she recognizes him by his nose—which has followed her around for years in the corner of some of her old vacation pictures.

"Scott!" she says. "Is it really you?"

"Heather!" he says. "Is it really you?"

They hit it off. They decide to try again. And one day, Heather makes Scott sit down because she has something very important to tell him.

"There's this doctor," she says. "He has this blender . . ."

Heather is a mother at 60. And not a moment too soon.

Isn't that a nice story? It's better than the stuff you read about teenage pregnancies.

I have a hunch, however, that not many 60-year-old women are going to be enthused about the ending. And that's too bad.

If more kids were raised by 60-year-old women, the boom boxes that go past my house would be playing Percy Faith instead of Nine Inch Nails. And what a blessed event that would be!

—May 5, 1997

Wackiness in the army

I've got an old Army commission hanging on my wall. To you, understandably, this is no big deal. But it's something I'm quietly proud of. Maybe that's why I'm in a stuffy, irritable mood.

So today, please do me a favor. Indulge me. Just let me get this off my chest. Then we'll go on to other things.

Lt. Kelly Flinn was an officer who slept with an enlisted man. Then she slept with the husband of an enlisted woman. The enlisted woman complained to her sergeant about it, and the sergeant passed the complaint on up the line. When confronted by her superior officer, Lt. Flinn lied.

Gen. Joseph Ralston was an officer who, more than a decade ago, had an affair with a civilian woman. Gen. Ralston was separated from his wife at the time. He later divorced her.

Yesterday, after a weekend of incoherent babbling by self-serving propagandists, Gen. Ralston was forced out of the running for chairman of the Joint Chiefs of Staff. The braying that surrounded his moral lynching went like this:

"If a female officer gets punished for adultery, a male officer ought to be punished, too. Otherwise, Lt. Flinn was the victim of a sexist double standard."

In fact, there was no double standard at all. The stories of Flinn and Ralston are two entirely different stories. Pretending that they are comparable is a lie. But, hey . . . what else is new?

A columnist in *Time* magazine managed to write a whole column defending Lt. Flinn without mentioning her involvement with an enlisted man. Or that Lt. Flinn's paramour was the husband of a female airman. Did the *Time* writer know these things? Of course she did. But in this racket, the preferred way to lie is to leave stuff out.

Then, some kind of activist female showed up on one of the blab shows over the weekend to pose this question:

"What's the difference between Flinn's adultery with a civilian soccer coach and Ralston's adultery with a civilian woman? Adultery is adultery, isn't it?"

The answer is no. In the military, adultery ain't adultery. Gen. Ralston's affair wasn't complicated by rank. But Kelly Flinn poached the husband of a woman who was required to salute her if they passed on the parade ground.

My Army wasn't sexually integrated. When women entered military units, they demanded to be treated as equals. In fact, for integration to work, they have to be.

So assume that Kelly Flinn was a man. Assume that you are Lt. Flinn's commanding officer. You hear that Lt. Flinn had a brief fling with an enlisted woman. This is a violation of military law. But Lt. Flinn is a hot pilot. So maybe you let it go.

And then the you-know-what hits the fan. Now Lt. Flinn is having an affair with the wife of an enlisted man. The enlisted man complains to his sergeant. And the sergeant passes the complaint along to you.

If you've got any brains, you're aware that every enlisted man on the post knows about this little melodrama and is waiting to see what you're going to do about it.

Officers get a lot of privileges in the military. Their accommodations are superior. Their food is usually better. They have little clubs that enlisted men cannot enter. A snot-nosed 22-year-old second lieutenant can look at a 40-year-old sergeant with a chest full of combat ribbons and say: "Stand at attention when I'm talking to you and call me 'sir'!" And the sergeant is supposed to grit his teeth and do it.

For an officer to abuse these privileges is the worst kind of sin. It violates the trust between officers and enlisted men and, without that trust, the whole command structure falls apart. And when that happens, sometimes people die.

And isn't bedding down the wife of an enlisted man and leaving him to feel frustrated and powerless a kick in the teeth to that trust? . . . Huh? . . . I Can't HEAR You!

If you're Lt. Flinn's commanding officer, you've got a big problem. So has Lt. Flinn. If he lies to you about it, you throw the book at him. I would.

Now let's take the case of Gen. Josephine Ralston, who is, hallelujah!, the first woman ever under consideration to chair the Joint Chiefs of Staff. Her qualifications are excellent, her career first-rate.

But then she admits that, more than a decade ago, she had an affair with some civilian fella. She was separated from her husband at the time and she later divorced him.

Are you really going to say: "Sorry, ma'am. But we just kicked a male lieutenant out of an Air Force base in North Dakota for having an affair with an enlisted man's wife and lying about it.

That's exactly the same thing you did. So if we give you the job, we'll be guilty of a pro-female double standard."

Ridiculous! But then, we're becoming a ridiculous country for all our grim attempts to be serious.

This week, a man lost his job because of this wackiness. I don't expect the wackiness to stop. But it makes me feel better to talk about it.

Are you still here? Well then, as you were. Carry on.

—June 11, 1997

So long to Woolworth's

I haven't been in a Woolworth's for a couple of years, but as soon as I heard it was leaving, I missed it. Or at least, I missed the way it used to be.

So did everybody else. News columns have been filled with the bric-a-brac of Woolworth nostalgia. In the showcase of memory, there's a little souvenir for each of us.

Where else, under one medium-sized roof, could you find curtains, curtain rods, cards of buttons, nine miles of thread and yarn, a little display of cheap basic tools, a Scout knife with four blades for 79 cents, a 39-cent diamond engagement ring, an Ingram or Westclox pocket watch, a Gilbert alarm clock or a screen for the window?

Or a minced-ham sandwich on toast; plain, chippable white china; dress patterns; dish towels; lipstick and rouge; comic books; Little Big Books; toy soldiers; an ice cream soda; caps; toy guns in holsters; tablets of plain, serviceable stationery with faint blue lines on it; or a strainer for the sink?

Or genuine cowhide wallets with cowboys on them, change purses with snaps, little wheels with plungers on them that shot sparks when you pressed them, bras, egg beaters, rubber racing cars, shoe polish, 45-rpm records and a whole candy case full of

muddy brown chocolate, including those hard, little chocolate
stars that may not have been Godiva but you didn't say no to
them?

Where else?

And where else will city kids first interact with the animal
kingdom? And hear the sudden, startling, sharp whistle of a
parakeet that lured a child to the nature preserve at the rear of
the store where two birds, three turtles and a tank full of fish
were on exotic display?

You could buy a thick glass bowl and one goldfish. You could
take the goldfish home in an ice-cream carton with a wire handle on it. You could name the goldfish Jerry and crumble smelly
fish food wafers into the bowl, and Jerry would nose to the surface to consume them with tiny smooches of his goldfish lips.

And then, as days went by, you could watch Jerry slowly dis-
appear in the gathering murk of his ecology, until soon he went
to heaven, pausing on the way to float on the top of the water.
Then you would assist his journey by giving him a solemn
funeral in the toilet, with you and Mom as the only mourners.

Mom! Almost forgot her birthday, and you've got 79 cents to
spend. How about a genuine oriental flower vase that says Japan
right there on the bottom? How about a handkerchief or a head
scarf? Or a key chain with a four-leaf clover or a real penny in it?
Or how about a bottle of Evening in Paris perfume, which had
to be one of the finest perfumes made since it came in such a
splendid, midnight-blue bottle?

All of these treasures were available right in your own neighborhood. But that's not all. That's nothing compared to what
was waiting for you if somebody took you downtown.

If you went downtown and walked a little distance from Public Square—past the old, tall blind man with his hand out;
through the wonderful rich aroma of warm salted nuts filling the
air from one small store—then you came to FOUR DIME
STORES ALMOST IN A ROW!

Big ones with more than one floor! Kresge's, Grant's,
McCrory's and, of course, Woolworth's. Unnnn-beeelievable.
And with astonishing refinements of sophistication never seen
in the provinces.

Why, at one counter they had a live lady sitting at a real piano. If you wanted to buy a sheet of music, she would play it for you first. So that you wouldn't go home thinking you'd purchased "How Soon? (Will I Be Seeing You)" only to find, when you sat down and played it, that what came out was "Flight of the Bumble Bee."

And if you wanted a potato peeler, you didn't have to just buy one and hope it worked. No. There was a young man behind another counter peeling potatoes with lightning speed while he kept up a steady testimonial to the virtues of his instrument. All of this. And downstairs, you could even buy furniture. Of a sort.

Well, it's all been leaving, and soon it will all be gone. The lady at the piano—where is she now? In a karaoke bar, soddenly reliving past triumphs? And the young man with the potato peeler? What of him? Is he the guy who calls you while you're eating dinner to ask you if you need new storm windows?

The lunch counter went to McDonald's. The toys and tools went to Kmart. The goldfish? Upstream, I hope, and safe from the lethal curiosity and transitory infatuation that is most dangerous when masquerading as love.

Just like people we thought would be around forever, businesses leave us, too. But wouldn't it be nice, just for a day, to walk down a street with a Kresge's, a Hough Bakery and a Clark's Restaurant all in a row? And a Woolworth's, too?

Why, you'd feel like a million-dollar baby.

—July 23, 1997

....

Jimmy Dudley's special voice

If I've got my physics straight, the voice of Jimmy Dudley, floating on radio waves, is moving at a soft drawl through the distant stars.

Perhaps intelligent life is listening, headphones clamped to feelers, trying to make sense of Earth from broadcast signals newly arrived after a long, long journey through time and space:

"Williams takes a strike . . . it's three and two, the string is out . . . Lemon checks the runner at first . . . here's the pitch . . . a sharp ground ball to Boudreau at short . . . he flips to Gordon for one . . . over to Robinson . . . it's a double play!"

It would be a nice place to visit, that distant planet where 1948 is today and baseball is still a radio game. Maybe there is a front porch there, and Dudley's calm and gentlemanly description mingles with the conversation of crickets as the light leaves the sky and fireflies wink solemnly back at the orange glow of the radio dial.

There were many voices on front porches in those days because that's where people gathered to tell stories. Jimmy Dudley was a gifted storyteller. He sat in the corner and spoke through the radio and told the story of the ball game. When you listened, your mind supplied the pictures—the emerald green grass shining under the lights, the outfield fence beneath a baseball that was going . . . going . . . gone! The long trudge in from the bullpen. You saw it all. Or thought you did.

When Dudley began broadcasting Indians games, television was still a gimmick. If you went to a bar or an appliance store, you could see a gray and fuzzy pitcher at the top of the picture throw a baseball to a gray and fuzzy catcher at the bottom. Dudley's game was better. You could see more. You could see everything worth seeing.

Then, gradually, television took over. It took over everything, baseball too. It showed you things that were not worth seeing at all, because that is its stock in trade. It bombarded you with images that Dudley would have ignored—mascots in chicken suits dancing atop dugouts and camera-hungry fans doing the wave. Brainless little diversions that cluttered up the story.

When radio became television, we left the front porch, which pined away in our absence and grew smaller and became a stoop. We moved indoors and switched off the imagination projector in our brains. We stopped talking to each other and stared at a screen, waiting for something to happen.

That's when we discovered that baseball was a slow game. We hadn't known it before.

Television wants a lot to happen in a hurry. It wants tension and hype and little ecstasies of frequent mayhem. Wrestling became its first darling, but wrestling was abandoned as ridiculous. Football replaced it.

Baseball, fighting for attention, prostituted itself with designated hitters and interleague play. It became vaudeville for millionaires and grew too big and flashy for the front porch. Americans didn't own it anymore. In the age of television, Americans began to realize they owned very little.

On the distant planets, they know none of this yet. The signals that reach them are signals of the America that used to be, not the America that is. And if the quiet and mannerly voice of Jimmy Dudley is reaching their ears, they will think us a better and more relaxed and less desperate people than we are.

Jimmy Dudley was taken into the Baseball Hall of Fame this week. He is 87 now and was too ill to attend the ceremony. In this town, where he told the story of baseball for 20 years, there are many who never heard him and some who never heard of him. And then there are some who, appallingly, think that "Garfield one, two-three, two-three" was all he ever said.

But even if I've got my physics wrong and his voice is not traveling among the stars, a lot of us can coax it back from the timeless vault of memory. Along with crickets and fireflies and Philcos and the other souvenirs we carry along to soothe our journey until the string is out.

—August 6, 1997

....

Hall of fad?

Our Rock and Roll Hall of Fame and Museum, we read, is looking for solutions. Well, who isn't?

I certainly am. Every night, in my basement, while the world is asleep, I work on perfecting my noise-seeking, anti-boom box missile, otherwise known as the Thud Scud.

By next summer, I want to be able to seek and destroy the

coffin-sized speakers that go thudding around the neighborhood in the back of pickup trucks driven by the baggy-pants, bill-in-the-back youth culture. So far, no luck. I launched one pandemonium-seeking warhead and it headed straight for Congress.

The balmy nights remain athrob with rock. But over at Rock Central, in the eye of the storm, things are ominously quiet. This year's attendance may total almost a third less than last year's. And the hall is in the hole.

It lost a wad of money on its psychedelic exhibit. It couldn't find a local company willing to lend its name to a celebration of the creative effects of illegal drugs on loud noise. Musical junkies have fallen from fashion and are bad for the corporate image.

The last purge left the rock hall in the hands of David Abbott and Lee Howley, fine men who, I happen to know, are possessed with ability and insight. An example of this insight made print the other day when the two men commented on improvements in the hall's neighborhood that might help attendance.

"They would like to see hotels, restaurants, a new convention center and shops to add life to the area," the story said.

Well, sure. The logic is unimpeachable. Why, if you surrounded a used Yugo dealership with hotels, restaurants, a convention center and shops, you could sell Yugos like Starbucks sells coffee.

My recollection, which must be wrong, was that it was supposed to work the other way around. The appearance of the rock hall was supposed to be the resuscitator that added new life to hotels, restaurants and shops. I wonder about a new convention center, though. That would give us three. And everybody seems to convene in Las Vegas these days.

It is a waste of breath to say so, but, if the rock hall needs help, help should come from the billionaire rock barons who could defray all expenses with their pocket change.

But the last we saw of them, they blew in for a one-night-stand induction ceremony, squinted at the town as if it were a bad blind date, then left us, muttering only vague and unbankable promises ever to return.

Unlike New York or Los Angeles, our town lacks an excessive population of exhibitionistic hipsters who like to lurk, garishly clad, around "happening" venues. Our town barely heard of Gianni Versace before his tragic death, and then, many of us thought he was a race-car driver.

And there is another fundamental problem. "Fame" in the rock world doesn't mean the same thing as "fame" in, say, the baseball world. In entertainment, fame is transient, subjective and forgettable. In sports, fame is permanent, objective and haunting.

A friend of mine became suddenly old at 38 when he took his niece to the rock hall to show her the sights.

"She is a popular music fan," he told me. "So I took her up to one exhibit and I said, 'Look, there's Pink Floyd,' and she said, 'Never heard of him.'"

This does not happen with baseball fame. As every baseball fan knows, every year a handful of players sets out to exceed the home run exploits of Babe Ruth and Roger Maris. Ruth and Maris, though older than Pink Floyd, are still very much in the game. Their Hall of Fame is not a Hall of Fad.

When Babe Ruth was hitting his home runs, the huge superstars of the music scene included such groups as the Coon-Sanders Nighthawks, Helen Kane (the boop-boop-be-doop girl), Jean Goldkette and his orchestra, and Johnny Hamp's Kentucky Serenaders. How marketable is their fame today? Why, it's hard to find a Mario Lanza record without a search warrant.

If rock goes the way of swing and tomorrow's youth turn to opera, we will have a very strange-looking building on our hands. The record moguls won't care. They will be busy cranking out videos of a topless Carmen.

But it will make the summer nights a little sweeter. Imagine the strains of the duet from "Lakme" wafting out of the back end of a pickup truck driven by a couple of kids who look like Beavis and Butt-head. Now there's one for the Fantasy Hall of Fame!

—August 11, 1997

Making peace with the Boomers

I think I have begun a peace process with the baby boomers. If it's successful, there's hope for peace anywhere. I have resented the baby boomers for 30 years. But if you read this column, you know that.

My small generation of Depression-born kids was powerless against them. Their overwhelming numbers rolled over us like a blitzkrieg—a historic analogy it is sometimes necessary to explain to them.

We were raised to obey our parents, listen to the wisdom of our grandparents and do what we were told. When the boomers invaded our "space"—arriving disguised as little brothers, nieces and nephews—we welcomed them with friendship and small trinkets, such as rattles and teething rings. We thought we could co-exist with them. We didn't know they were bent on complete domination.

They changed everything they saw to suit themselves and never asked permission. They threw out all music but rock, ripped up the old rules of sexual behavior, sneaked new drugs into the culture and introduced dirty words into public discourse. They banished the waltz and the fox trot and showed off for each other on dance floors, jerking and twitching like mating peacocks. They installed telephones in their cars, held business meetings at breakfast and met with a Stairmaster at lunch.

Whenever we, their immediate elders, raised objections to this behavior, the boomers told us to "quit whining" or "get with it." Usually though, they just ignored us. They were driving the wagon and, if we didn't like it, we could get off and hobble.

But now, finally, we may have found common ground. The baby boomers are getting old. They will treat advancing age like they have treated every other natural phenomenon—as if they invented it. And since, from birth, they have believed that everything they did was cool, being old is bound to become cool, too. More than cool, in fact. Hip!

The other night, I saw a TV commercial for a brand of false-teeth glue. In the past, such commercials featured some old grandpa trying to gnaw on an ear of corn. The implied message was obvious. "Here's another example of how age stinks!" it said. "Why doesn't somebody put the old guy out of his misery and buy him some good false-teeth glue?"

But the new false-teeth glue commercial sings a far different tune. It opens with a breathtaking shot of a boomer couple galloping on horseback across the plains of Colorado.

A close-up reveals that these boomers are not young. You can tell because each sports a head of beautiful silver hair so lustrous and enviable it would make a demoralized Fabio rush out and buy a babushka to cover his shame.

Time has hardly laid a finger on this flawless couple. They are wrinkle-free, clear-eyed and bulge-proof. The ravages of age have missed them, except for that fairy's kiss of a hair wound. But each knows the other's little secret. False teeth. Yes, they have reached the stage when they must wear false teeth.

And they are delighted about it. As they canter along, they reward each other with wide, dazzling, Christie Brinkley smiles. Their false teeth are obviously their prize possessions. A gain instead of a loss. An enhancement instead of an extraction.

But, oh-oh, here comes a stone wall. Over they go, false teeth and all. As they hit with a jolt, he smiles at her. His teeth are still there. She smiles reassuringly back. Her teeth are still there, too. He gazes proudly at her indomitable dentures like Francis Scott Key glimpsing the star-spangled banner. Their false-teeth glue has done its job.

Emboldened, she reaches into her saddlebag and produces an apple. Smiling brazenly at him, she takes a huge bite. "Ker-rrr-unch!" Smugly, she shows him her teeth are still in place. He favors her with a final flash of his own chompers. Who says age brings infirmities! They wheel their steeds and race toward a distant, picturesque ranch house where, out of sight, they will presumably swallow three Advils and bathe in Epsom salts.

The boomers have always seen themselves as glamorous. Now they are bound to make old age glamorous, too. Nursing homes will become as fashionable as Club Meds. A walker will be a mark of distinction, like an ebony walking stick. Old, at last, will be in. Young will be out.

And for those of us who got there ahead of them, finally . . . finally! . . . there will be a payoff. As they arrive, toothless and saddle sore, from their gallop through life, we will speak to them of painkillers and Metamucil and greet them, at last, as brothers.

—September 15, 1997

....

Two different Americas

Some years back, my Channel 5 pal Leon Bibb was working weekends at a TV station in Toledo. On the night of the station Christmas party, Leon was busy with the newscast. So the party had already started when he got there.

The party center was one of those sprawling places which, like a funeral parlor, was equipped to hold several events at once. Leon parked his car, hurried inside, and was greeted by a harried hostess.

"I'm here for the TV station party," he told her.

"You're late!" she said sharply.

Her exasperation seemed a little odd. Mechanically, Leon started to explain the reason for his tardiness. But the hostess cut him short.

"Oh, well," she said. "You're here now. Follow me."

She turned on her heel and set off at a brisk pace down a hall-way. Leon followed. He assumed she was leading him to the party room. Instead, she banged through a set of double doors and Leon, following like a caboose, found himself standing amid the frantic clatter of a busy kitchen.

"Take your jacket off," the hostess ordered. "You'll find an apron over there on that rack. Then report to the dining room to bus some tables. They've already started serving dinner."

Leon stared at her. Then a glimmer of dawn broke through and chased the mystery away from this wacky scenario.

"Perhaps I didn't make myself clear," he told the woman.

"When I said I was here for the party, what I meant to say was that the party is here for me."

"And what did she say to that?" I asked when Leon told me the story.

"I don't remember that she said anything much," Leon said. "I do remember that she was very embarrassed."

We both laughed. But we were laughing from different directions. I understood the story. I understood its implications. It was a story that ended well because my friend Leon got the last laugh.

But it was not a story that could have happened to me. When I walk into a party center, nobody assumes I'm a waiter. Leon's America and my America have not been the same America.

This is a simple fact. It is not a bleeding-heart-liberal sermon. When I was a young man, I was free to travel through America at will, and with little apprehension. When Leon's family wanted to visit relatives down South, they would leave Cleveland in the wee hours, gas up in Cincinnati and make most of the trip in the daylight. It was unwise for a black family to travel through segregation country after dark.

Time, it is said, heals all wounds. But time takes its own sweet time. We tend to measure the passage of time with the short yardstick of our own brief span of years. That's why my voice mail predictably fills up with calls from people anxious to say that they are "sick of hearing about slavery," "sick of hearing about segregation," "sick of hearing about the Holocaust."

I am sick of hearing about none of these things. The last two occurred in my lifetime and they are part of my experience on earth. The study of human evil is not an irrelevant pursuit for human beings. I'm sick of hearing about cancer too, but blocking my ears won't make me immune to its ravages.

What I am sick of, though, is the exploitation of race. The harsh rhetoric. The confrontation. The charges of racism and reverse-racism that fly back and forth. The flawed—obviously flawed—idea that preaching division will unite us. The confusion between equality of opportunity and equality of outcome.

The politics of race are no different than the politics of anything else. The strategy of politics never varies. It's always, "We're right and they're wrong." The goal of politics is immutable. It's always "Gimme."

In our talks about race over the years, Leon and I have gone around this shallow noise. We've taken a far bolder tone. We've risked telling each other how we really feel, what we really resent, what we really fear.

This is the way friends behave. They respect each other, they root for each other, they are curious about each other. They are careful with each other's feelings. They try their best to walk in each other's shoes.

America is not the same for each of us. But what unites us is so much more than what separates us that we can deal with what separates us. And work it out.

Let's see how much of that spirit finds its way into the president's town meeting in Akron today. By tonight, we will know. Will it be good for what ails us? Or will it be just another political side show where honesty, arriving late, is again mistaken for a busboy?

—December 3, 1997

Living too long

Now science is telling us it may be able to monkey around with our cells and stop the aging process and fix us so we can live as long as 200 years.

Time to buy some new underwear.

Unfortunately for some of us, the technique may take 15 years to develop.

So, in 15 years, when I'm 74, I may be able to stop my aging process and stay 74 for another 126 years.

Frankly, that's not the best offer I've had all week.

I think I'd feel like a man on a bus who had ridden past his stop.

It seems a shame to halt the aging process just when I'm getting used to it. Mastering the process isn't easy.

Here are a couple of ways to tell if you've made it:

When you open the newspaper in the morning, do you turn first to: (1) the sports page so you can root? (2) the obituary page so you can gloat?

When somebody you know gets his name in the paper, is it more likely to appear in: (1) Denise Dufala's column? (2) the death notices?

When you get together with your friends on Saturday night, are your liveliest conversations about: (1) whether the Denver Broncos are better than the Green Bay Packers? (2) whether FiberCon is better than Metamucil?

When you see a list of "Hollywood's Hottest Stars," have you heard of: (1) most of them? (2) none of them?

When your doctor retires and you meet his replacement, does he remind you of: (1) Marcus Welby? (2) Opie Taylor?

If somebody mentions Marcus Welby or Opie Taylor, do you say: (1) Never heard of them? (2) Oh yeah, they're among Hollywood's Hottest Stars?

If you answered "2" to all of those questions but are reluctant to admit it, you are grappling with the aging process. If you answered "2" to all of those questions and don't care, you have mastered it.

And once you've mastered the aging process, it doesn't bother you anymore. In fact, you often view the aging process and its inevitable destination as somewhat of a relief.

When my friends and I get tired of talking about whether Advil or Tylenol is better for aches and pains, we often spend a joyful half-hour happily looking forward to things we won't live to see.

"Did you see that nut on television saying he was ready to start cloning human beings?" one of us will say.

"Yeah," another will say, "I sure hope I won't live to see it."

"Social Security looks like it's in big trouble," somebody else will say. "What's gonna happen when all the Baby Boomers retire?"

"I'm glad I won't be alive to find out," somebody else will say.

It isn't that we don't like life. In fact, once you've mastered the aging process, life can be more pleasant and stress-free than it ever was before. We are all very glad to have seen what we have seen. But most of us think we've seen the best of it. And we don't really care if we see an awful lot more.

Now here comes science butting in and talking about stopping the aging process so we can all just go on and on. Suppose that happened?

Do we really want to stick around to see a *Jerry Springer* show titled "I'm in Love With My Mother's Clone"? Or to see another special called "The Rise and Fall of Adolf Hitler" on the Arts and Entertainment channel? Or to listen to Bill Clinton explain that U.S. troops will be extended in Bosnia for the 34th time?

And where would they put us all? Westlake is filling up fast and there's hardly room in Medina County for a cow to graze anymore. It's hard enough as it is to go to the store to buy a loaf of bread without standing in line behind three people buying lottery tickets.

I don't need to stick around to see the girl who replaces the girl who replaces Madonna. I saw Judy Garland once, live in the Rainbow Grille. That was good enough for me.

It might be a fascinating sight to watch the fire marshal wheel over a birthday cake with 200 candles on it. But you know what? I think I'd rather just blow.

—January 16, 1998

Taking the romance out of Valentine's Day

Pat Fortner from South Euclid called to ask if Valentine's Day is politically incorrect.

Tell me more, I said.

So Mrs. Fortner explained that her daughter had brought home a note from her fourth-grade teacher. The note said that this year the class would not celebrate Valentine's Day.

Instead, the normal Valentine's Day party would be dedicated to the theme that the winter season is halfway over.

"I guess instead of saying 'Happy Valentine's Day,' the kids are going to say 'Happy Winter Is Halfway Over Day,'" Mrs. Fortner said.

She stressed that she didn't think this was a big deal. But she thought it was an intriguing small deal. Was it the beginning of a trend, she wondered?

Her question took me back in time. It took me all the way back to my own fourth-grade days, which is quite a trip.

As I remember the drill, you went over to Woolworth's and bought a bag of cheap valentine cards with clever little verses on them. Clever, that is, if you were 10 years old.

For example, there might be a drawing of a little girl sitting in a pine tree. And the verse might read, "I'm pine-ing for you to be my valentine."

Pretty creative stuff, we thought. Not as good as Shakespeare, maybe. But more intellectual than your average rap lyric.

At the appointed moment, the teacher would give a signal, and we would all get up and mill around the room. There would be about five minutes of mass confusion, bumping and giggling as we put our valentines on the desks of the kids we were pine-ing for.

Then we would go back to our own desks and sort through the pile to find out what kids were pine-ing for us. The resulting audit often led to moments of heartache and despair.

The prettiest little girls and the baddest little boys usually got the biggest stack of valentines. The nerdy, quiet little boys and the awkward, shy little girls generally got an embarrassingly small stack. Then there were those of us in the middle—snubbed by some we pined for, sought after by some we disdained—an introduction to a pattern that would follow us for the rest of our lives.

Next would come much whispering, gossiping and tee-hee-ing:

"Tommy likes Suzy."

"No I don't, either!"

"Well, Betty likes you. She told me she did."

"That's a lie! She never said any such thing!"

Thinking back, I remembered that Valentine's Day, in the fourth grade, can be a traumatic experience. And maybe we never really outgrow it when we get to be big boys and girls.

On National Public Radio the other night, a commentator

remarked that a story currently much in the news reminded her of the carryings-on in a grade-school class. And, remembering Valentine's Day, I think she had it exactly right:

"Billy likes Monica."

"No I don't, either!"

"Well, Monica likes you. She told Linda she did."

"That's a lie. Linda just said that because she hates me."

"Well, that's what Linda told Ken."

"So what! Hillary says Ken's got it in for me."

Even when some people get old enough to shave or wear mascara, a lot of their pine-ing transactions continue on a fourth-grade level. Valentine's Day looks soft and fluffy on a greeting card. But it doesn't always look so hot when it hits the headlines.

Maybe that's why Pat Fortner's daughter isn't going to celebrate Valentine's Day with her classmates this week. Maybe her teacher is afraid that fourth-grade children might have almost as much trouble dealing with Cupid as adults do. Of course, that's only my guess. Not a firm opinion.

But I do have a firm opinion about celebrating "Winter Is Halfway Over Day" in Cleveland in February.

My opinion is that the teacher must be from out of town.

—February 11, 1998

....

They don't throw like girls

The first warm day of the year is like a sweet sip of the Fountain of Youth.

It brings back memories of Orangeade on the back porch. Of the fresh smell of a thunderstorm in the soft summer air. Of the way the top of my head used to look without a bald spot.

On the first warm day of the year, I took a walk around the neighborhood. And I saw a sight that made me feel young again.

Over on a school baseball diamond near my house, a girls softball team was practicing. So I stopped to watch, being careful to hide behind a nearby tree.

Why did I do that, you ask? For two reasons.

First, you don't want to be caught hanging around a schoolyard these days, watching a bunch of girls. People get funny ideas. Such are the dreadful times we live in.

My pal, Leon Bibb, was visiting relatives in Toledo and he went over to a school to pick up his niece. While he was waiting by the schoolyard fence, a little girl came boldly up to him.

"Are you a stranger?" she asked.

"I guess I am, in a way," Leon said. "I'm from Cleveland."

At that, the little girl gave out a scream and turned and ran away.

"My momma told me never to talk to strangers!" she yelled as she fled. And Leon was left to nervously wonder what anybody viewing this scene might have thought he had said to her.

So that's one reason I hid behind a tree. The other reason was courtesy. I didn't want the girls on the softball team to see me laughing. And I was sure I was going to start laughing any minute.

In my youth, the sight of girls playing softball was as comical as anything you could see. Providing Abbot and Costello weren't playing at the neighborhood picture show.

For instance, there was nothing in the annals of sports looniness funnier than watching a batter on a girls softball team hit a home run. This was a feat that was usually accomplished without the ball ever leaving the infield.

First, the girl softball batter would take a mighty swing and hit a little dribbler, which would dribble Bill Buckner-esquely beneath an eager infielder's glove.

"Run! Run! Run!" her teammates would squeal. And, after carefully watching the ball until it had rolled to a stop, she would timidly hurry to first, beating a throw that eluded the first-baseperson.

"Run! Run! Run!" they would squeal again.

And off she would scamper to second, where the throw was dropped. Then on toward third, where the throw was dropped.

Then into the plate, where the throw was dropped. Then back to touch third base, which she had missed. Then back to the plate again, where the throw was again dropped. Safe!

This whole complex choreography took less than five minutes. And it was accompanied by more shrieks of ecstasy than Leonardo DiCaprio would get if he suddenly turned up at a Gap store in a mall.

To me, that was girls' softball! And that's what I expected to see as I peeked around the tree on the first warm spring day of my 59th year.

But that's not what I saw at all. These girls were . . . awesome! That's the only word for them.

They could hit, they could field, they could throw. And I mean throw! No stiff-elbowed, little over-the-top hand-grenade hurls that sent the ball in a short arc until it landed, "plock," on the ground and lay there motionless. These girls were throwing BBs.

They had all the moves, too. And they were serious about it. I could tell because they wore sweatshirts with serious sayings on them like:

JUST DO IT!

And:

IF YOU DON'T PLAY TO WIN, WHY KEEP SCORE?

I watched these girls of summer in amazement. And I knew they could have creamed any all-boys baseball team I ever played on. Including the Fisher Foods-Cleveland News, Ken Keltners of Class F—the team that left me happily wearing a ring. Until my mother made me wash my neck.

Standing there in the soft, warm afternoon, I realized that I would have to revise my whole opinion of girl softball players. My notions were completely out of sync with the times. It was the kind of experience that might make somebody else feel like an old man.

So why did it make me feel young again?

Are you kidding? Do you know how long it has been since I changed my mind about anything?

—March 30, 1998

Another comeback

No wonder we're called the Comeback City! It seems like only yesterday we came back and now we're coming back again. Apparently when we came back before, we didn't come back far enough.

Take Euclid Avenue, for instance. When we came back the first time, we neglected to bring Euclid Avenue with us.

"Uh-oh," said those of us with longer memories. "I think we forgot something."

Euclid Avenue used to be something people came back to. Four big department stores. Nice restaurants, shoe stores, jewelry stores, clothing stores. Some big, fancy movie theaters— uniplexes.

Even the signs were coo-well. The windmill turning outside Mill's Restaurant. Robin Hood shooting neon arrows at the front door of the Sherwood Inn. The marquee on the Statler Hotel that announced that Sammy Watkins and his orchestra were playing nightly.

When people thought of Downtown, Euclid Avenue was what they thought of. Then we went away and when we came back, Euclid Avenue was missing.

This confused the tourists who had come flocking here to behold our comeback.

"Where's downtown?" they asked as they stood on the sidewalk of the former Euclid Avenue, which was now masquerading as a street in Mother Teresa's neighborhood of Calcutta.

"Whaddaya mean?" we replied with some asperity. "Why, the Rock and Roll Hall of Fame and Museum is that way. And the Flats are that way and down about 40 feet. And the ballpark and basketball arena are that way. And the . . ."

But the tourists remained perplexed.

"Where's the main street?" they asked. "Isn't there a street with, like, stores on it?"

"Oh!" we said, catching on. "Main Street! It's in the basement of that big building over there. We call it Tower City. It's really very nice."

They weren't impressed. They would go back home to cities like Chicago and walk down Michigan Avenue and laugh about us with their friends. "You know where they keep their Main Street?" they would say. "They keep it in the basement of a building."

Nuts! Back to the comeback drawing board.

The comeback drawing board occupied the top half of page one last week. On display were dreams for the newest comeback, otherwise known as Come Again. Or the Second Comeback.

That's just a little joke.

Actually, the name for the new comeback is "Civic Vision 2000 and Beyond." Its hoped-for completion date is 2008. So perhaps you wonder why they didn't call it "Civic Vision 2008."

That's easy. Back some years ago, everybody fell in love with the sound of the year 2000. It had a nice ring to it. It was hot. So everybody who planned things used it in the titles of their plans. A title like "Goals 2000" was very exciting on the cover of an 865-page plan for education reform written in the language of bureaucratese.

But suddenly the year 2000 was breathing down our necks. And it was pretty obvious that none of the Visions 2000 or Goals 2000 was going to be finished on time. Why, some had barely gotten started.

The nice thing about "Civic Vision 2000 and Beyond" is that it preserves all the cachet of "2000" while remaining comfortably vague. If the dreamed-for "multimodal transportation hub" isn't available for multimodality until the year 3457, so what? That still meets the deadline of "Beyond," which means from now until the meteor hits.

Don't take this as negative. The dreams for the Second Comeback sound wonderful. There's even a dream of bringing Euclid Avenue back this time.

I just wish some of us seasoned comeback travelers had been consulted. We might have had some ideas on what to pack this time that we didn't pack last time.

If I were packing for a Second Comeback, I'd bring along a Hough bake shop. I can still taste their cakes and those little cupcake things that had the raisins in them.

I'd bring a couple of Clark's Restaurants, too, with their

knotty pine paneling and their chicken croquettes covered in yellow sauce with parsley in it. And Kornman's, a restaurant for people who eat plain and don't need the waiter to recite the 17 herbs hiding in the dill butter.

A Richman Bros. would be nice. You could go to anybody's funeral in one of their suits and their fussy tailors didn't tack an extra hundred bucks on for fussing.

I was happy to see plans to bring the Euclid Beach merry-go-round back. Now let's see if we can find the rest of the park. A great old movie theater like the Hipp would be nice, too—with ushers and actors up on the screen who are bigger than I am.

And, before I forget, this time, when we come back, we really ought to bring the schools with us.

What can we lose? They keep coming back to haunt us anyway.

—May 18, 1998

Sinatra still sings

They buried a man in California this week, but they didn't bury Frank Sinatra. Rock 'n' roll couldn't bury him. Disco and rap couldn't. Elvis and the Beatles couldn't. What good is a shovel?

Singers have careers. Sinatra had an age. The Age of Sinatra began 60 years ago. One week of eulogies did not end it. Tears were only a small intermission. The funeral wreath was only a comma.

If there must be a wake, then hold it this way:

Very late tonight, when the house belongs to you and the ghosts, put a copy of "Only the Lonely" on the machine. Listen. And as you listen, try to detect a syllable that isn't perfect. Or what he thought of as perfect—which is another way of saying the same thing.

The brassy songs of his middle years sold best. He was a man reinventing himself with a little push of swagger and bravado.

It's what men in their middle years do. It's a phase. It passes.

The man is defeated. He surrenders and stops reaching back for his youth. And that's when he finds it again. The best of Sinatra was what he did early and late—the songs of a young man dreaming, the songs of an old man remembering.

Those two notes, one sweet, one sad, octaves apart, make the harmony of our lives. We cry sad tears of delight at their painful beauty. "Once upon a time, the world was sweeter than we knew," Sinatra sings on his album *The September of My Years*. The jury of ghosts in the darkened room agrees. It is one of the Great Forlorn Truths.

I met him in a stack of my father's 78s. You dropped them, they broke. Sometimes, the edges chipped like teacups. More than 50 years ago, this was. "I'm mad about good books, can't get my fill," he sang, "and Franklin Roosevelt's looks, give me a thrill." At age 7, both things were true of me, too.

After that, he was with me all the way. During the war—which means The War—his songs yearned. There were such good times ahead of us, he sang, if only we could get there. Then we got there and many of the vague, shimmering dreams melted like a mirage.

I tried to be hip when he was hip. I climbed a hillside in a rented tux to watch him open Nick Mileti's Coliseum. The traffic jam made us abandon our cars on the interstate. Inside, the blend of Vegas and Richfield, Ohio, was like a badly mixed drink. "I am not hip," I told myself sadly. It was a jaded era. "Strangers in the night," Sinatra brayed. And we almost were.

Now we know, happily, that he hated the song. It was just something he sang for money. That came out this week. A lot came out this week. Everybody wanted to be sure to get it all in. The gangster business, the flashes of cruelty, the dirty linen under the custom tailoring.

Well, it's noted. I don't care about that. I didn't know the man. But he knew me. How else could he summon my ghosts to my darkened living room? How else would he know about the great mystery of what to do with your life—the life you've already lived, I mean. Do you take it out and look at it like a souvenir? Or do you report it stolen like a watch?

He was a man of natural class, who only lost it when he tried to fake it. The class is there in the overwhelming honesty of his art. When it wasn't just for money. When he was showing us the possibilities. For that is what a great artist does. He shows us the possibilities and dares us to understand them.

Before the era of shock and schlock—of singers who dress for Halloween and shriek of atrocities and fancied injustices—before the era of anti-class, there was class. It is an endangered quality now. He took a huge portion with him. I don't know who will replenish the supply. I don't know if anybody makes it anymore.

I held my wake last night. The old 78s are long gone, lost to time. Eight-tracks replaced them, then cassettes, then CDs. Sinatra sang on all of them. He sang into a cardboard megaphone and he sang through technology brought back from the moon.

The generation that started when he did, so optimistic and innocent, looks back now trying to understand what has been lost and why. But he stayed with us until closing, comforting us by explaining that loss is part of life. And that beauty, when lost, is never gone.

And then he died to prove it. Listen, you'll see.

—May 22, 1998

....

Blowing political smoke

My mother has X-ray eyes. She used to have them, anyway. She hasn't mentioned them for years.

Back when I was in college, she would draw a pair of eyes at the bottom of her letters to me. These eyes would appear uncaptioned. But their meaning was obvious.

"Watch your step," the eyes would warn. "I know what you've been up to this week."

Since almost every week I was up to something that wouldn't

have sold well at home, the message of the eyes was always accurate. A good parent knows what her kid is likely to be up to. If she doesn't know for sure, she can guess with a degree of accuracy that would shame a psychic.

In the '90s, parental X-ray eyes have grown a little nearsighted. For example, with both parents working, it's not easy for them to know if their kid is illuminating his after-school hours with toxic exposure to *The Jerry Springer Show*.

Parenting gurus warn parents to peer over their kids' shoulders every time they use the Internet. You're supposed to sit there with a shotgun, prepared to exterminate any erotic ladies or child molesters who might suddenly appear on the screen if the kid sends his search engine off in quest of information about "sextuplets."

Thanks to an improved delivery system, many dangerous guided missiles of American culture have managed to slip past parental defenses. But there is still one worrisome act that a kid can't hide from the X-ray eyes of his parents. Not for very long, anyway.

A parent knows when her kid is smoking cigarettes.

There is the hint of tobacco breath lurking beneath the camouflage of Juicy Fruit gum. The whiff of tobacco smoke in the bathroom accompanied by the circumstantial evidence of three burnt matches in the toilet bowl. Cigarette butts in the car ashtray. A cigarette pack discovered under the BVDs on laundry day.

And then it's confrontation time:

"Kevin, are you smoking cigarettes? Don't lie to me now. I'm your mother, and you know I have X-ray eyes."

"Aw, Ma. Lots of kids do it."

"I don't care what lots of kids do. If lots of kids went and jumped in the lake, would you go jump in the lake?"

To save space, we will skip the rest of the conversation. The lecture on lung cancer, fetal injury, premature birth, low birth weight. The threat of grounding or restricted use of the VISA card or the family Chevy. The bribe of a Walkman or a pair of designer tennis shoes in exchange for abstinence.

But no parent, not even a parent at her wit's end, ever threatened her errant kid by saying:

"Kevin, unless you stop smoking right now, we're going to send $1.10 to Washington for every pack of cigarettes you smoke!"

Only the Great White Father in Washington could dream up such a scheme of parental discipline. Somehow, when we weren't looking, the president apparently adopted the nation's children. And he wants to show his love for them in the traditional Washington way. By levying a tax.

"This is going to hurt you more than it hurts me," the president murmurs, playing a telling topsy-turvy with the time-honored parental line. At least he's honest about it. Compassionately picking the pockets of the nation's smokers would net Washington extra billions to spend on a grab bag of pet programs.

When the tobacco bill died in the Senate, the First Dad got very angry. He blamed the Republicans and the tobacco lobby for spending evil dollars on an ad campaign to defeat goodness and corrupt children.

And, of course, the tobacco companies did have their own agenda. They spent $40 million on self-serving television ads that called the tax a tax. Which, self-serving or not, is merely calling a spade a spade.

When I last checked, Washington was still subsidizing tobacco farmers. Tobacco was still a legal substance in America. Great civic projects, here and elsewhere, were being funded by tobacco taxes.

Government, in short, has nicotine-stained fingers. It preaches against tobacco addiction, but it can't break its own addiction to tobacco tax revenues.

But that isn't the point. The point is that any realistic American has learned the hard way that sending more money to Washington is no way to deal with a problem that can only be dealt with in individual family settings.

America doesn't need X-ray eyes to detect political smoke. Ordinary nostrils will do. And when it comes to blowing political smoke, Washington is the only town left in America without a no-smoking section.

—June 19, 1998

Memories of a heat wave

I remember how the old neighborhood awoke in the sticky sunrise to find itself in a heat wave.

Those were the days before the TV forecasters treated climate change like a nuclear attack. Weather crept up on you then. The heat stole in silently, at night, and burglarized the life from the air.

Wake into it with me.

The green maple leaves are too dazed to move and the birds have canceled their concerts. But we kids are up and out and prowling about in the fevered morning.

At the end of the street, the old gray horse droops in the traces of the Shaker Grove Dairy milk wagon. The milkman often leaves him there, unattended. This horse does not welcome attention. He is not a horse for petting. Children annoy him. Life annoys him. He shows us the whites of his eyes and broods in the hot dawn about theology, destiny and glue.

In the back of his wagon, the metal crates of milk bottles are covered with shards of ice. We take some of these and distribute them and suck their cool flavor of petty larceny. But we wouldn't steal a bottle of milk on a dare.

There is little to do with the listless day. Our mothers are terrified of polio. They think it comes from getting "overheated." Newspaper clippings listing the warning signs of polio are thumbtacked to kitchen cupboard doors.

The refrigerator magnet has not yet been invented.

"Don't get overheated," the chorus of mothers warns us shrilly. It is an irrational order in a heat wave. Swimming is out. The mothers are convinced the polio germ lurks at the bottom of swimming pools. Immersion in the polluted lake is unthinkable.

So we run through the lawn sprinkler. There are no inflatable, backyard plastic pools to splash in. Plastic does not yet cover the Earth like Sherwin-Williams paint. It is the lawn sprinkler or nothing.

Our bathing suits are scratchy wool, navy blue with a little white stripe down the side and a little white belt. When they are dry, they are torture.

When they are wet, they are worse.

The anticipation of running through the sprinkler always far exceeds the event. We stand around the sprinkler in a tense circle. One by one, we screw our eyes shut and dash through the sting of the spray. We each do this seven times and then the magic is evicted from the experience. We peel off the gruesome, wet bathing suits and confront the parched and empty afternoon.

If we had a nickel, we could buy a popsicle. If we had 6 cents, we could buy a Fudgesicle. If we had 7 cents, we could buy an Eskimo Pie. Since we are broke, we can have a gulp of ice water from the bottle in the refrigerator. We can tiptoe in and hoist the bottle to our lips and then . . .

"ARE YOU DRINKING STRAIGHT FROM THAT BOTTLE AGAIN . . . HOW MANY TIMES DO I HAVE TO TELL YOU TO USE A GLASS!" our mothers yell. They always catch us. Why don't they ever catch our fathers?

Dusk comes down like a flatiron. Electric fans whisper an empty promise and push hot air around the room. Only God and the movie theaters can manufacture coolness. Nobody's house has air conditioning. Nobody's car has it. Limp banners hang from the movie marquees. Blue penguins relax on a field of ice above the words "Cooled By Refrigeration." It is the only place to go to escape the heat. Unless you've already seen the picture.

We drink Orangeade on the porch and rock slowly in the porch glider to make a breeze. Everybody has a porch glider. They cost about $40. (But in the years that are yet to come, they will leave us, along with the milkman's horse and the wool bathing suit. One day, I will see an ad for one in a fancy catalog with a 500-buck price tag on it.)

At bedtime, I lie with my head at the foot of the bed and my nose against the window screen. Our neighbor is sprinkling his lawn and smoking a cigar. I hear the spritz of the water and smell cigar smoke and the dry dust on the screen. And there is another smell—a live, plant smell. I fall asleep with the smell teasing my nostrils.

It comes from the wooden windowsill which, on hot nights, remembers it had once been a tree.

—July 1, 1998

We the People

Homeless, not hopeless

Wow! If you've misplaced anything, call the Clinton administration. Guess how many homeless people they found on the streets of America we didn't know were there?

Aw, you'll never get it. Six million, four hundred thousand. That's right. The Republican administrations estimated there were 600,000 homeless. But Donna Shalala went out and counted and came up with 7 million.

That's the good news. At least, it's good news for a fellow named Fred Karnas, director of the National Coalition for the Homeless. He was crazy about Shalala's new math homework.

Her study, quoth he, "doesn't just talk about mental illness and substance abuse. It also talks about housing and poverty and racism. It really does say what we've been trying to say for a long time."

It also talks about money. And boldly, I might add. If I asked you how much money it would take to clear up mental illness, substance abuse, housing problems, poverty and racism, you might say you were clueless. But Donna Shalala knows. It'll cost us $40 billion a year if we do it on the cheap. I supplied the word "us." Shalala left it out. They have a habit, in Washington, of acting like money just arrives. Probably because it does.

Here's the bad news, though. Since we are a deadbeat government, the money will have to come from somewhere in particular. There is some talk about getting it by eliminating the tax deduction for interest on home mortgages. Right now it is whispered talk. Shalala probably fears, rightly, that if she said it out loud, she might find herself out on the street. Thereby raising the number of homeless to 7 million and one.

Every time I write about homelessness, I am accused of

heartlessness. Clergymen send me letters advising me to soak my soul in some kind of fabric softener. Once I was taken to lunch and lectured sternly by a nun. She implied that my hope of a glorious hereafter was in serious jeopardy.

So I'll tell you what I did.

I asked a very compassionate friend of mine to find me two homeless people whose stories would turn me to mush. He hurried away, his eyes glowing with the hope of my redemption. Soon he returned with two women, taken from a homeless shelter.

The women were in their late 20s. One was white and one was black. I will call them Nancy White and Nancy Black. My compassionate friend told me that Nancy Black was not only a victim of homelessness but had, as a result of her homelessness, suffered an attempted rape. Then he left us, wearing the smug air of a man who has played an ace.

Nancy White told her story first. She had come to Cleveland from Florida, where she had had a job in construction, which she had quit. The reason she had come to Cleveland was that she had met some guy from Cleveland who had told her that if she ever came to Cleveland, she could live with him.

But when she got to Cleveland, she couldn't find him. He was not at the address he had given her. Had she made any attempt before she quit her job to call him first and tell him she was coming? No. She had just quit and come up? Well, he had said she could.

Was there any place on earth she could go and live? Well, her father would probably take her in. Where was he? He was in Tennessee. Had she told anybody in Cleveland she could go to Tennessee? No. Had anybody asked her if there was someplace she could go? No.

That was Nancy White's story. I checked the rime around my heart for any signs of thaw. Negative. Ah, but there was still Nancy Black to be heard from.

Nancy Black had come to Cleveland from Louisiana. Why? Well, she too had met a guy from Cleveland who said she could come up and stay with him. But when she got here, he too was nowhere to be found.

Now this WAS interesting. Could it have been the same

fella? No, the address was different. Could there be some kind of society of Cleveland men who sprinkled the southland with shack-up IOUs? Nancy Black didn't know.

Well, how about the attempted rape? The way that happened was that Nancy Black had gone to a bar and a couple had invited her to go home with them. And when they got home, the couple had invited Nancy Black to sleep in the same bed with them. In the middle. And in the middle of the night, the man had rolled over on top of her and Nancy Black had fled through a window.

Was there anyplace Nancy Black could go to find a home?

Oh yes. She had an aunt in Houston who was ill with cancer. This aunt had always liked Nancy Black and very much wanted her to come down and nurse her. Nancy Black had always liked this aunt and very much wanted to go.

Had she told anybody at the shelter about this aunt?

No.

Had anybody asked her if there was someplace she could go?

No. They had just said to sit over there and fill out this form.

I thanked the Nancys and they disappeared back into the crowd of between 600,000 and 7 million homeless, depending on how you vote.

Now there are no funds in the Shalala piggy bank earmarked to address the problem of the Nancys. They were not mentally ill, they didn't abuse substances, they knew of homes they could live in. They were not victims of racism. They were poor, but then they had both quit jobs.

You might say they were hopelessly dumb. I won't. I'm in enough trouble already. Besides, it isn't true. The Nancys were not a couple of Einsteins, but they had adequate brains.

What they lacked was judgment. Any sense of cause and effect. Bad things happened to them because they lacked the ability to see that, if they behaved in a certain way, bad things would.

This is a massive problem in America and it seems to be getting worse. I would cheerfully give a portion of my mortgage-interest money to correct it. But it never makes the list of fashionable ills. There is no money in reason. There is no National Coalition for the Development of Common Sense.

Throw money at the two Nancys and it would bounce. It would probably bounce back into the coffers of bureaucratic organizations that feed on problems rather than examining them.

I would have put one Nancy on a bus for Houston and the other on a bus for Tennessee. And saved the country money in the bargain. If that be heartlessness then, clergymen, lick your stamps.

—February 18, 1994

....

Bill Clinton steps in it—again

I'm still trying to understand Bill Clinton, prodded by the suspicion that I've only got another year to do it. Parts of him are still obscure to me. But I'm pretty sure that he's the kind of guy who, if you walked through the park with him, would be the one who would get the doggy mess on his shoe.

"Darn," he'd say. And then the very next day, he'd go into the very same park and step in the very same pile.

You can't hate a guy for that. But it does make you question his awareness. Why step in something when, with just a little care, you can walk around it? Or, scraping off this nasty metaphor, why go to Russia to celebrate V-E Day?

Clinton is having more trouble with the end of the Second World War than Eisenhower and MacArthur had. A couple of weeks ago, he irritated veterans by suggesting that they remove the "J" from commemorations of V-J Day to soothe the feelings of the Japanese. The snarling response from the men who remember their hard-won victory forced the White House to back off a little. But it was a stupid controversy for the president to have started in the first place.

Last spring, there was a lot of muttering when Clinton flew to Normandy to speak at the festivities surrounding the 50th anniversary of D-Day. Some veterans felt that controversy surrounding his draft-evasion techniques during the Vietnam War made him a poor choice to commemorate martial exploits.

But he went and he brought it off well. His speech was graceful and it was politely and respectfully received. And if he had not entirely mended his fences, he had at least proved that, as commander in chief, he could navigate across the subject of military service without stubbing his toe.

Having accomplished this, he could have easily just gone with the flow during the rest of the World War II celebratory events. It was not his war. It belongs mainly to the men and women who fought or suffered through it. To them, it is a very big deal—for many, the watershed event of their lives' geography. But Clinton wandered off the obvious path and stepped in what he continuously steps in. Then he tracked it all over V-J Day and the vets started to wrinkle their noses again.

This left him one more theater of war to blunder around in. And he didn't hesitate. He announced plans to spend V-E Day in the company of our erstwhile allies, the Russians.

Now, it is true that the Russians endured tremendous suffering at the hands of Hitler's armies. The suffering came after Hitler double-crossed Moscow, which thought it had signed a nonaggression pact with Germany. But, after they were in the war, the agony for the Russians was horrible. Finally, they pushed Hitler's troops back and, by our agreement, became the first troops to enter Berlin.

But having marched across many nations to get to Berlin, the Russians pronounced these liberated countries their own spoils of war. If we had operated the same way, we would have liberated France and then claimed it was ours, built a Disneyland and installed Julia Child as its puppet ruler. The countries the Russians "liberated," they kept in chains for almost 50 years. V-E Day sent Poland, for example, from one kind of oppression to another.

I always feel silly putting this stuff in columns. Then I remind myself that the school system is busy bashing Christopher Columbus and that MTV has no history department. But I would not insult Arkansas by suggesting they don't teach these things in school down there. Surely, the president is aware of them. Somebody should have wedded his knowledge to his itinerary.

It would have been so easy for him just to pop over to London and enjoy a V-E Day celebration comprised of quotes from Churchill and Roosevelt. He could have hummed through a couple of choruses of "White Cliffs of Dover" and listened to Vera Lynn sing "We'll Meet Again." Then he could have gone on to Paris and spoken a few praiseworthy words in French, which always leaves them eating out of your hand over there. V-E Day would be over and he would have gotten out of it with clean shoes.

But he's going to Russia, which happens right now to be involved in the sale of some nuclear reactors to Iran. Because of events too recent to warrant a reminder, we feel a little squeamish about that. We have told Boris Yeltsin so and he has told us to go stick it.

There have been some indications that the president plans to spend V-E Day persuading Yeltsin to reconsider. This is a worthy errand conducted with the president's customary atrocious timing. Red Square is the wrong pew for an American president on V-E Day. Berkley Square is a far better venue.

Next year, the president may find himself running against a man who left the use of his arm on a European battlefield. Bob Dole and his comrades lucky enough to survive left Italy to forge its own destiny and came back home to heal. Comic strips and comedians have a lot of fun claiming that Dole is trying to cash in on his war injury. In fact, he only mentions it when he's asked about it, and then it's obvious that the pain of it sears him yet.

There are plenty of people in America who know the difference between an honorable wound and a cheap shot. It's true that such people are getting old and gray and that their notion of sacrifice is considered, in some quarters, quaint and unhip.

But, in the president's quest for diversity in the White House, he ought to import a couple of them to advise him on how to keep his loafers out of the goo. "Watch what you're stepping on" is all they'd have to say. Isn't it that easy, or am I missing something? Somebody is.

—April 10, 1995

Uncle Sam's vacation

Dear federal employees: Congratulations and welcome back to work. The rest of us are very happy for you.

While you were sitting at home, we felt sorry for you, but in a limited way. We know most of you work very hard, and the money you spend enriches the private businesses in our community. You are our friends and neighbors, and we wish you well.

If you felt we had rationed our sympathy, you were right. In a country that lives from paycheck to paycheck, your furlough caused you anxiety and grief. A caring media filled the news with little human interest stories about you, worrying about your mortgage payments and your telephone bills. Your few weeks of nervousness got you a lot of coverage.

But the rest of us knew that YOU knew that sooner or later— probably sooner—it would end. That you would be back at your desks and paid in full for the time you were away. That in the meantime, banks would lend you money based on the certainty that your full salary would be restored. That everything would be the way it was again—the paycheck, the health care, the pension program. All of it.

A lot of us out here aren't so lucky. Steadily, almost stealthily, over the last few years, many of us have been sent home, too. Like you, some of us had been told we were no longer essential. The companies we thought would see us through to retirement downsized or merged or moved or just flat went out of business.

And when that happened, the TV reporters didn't come poking around to record our fears and anger. Our little tragedies were usually camouflaged on the business page. "Ajax Screw to Lay Off 200 Workers," the story said. And somewhere, hidden behind that number, were our individual stories of depression and grief and dashed hopes.

Oh, it's true that every once in a while some feature editor or producer would get the idea to mount an expedition and find out what on earth had become of us. What they usually found was that we were in lower-paying jobs with fewer, if any, benefits. Maybe the house was gone. No bank had been willing to bet on our economic resuscitation. It looked like a sucker bet, and, for many of us, it was.

Sometimes, the media would try to put a cheery spin on us. "Man, Fired From Middle Management, Turns Hobby Into Business," a story would say. And we would see Sam, down in his rec room, making pottery and talking about the joys of freedom from the pressures of the workplace.

But such stories rarely mentioned the dark side of self-employment. Sam pays all his Social Security now, and his pension and his health care. Unless it has been a great month for pottery, he's lucky if he has a pot left to . . . to save his pennies in.

I have used the words "we" and "us" in this little message, and some may think that's presumptuous of me. After all, I have a nice job—a couple of them, as a matter of fact. And so far, I have managed to pay all my bills and put a little aside, too. Not enough, but a little.

Ah, but I am very lucky and I know it. In the last 15 years, two of the publications that employed me have gone out of business. One of them we all thought would be around forever. And, while I was lucky, I have a lot of friends who are Sams. Good, talented, hard-working people who have had to settle for less and who, by now, know that less is all they are going to get. And that's just in my business. Multiply that by all the businesses and try to count the Sams.

While you were home last week, federal employees, some of your bosses were making big news. A congressional committee was investigating Secretary of Energy Hazel O'Leary, for example. She likes to fly around the world like royalty, lugging a bigger entourage than the one Prince Charlie brought when he came to town.

She did her best to justify her expenses, but her expense account still came up with $250,000 unaccounted for. The Sams get mad when they hear stuff like that. But she's at work today. Hell, she was at work while you were home.

And it's not just Hazel O'Leary. It's all the Hazel O'Learys. When you were waiting for paychecks, some of you blamed the

Republicans and some of you blamed the president. But you were paying the penalty for 30 years of Hazel O'Leary-style accounting that's going to leave our children in hock.

What kind of name would you hang on somebody who steals money from a child?

Well, it's over for the time being. It isn't your fault. We know that. But something's going to have to change. And you've got the key to it. You learned a lesson these last weeks that a lot of the people above you don't know. It's this: You can't spend what you don't have.

See if you can pass that up the line, will you? All the way to the top. To where the buck stops and is turned into confetti. Have a nice day.

—January 8, 1996

Saved to death

The other day, the government shot a wolf it was trying to help. This shows you that government welfare programs can be as hard on wolves as they are on people.

I have been following the wolf welfare program with astonishment and dismay, but until now, I've kept my trap shut about it. When it comes to wolves, I am an admitted ignoramus. If pressed for an opinion, my advice would be to leave them alone and hope they reciprocated. But as you will see, no matter how dumb you are about a subject, you are probably smarter than the government.

A year or so ago, the government decided to move some wolves back into Yellowstone Park. The last wolf moved out of Yellowstone about 60 years ago because the neighborhood had gone to hell. Every time a wolf went out to take a stroll or nibble on a sheep, some hunter or rancher shot him. So the surviving wolves wisely took off for Canada, like the hippies did in the '60s.

But animal lovers and the government wolf experts decided

the wolves ought to come back again. Probably this seemed like a nice idea at the time. But looking back on it, even a wolf illiterate like me can see that it had at least two unfortunate flaws.

The first is that wolves know as little of geography as your average 11th-grader. If you tell a wolf he is in Canada, that's news to him. Even if you convince him he is in Canada, he doesn't care. Wolves have no patriotism. They go where they can get the best deal, like an NFL football team.

So the idea of moving wolves back to Yellowstone wasn't done to make the wolves feel better. It was done to make the animal lovers feel better. Animal lovers are always forcing their own desires and ambitions on animals and imagining the animals are percolating with gratitude and bliss. This may work on domestic animals like Chihuahuas or husbands. But a wolf has his own ideas.

Nevertheless, a government plane flew up to Canada and brought back 55 wolves. Naturally, the wolves did not come voluntarily. The sight of a federal agent saying he was there to help them understandably terrified them. They had to be drugged and kidnapped. When they woke up, some of them were in Wyoming and some of them were in Idaho.

Now, let us examine the next flaw in the plan. This is the flaw that mystifies me no matter how hard I think about it. Let's say I really wanted a wolf. Let's say I wanted one bad enough to fly up to Canada and abduct one. When I got the wolf home, wouldn't I expect it to behave like a wolf? Wouldn't I want it to? And wouldn't the wolf have a right to assume that since I chose it over, say a cocker spaniel, its wolfish personality would be welcome, or at least tolerated?

Of course. So the wolves woke up in Yellowstone and, being wolves, they went looking for some sheep to eat. And the next thing they knew, bullets were flying. It was *deja vu* all over again. The old neighborhood hadn't changed a bit. Except now the ranchers weren't just shooting at Wyoming wolves. They were shooting at wolves who were minding their own business up in Canada until the government went up to do them a favor.

To remedy this, the government got a new idea. The victim of this new idea was the unfortunate wolf way back in the first paragraph whose demise forced me to speak sharply on this matter. I will call him George, after a fellow named George Wolf I used to know.

George ate five sheep. The sheep owner was furious. The government stepped in and put George in a box and moved him across 2.2 million acres of park and let him out. And George found his way back across those 2.2 million acres to the same sheep ranch and ate another sheep for dessert.

When Lassie used to accomplish similar feats of navigation, Timmy and Timmy's mom would smother her with hugs and words of praise. But when George made the trip with a little flurry of his personality thrown in at journey's end, the government shot and killed him.

Maybe I'm not a wolf expert, and maybe I don't know much about animal feelings. But I have to believe that George must have been pretty surprised, in his last moment, when he realized that the very government that had pledged to save him from extinction was about to render him personally extinct.

A Canadian wolf can't comprehend such things. It takes an American taxpayer.

—February 7, 1996

Goodbye to a friend

I knew he was dying and I should have called him.

Brent Larkin did call him and the two of them had lunch, and Brent reported back to me that the news was very bad. So I thought, "I'll call him. Just as soon as I can figure out what to say to him."

It was never easy, figuring out what to say to him. He was no fan of the media, though he worked in it awhile. At his news conferences, he chewed on hostile reporters with relish, like a man eating hors d'oeuvres. The media was a catered snack to him in the heady days when life was a party thrown in his honor. The party's over. It was over years ago.

Once I made the mistake of telling him what I thought had gone wrong in his life.

"If Hubert Humphrey had been elected in '68," I said, "you surely would have been a candidate for a Cabinet post. But he lost and there wasn't anywhere for you to go."

Being black, I meant. For in those days, a black man had no hope of election to statewide office. He had to stay in his own county, near his own ethnic power base. Hall of Fame politicians stuck in the Negro Leagues.

He didn't like my analysis and a chill fell over the dinner table and he stayed sore at me the rest of the evening. Because I was right? Because I was wrong? Because, right or wrong, I had carelessly opened an old wound in his pride? I didn't know, and now I'll never know. The Q and A is finished and I missed my deadline.

I was his friend, but I didn't pick up the phone and call him. When he signed his book for me, he generously wrote: "To my friend, Dick Feagler, whom I admire and respect as a journalist and whose wit and insight make him a standout among those who would comment on the vicissitudes of mankind!" But when it was my turn to say something back, I was tongue-tied. And now that I know what to say, it's too late.

Tomorrow, my voice mail will be full of calls from his enemies. They will take me to task for not commenting on his vicissitudes, which were many and often trying. They will demand the truth and I am ready for them. They will ignore, in their pettiness, that a man's life is the sum of many truths. From this man's life, I will choose only three and I will splice them together and then play them backward, like a tape on rewind.

There is the truth of California in 1968. My friend is out there campaigning for Humphrey, but the Democrats have called on him late and left him time to do little. But my friend is at the top of his game and, at the top of his game, he is so magnetic that when he enters a room, its occupants move toward him, irresistibly, as if the floor has been tipped in his direction.

At a university, a cafeteria is packed with students, black and white, who greet him like a rock star and gaze at him adoringly and lunge for autographs. He is criminally handsome and impeccably dressed and he moves like a dancer, and the eyes of the white students shine with excitement and the eyes of the black students shine with hope. He is a man who, near the end of a harsh and cynical decade full of death, can kindle hope and enthusiasm in the eyes of young people by talking about the system. That is the truth and I saw it. And I have rarely seen it since.

Next, the year before. In the small hours of morning, the vote count reveals he has done something no black man has ever done before in the history of the country. And he has done it here! In this city! God, we are proud, most of us. He stands at the podium with his arm around his wife and his eyes glinting with tears of triumph, and nobody wants the cheering to end. We thought we were onto something; he thought so at 40 and I thought so at 29. Were we right? Were we wrong? The promise of that night got lost in the vicissitudes. But it happened. That's the truth.

One last picture.

It is two years earlier, 1965. My friend's name is not yet known on the campuses of California and his picture has not yet graced the cover of *Time*. He is running for mayor in an election he will lose. There are no groupies, no autograph seekers. It is night again and he is driving himself around the city from ward club to ward club and I am in tow as his only passenger.

The wisdom is, he hasn't got a chance because he is black. He knows he will probably fail, this time. He is confronting a hurdle no one has leaped. He wonders if he is just going through the motions. So do I. We are both young men with young men's dreams and we cannot see the future. All we can see are the blighted, run-down storefronts of lower Kinsman, their doors barred, their doorways trash-laden.

At a traffic light, a cab pulls up next to us. The driver is an old black man. He recognizes my friend instantly. He leans over and rolls his window down.

"You're gonna do it," he says.

"Maybe," says my friend.

"No maybe," says the old man. "You're gonna be the one who

opens the door. You'll do it." Then the light changes and he is gone.

My friend grins at me. "What do you think?" he says. "Think he's right?"

I should have called him before he died. We should have sat together in the dusk of age, sharing our individual burdens of wasted years and youthful illusions long gone. And what I should have said to him was, "You did it. You really did."

So long, Carl. See ya.

—April 5, 1996

....

Eleanor, Hillary, and Fess Parker

I wasn't sure whether to write about Hillary Clinton and her guru. So I turned to Eleanor Roosevelt for advice.

"What do you think I ought to do, Eleanor?" I asked. "Is this wackiness worth a column? Or should I leave it for Jay Leno?"

"You have to do what you think is right," Eleanor Roosevelt told me, in that high-pitched voice that was unmistakably mine. "It is crucial to set a course and hold to it."

Heavvvvy! That is exactly the same thing Eleanor told Mrs. Clinton, according to revelations in a new book by *Washington Post* Assistant Managing Editor Bob Woodward.

Woodward claims that, at the prompting of New Age (why do you capitalize that?) guru Jean Houston, Mrs. Clinton shut her eyes and imagined a conversation with Mrs. Roosevelt. Houston believes that Eleanor is Hillary's "archetypal, spiritual partner." Houston's own, "archetypal, spiritual partner," she thinks, is the Greek goddess Athena. Mine is the bank that holds my mortgage.

According to Woodward, Hillary, with her staff around her and a tape recorder running, asked Mrs. Roosevelt why people were always putting her down. And then Hillary "speaking as Mrs. Roosevelt," answered in the manner indicated above. But both Hillary and Hillary-Eleanor forgot they were on the record.

So the talk shows got hold of it and naturally they are having a field day with it. Most of them don't like Hillary anyway. Now, thanks to Woodward, they have a new nugget to add to their grievances. They think Hillary may be some kind of nut.

Woodward himself has had some experience with strange and improbable conversations. In a previous published incarnation, he wrote of a conversation he had with CIA head William Casey when Casey lay on his deathbed. Nobody at the time could figure out how he got in to see Casey. Some people thought he hadn't gotten in at all and that Casey was speaking through Woodward's mouth, just as Eleanor spoke through Hillary's and mine.

Then, of course, there was the notorious series of conversations Woodward and his teammate Carl Bernstein had with Deep Throat about the Watergate break-in. We never found out whether Deep Throat was a real person or whether he (she? it?) was some kind of archetypal, spiritual partner with a grudge against Nixon. Maybe it was Oliver Stone.

Talking to themselves is nothing new in Washington. In fact, that's all they do there. All you have to do is watch the Sunday talk shows and you'll hear babbles of incestuous conversations emanating from the mouths of the spirutally aligned.

But dragging in characters from history is a new idea. If the guests show up lugging two or three star-quality spiritual partners with them, all fighting to get a word in edgewise, the McLaughlin Group will seem as orderly as a Quaker meeting house.

In the Old Age, if people wanted advice, they went to their priest, minister or rabbi. But there was a serious drawback in this. Often the priest, minister or rabbi told you stuff you didn't want to hear.

The nice thing about rapping with a New Age spiritual partner is that, when you get through, you always feel real neat about yourself. You're ready to go out and be all that you can be and dream the impossible dream, even if you sleep through your dental appointment.

That's why New Age gurus are popular with egomaniacs like movie stars, rock singers, and the upper-management elite of big corporations. I know executives who have gone off and locked themselves in a Holiday Inn for a couple of days to get their self-actualization tuned up by a passing gypsy. They come back delighted with themselves and full of idiotic plans and hallucinogenic visions. Their employees know enough to hide in the can until the spell wears off.

If Hillary had taken her troubles to an Old Age spiritual partner, she might have found herself in a conversation about the Whitewater files or the travel office firings or the stack of confidential files the White House ordered from the FBI. Such a conversation might have made her gloomy and perhaps even repentant. Old Age spiritual partners are big on confession and repentance, which is why they are fading from fashion, especially in Washington, where confession and repentance are regarded as cardinal sins.

But Eleanor Roosevelt wasn't nosy. In fact, if you read carefully, you'll see that she didn't even answer the question Hillary asked her. Come to think of it, she didn't answer mine, either.

All Eleanor told Hillary and me was to do what we think is right, set a course and hold it. That's the same thing Davey Crockett, speaking through the actor Fess Parker, told me when I was just a lad.

"Be sure yer right, then go ahead," Davey (via Fess) told me as I sat in front of the TV set watching the *Walt Disney Show.* "By golly, I will!" I said. But I soon found out that the trick was in knowing when I was right and when I wasn't.

In the New Age movement, you're right if it feels good. And writing about Hillary hobnobbing with Eleanor doesn't make me feel good. I'd feel a lot better if the conversations coming out of Washington were about saving Medicare and Social Security and fixing welfare and curing education.

These are the things that worry Washington's real archetypal, spiritual partners, otherwise known as the taxpayers. I'm pretty sure I'm right about that. There's nothing surprising about Hillary's solo-duet with Eleanor. In the White House, they've been talking out of both sides of their mouths for years.

—June 26, 1996

We drove American troops to death

When body bags come back from foreign shores, the decent thing to do is pause in our busy lives and honor the fallen.

We used to say that the fallen fell to keep us free. But lately it's become a little more complicated than that.

What we usually say now is that the fallen fell to preserve our American values. And, in the case of the young airmen who died in Saudi Arabia, that is surely true.

We Americans value oil. We value all-terrain vehicles and jet-ski sleds. We value a car in the garage for Daddy and one for Mommy and a beater in the driveway for Junior.

We value rush hour, no matter how much we curse it. We value sitting motionless in our autos on clotted freeways, listening to the drive-time radio jesters amuse us with their droll and salacious wit.

Peer into the creeping cars surrounding you some evening at 5:30 and you will see that most carry a single occupant. Decent commuter rail systems would free our clogged traffic arteries like blood thinner. But we don't want decent rail systems. They would rob us of independence. Not that it's easy to achieve Independence, or Brecksville either, with I-77 a nightly parking lot between downtown and I-480.

The body bags are coming home from a culture where women are discouraged from driving a car. At the beginning of the Gulf War, a group of Saudi women staged a drive-in. They drove through Saudi streets demanding driver equality. They kept their veils on during their protest. They didn't want to appear unreasonably rabid. But their protest was too extreme for one Saudi journalist who was quoted as saying: "I can't imagine looking over at another car and finding my sister at the wheel."

Saudi culture shields the squeamish from such shocking sights. But American troops are not over there to defend the Saudi way of life.

They are there, in large part, to defend the American way of cutting the grass on a cute little gasoline-powered tractor. The American way of whacking weeds with a gas-powered flail. The

American snowmobile is on the line in an arid desert kingdom. The American dirt bike is fighting for its life over in the sands.

Our allies, the Saudis, are having family trouble. Their king suffered a stroke last year. In meetings, his mind wanders back to the happy memories of his youth. The royal family is seen as corrupt by many Saudi citizens. Militant Islamics are saying the government is too cozy with America. We could say "so long" were it not for oil. Oil does not calm the troubled waters of the Middle East. But oil forces us to sail in them.

Once we talked of conservation, but such talk faded away. Now, anybody who suggests we ought to conserve energy is branded as a tree-hugging liberal. We are not a careful country. Conservation is no virtue here. Prudence is labeled paranoia. We are not big on long-term plans. We have a heritage of using up the landscape and moving on.

Under Jimmy Carter, the oil scare scared us big. We created a Department of Energy to shoosh it away. Now, the energy secretary is under fire for burning too much gas in movie stars' planes on junkets. Lyndon Johnson tried to teach us to turn out the lights before we left the room. Now Cleveland Electric Illuminating Co. is offering bonus points for customers who use the most electricity. If you collect enough, you get free electrical appliances.

But this is a column of respect, not of whining. It is not meant to foster guilt for the dead. Simple tears always short-change the flag-draped coffins. And, while it is customary to thank the military dead, such thanks is often vague, as if we weren't sure what we were thanking them for. That's not good enough.

We stuck a long straw into a sand dune in a troubled country. We want to sip enough oil to quench the thirst of our gadgetry and to keep the prices low at the pumps. Young men and women are sent to protect our lifestyle, and this week some of them died. A gasoline truck exploded like a blockbuster and killed them.

Their names are on the newscast, which is filled, nightly, with impersonal death. But the deaths in Saudi Arabia are personal. The dead died where we sent them. The least they deserve is a moment of thoughtfulness out there on the freeway in drive-time.

—June 28, 1996

He's ba-a-ack

Dennis again!

In the wee, witching hours of Wednesday morning, that unmistakable elfin face suddenly filled the television screen. The patent leather hair. The shoe button eyes. The slightly mad, "What-me-worry?" grin. It was him, all right. Dennis the Undead.

The head floated there for a while, disembodied. Dennis was asking for a box to stand on, to hike himself up for the camera. No box could immediately be found. It was better that way. It was spookier.

In the bad lighting, the head looked perfectly preserved. It did not seem to have aged an hour in 17 years. But this was in keeping with the laws of the supernatural. Read Stephen King and you know these things.

What else was going on at this astonishing hour? Were the chandeliers at the Union Club wildly vibrating, their crystal pendants exploding in a puree of ground glass? Were the computers in the city's large banks in a state of meltdown? Had Tony's Diner risen from the weeds to serve meatloaf once again to the out-of-town press, lured here by a story of civic chaos?

The head turned toward me. The eyes gleamed. The lips moved.

"I am now your congressman," Dennis said.

And then I remembered the zapper. I was sitting on it. I grabbed it and aimed it at the TV and pushed a button. Dennis vanished. David Brinkley appeared, muttering oaths about the president of the United States. I relaxed. "None of this is happening," I thought. "It must all be a dream. Brinkley wouldn't say those things. And Dennis can't be back. I was there the night they buried him."

And I was. Here is some of what I wrote, back in 1979:

"The town was a hit-man yesterday. It terminated Dennis Kucinich with extreme prejudice. It voted bitter. It knew what it wanted to get rid of and it turned out to do the job.

"The city knocked Dennis Kucinich down and that left George Voinovich standing alone. And so he became the mayor.

"'What I need now is time,' Voinovich said. 'I have to have time to find the right people. I've got to keep the people around me from panicking. I have to find a finance man. I have to have a guy who has some credibility with the banks. A guy who can walk into the banks. That's the first job and the tough job. Finding people to straighten out the finances.'

"When Dennis left the Voinovich ballroom, there were some city policemen on the sidewalk in front of the Cleveland Plaza Hotel. The Kucinich car had difficulty pulling out into traffic. One of the cops left his friends and walked into the street.

"'I'll get you out of here,' he said. He put his fingers in his mouth and whistled. 'I'll stop traffic for you,' he sneered. He held up his arm and oncoming traffic stopped.

"'Now go!' he yelled. He kicked the bumper of the car. 'Go!' he bellowed. 'Go, you S.O.B.!'"

That was the eulogy I wrote for Dennis' political funeral. And if you think it's harsh, get this. I liked him. Maybe that will give you a sense of the state of mind of the Comeback City at the end of Dennis' stewardship.

His political career went into a well-marked grave. But time is a great eraser. And time has been kind to Dennis while he's been floating in the political nether world. The world where the restless spirits of ejected politicians scratch at the windowpane, trying to rejoin the living.

The light plant he saved is a candle to his memory. The anarchy he created is half-forgotten. His job description was mayor, but he barked at the businessmen until they finally turned and bit him. He was on a populist mission, carrying his slingshot, ready to play David for anybody who thought he was getting screwed. That's the act he left with. And the one he packed for the second coming.

For it's all true. Brinkley did cuss and Dennis did come back. And he's my congressman. And here we go. I vastly prefer this incarnation. At least he's not running things. Agitators cannot govern. Governing demands compromise. The previous Dennis refused to accept that. Zeal and uncompromising righteousness swept him into the mayor's chair. And the same qualities ushered him out at the end of a cop's flat foot.

In 1979, I wrote a column called "So Long, Dennis." At the end of it, I said:

"You had the heart but you lacked the humility. To you, that was weakness. You never learned humility, but you'll get a lesson in it on election night.

"When it comes, treat it like a gift. When you come back, bring it with you."

A little pompous of me, I agree. But not unkindly meant. His return was a long time coming. He is bound to make life interesting. Perhaps the mellowness of years has brought the gift of humility to both of us. I get plenty from you. He'll get his from the Republican Congress.

—November 8, 1996

....

Saying lots of nothing

"Fellow citizens, the future is up to us."

So read the USA Today headline above the text of William Jefferson Clinton's second inaugural.

Instantly, I recognized that as something I had once said.

Seizing the newspaper, I read on with a mounting feeling of disquiet and suspicion:

"Guided by the ancient vision of a promised land, let us set our sights upon a land of new promise."

Aha! This was obviously a crafty reworking of a line I had once written that went like this:

"The past is history, the present is reality, only the future will unlock the secrets of those things which are yet to come."

Could it be? Could William Jefferson Clinton be a plagiarist? This was a serious charge. I needed more evidence. I read more of the inaugural text:

"A government that is smaller lives within its means and does more with less. Yet, where it can stand up for our values and interests around the world and where it can give Americans the power to make a real difference in their everyday lives, government should do more, not less."

No question about it! This was a rather clumsy rewrite of my line, originally crafted this way:

"Government should become less and do more with less. Except in those cases where it should do more, not less. In those cases, doing less should never stand in the way of doing more. You have my word on it!"

That was all the evidence I needed that William Jefferson Clinton was pirating from me. And don't you scoff. I have a witness.

Years ago, I made a bet with John Halprin, a producer at a television station where I worked. I bet him $25 I could deliver a television commentary that said nothing at all.

I don't mean, you understand, a television commentary that was merely dumb. Or badly reasoned. Or wrong-headed. Those are easy to do. I do them all the time.

No. Our bet was that I could deliver a commentary that, while seeming to say something, in fact said nothing. Each ringing phrase, which appeared to be a call to arms, would in fact be a yodel. When encountering a metaphorical fork in the road, the commentary would urge its inspired listeners to march boldly in both directions. And nobody would catch on.

That was the whole point of the bet. If just one bemused viewer called the station to point out that the commentary, while crowded with "meaning," was vacant of opinion, I'd lose.

But Halprin and I were afraid somebody from management might have overheard our plot. We figured that if we purposely aired a commentary that was contrived as a prank, we might be fired for fraud.

So we decided to wait a year or so to try out our scheme. I set to work preparing the commentary so it would be ready when the heat was off us. But in that year, Halprin left to take a job at another station. And we never got a chance to pull our stunt.

But I still have my notes. Listen to this line, for example:

"There is nothing wrong with America that is not wrong with Americans. And let us never forget that there is nothing wrong with Americans that is not wrong with America."

Doesn't that sound suspiciously like this line from the inaugural speech?

"Government is not the problem and government is not the solution. We, the American people, we are the solution."

Of course, I'm not claiming that the whole inaugural speech was based on my flim-flam commentary. The commentary was only a minute long. The inaugural speech went on for about 20 minutes. So the president had to pad it with the vision thing. He put in the following 19 things he would like to see happen pretty soon:

Unity, diversity, illness cures, lots of computers, great schools, free college, no drugs, laughing children, nice parents, full employment, no terrorists, a balanced budget, plenty of Medicare and Social Security, no crime in the streets, no bickering, no poor people, world peace and lots of values.

All of those things, he said, are waiting across the bridge to the 21st century, if only we . . . as soon as we . . . if, starting tomorrow we . . . if, with the help of Congress, we . . . if all of us, individually, vow that we . . . if, calling on the spirit of our forefathers, we . . . and foremothers, we . . . if, all-together-on-three, we . . .

DO SOMETHING!

Speaking from experience, I'll tell you it was a great speech, no matter what some of the pundits are saying. And it looks like he got away with it, too, because after it was over, they gave him a big round of applause. Not to mention a big parade. Not to mention a big dance.

Not to mention that John Halprin owes him 25 bucks.

—January 22, 1997

North by north coast: a sports crime thriller

I never enjoyed football until we lost our team. But ever since then, I've found football riveting. Spine-tingling. Jam-packed with the kind of suspense that keeps me on the edge of my seat. So full of startling plot twists that I can't put it down.

"Gripping" is another word for what I now find football to be. To put it yet another way, football has become a masterful psychological drama that illuminates the dark side of the human soul. "Numbing," "heart-stopping" and "emotionally exhausting" are a few other things that football is. Did I mention "riveting"? Yes, I did.

For me, football changed forever the morning we woke up and found that the team was gone. At first, this seemed unbelievable. There must be some perfectly natural explanation for it. Perhaps the team had gone off to play in the Super Bowl. No. That was a perfectly unnatural explanation.

And then we found the note.

"We have taken your team," the note said. "If you ever want to see the Browns again, go down to the lakefront, dig a hole and put $250 million in it. No cops. Signed, the NFL."

Our first reaction was shock. Outrage soon followed. Then outrage was replaced by anger. Anger soon gave way to tears. Tears led to deep depression. Depression was transformed into grim resolve. Resolve translated itself into action. Action brought with it a sense of relief. Relief produced exuberance. Exuberance seemed to open the door to giddiness, which in turn ushered in temporary insanity. Temporary insanity brought its wallet.

So we went down to the lakefront, dug a hole and put $250 million in it. Then we waited to get the Browns back.

By this time, I was hooked. I had suddenly become a football fan. Before these events, I had always found football to be boring and predictable.

It was the same, year after year. A shaky season, followed by the playoffs. Much fuss, hoop-de-doodle and hollow optimism.

Then somebody fumbles the ball on the four-yard line and the other team drives 630 yards in the last three seconds of play and wins the game. Everybody had the plot memorized like the script of the *Rocky Horror Picture Show*.

Me? I like a good mystery myself. One of those vintage Hitchcock films, or a lavish and tasteful whodunit on PBS. A *Columbo* rerun will do. *Murder She Wrote* isn't much for plot, but the actors in it have emerged from puberty and behave like grownups.

So when we found the ransom note and argued about whether to pay it and then decided to pay it and dug the hole and put the money in, I realized that football had a familiar side to it that I had never known was there. Football was something I understood and enjoyed. Football was a felony.

I went straight to the nearest sports bar and struck up a conversation with a huge fat fellow, naked to the waist, with orange and brown stripes painted all over him.

"Are you a football fan?" I asked.

"Woof," he said.

"Woof once if you mean yes and twice if you mean no," I said.

"Woof," he said.

"I'm a football fan, too," I said. "I haven't been one for very long. That's because I never realized that football is really all about kidnapping and blackmail. That's something I'm an expert in from watching a lot of mysteries. And do you know what the first rule of blackmail is?"

"Woof-woof," said my new friend.

"Don't pay it," I said. "Because you can't trust a blackmailer. Once you start playing his game, he makes up his own rules. And pretty soon, you find yourself getting in deeper and deeper. You wanna hear the stats on that?"

Well, he was out of his depth. Overwhelmed by my superior knowledge of football, he whined softly, paid his bill and left. I certainly hope he has been reading the recent newspapers. Now there is talk of a new ransom note.

"Thanks for the hole and the $250 million," this note may say. "There has been a little change of plans. We're thinking about kidnapping somebody else's football team and giving it to

you. And here's what's rich. We're thinking of kidnapping the
team from the city that kidnapped the team from the city that
kidnapped your team. Pretty funny, huh? Signed, your pals and
accomplices in the NFL."

I ask you. Could Hitchcock have done any better when it
comes to startling plot twists? Hasn't this become a masterful
psychological drama that illuminates the dark side of the
human soul? Isn't it jam-packed with the kind of suspense that
keeps you on the edge of the seat you paid for twice?

Woof once if you feel like a fireplug.

—June 2, 1997

How to burn a symbol

"Our guest today on *Face the Media* is the Star-Spangled
Banner. Thank you for being here, Mr. Banner."

"You can drop the mister. Just call me Banner. I wave at
everybody, regardless of sexual orientation."

"Well, Banner, as you know, Congress is again trying to pass
a constitutional amendment to protect you from desecration."

"Is that right?"

"You mean you weren't aware of it?"

"I stopped keeping track. They do that every couple of years,
you know. It never gets anywhere."

"How do you feel about the present House of Representatives
voting to protect you, Banner?"

"I hate to say. It might sound a little rude."

"Please feel free to speak your mind."

"Well, it's a little bit like Pee Wee Herman volunteering to be
your bodyguard."

"But a lot of people say that a threat to you is a threat to our
freedom, Banner."

"They've got it backward. What they ought to be saying is a
threat to freedom is a threat to me."

"But what about people who actually set fire to you and burn you up?"

"Who? Name one."

"Cheryl Lessin."

"I beg your pardon? Who's Cheryl Lessin?"

"Why, Banner. Surely you remember Cheryl Lessin, that Cleveland communist woman who set you on fire a couple of years ago. Everybody was real worried that she might have hurt you."

"Take a good look at me. Do you see so much as a smudge?"

"Well, no. No I don't."

"Of course you don't. I'm still here. Haven't you ever heard that song written about me? 'The flag was still there,' it goes. And here I am, just like the song says."

"But, Banner, aren't people like Cheryl Lessin a danger to all you stand for?"

"Listen, sonny. I've survived people like Tojo and Hitler and Mussolini. I was ripped down over Corregidor and hauled up over Iwo Jima. I've had my ups and downs with world-class tyrants. Compared to them, Cheryl Lessin, whoever she is, has got about as much menace in her as a wet match."

"Maybe so, Banner. But what about all the good men who died and were wounded in your name? Doesn't an attack on you desecrate their memory?"

"You don't have to remind me of them, sonny. I was there, remember?"

"Well, of course, I didn't mean . . . "

"I think about them all the time. I fly over their graves. I fly over veterans hospitals, where some of them will spend the rest of their lives. I don't see too many visitors to those graves or those veterans hospitals. I don't see too many people coming and going. It's pretty easy to respect the dead and wounded with your mouth."

"So what you're saying, Banner, is you don't want a constitutional amendment to protect you from desecration?"

"No. What I'm saying is, I don't get a vote one way or the other. It isn't my country. I'm just the symbol of it. I'm fireproof. Nobody can burn me. But what they can do is cheapen me."

"What do you mean?"

"Listen, sonny. It's my job to fly over this country no matter what kind of country it is. What's important to me is to fly over a country I'm proud of. For 200 years I've been pretty lucky. But it's the people in charge that can ruin me. Look at my old colleague, the Hammer and Sickle, God rest him. It was his government that brought him down in shame, not some twerp with a Zippo."

"So you mean . . ."

"I mean if Congress wants to do something nice for me, they ought to quit grandstanding over the sexy issues and tackle the hard ones. The better the country gets, the happier I am being its symbol."

"And how happy are you at the present time, Banner?"

"I've felt better. But then again, I've felt worse. If the country's strong, I'm strong. And the stronger the country gets, the less I need protection. Nobody has to hang a sign on Arnold Schwarzenegger that says, 'Messing with this man is a constitutional violation.'"

"Well, thank you for being with us today, Star-Spangled Banner. You're a grand old flag. And, if you'll allow me to say so, long may you wave."

"You're welcome. And if Congress will only do what it was sent to Washington to do, my wave will be permanent."

—June 16, 1997

....

Last words from LBJ

Once, I visited a place where people listened to the voices of the dead.

It was a place called Lily Dale in New York state. Lily Dale was a spiritualist community. Its residents did not believe in the silence of the grave. The grave was merely a doorway, they thought. Loved ones passed through and wandered out of sight.

But they could speak to us as if they were speaking from another room.

I wrote some articles about Lily Dale and, since I was a non-believer, I wrote them in a lighthearted vein. For I was certain then that dead men tell no tales. But I was wrong.

Lyndon Johnson has been dead for nearly 25 years. But the other day, he spoke to us about the Vietnam War. What he said came from an Oval Office tape we had never heard before.

Johnson wanted to speak from beyond the grave. But he didn't want it to happen this soon. Before he died, he asked his wife to keep the tapes secret until at least the year 2023. She decided not to wait that long. For that, she deserves our thanks.

The young men who fought in Vietnam will be old men in 2023. It is better that they hear Johnson now, before the sharply etched inscription of memory grows faint and smooth. Perhaps they still remember him as the commander-in-chief who urged them into battle and assured them that their cause was necessary and right and unquestionable.

They may have a memory, as I do, of a macho Lyndon Johnson touring the rear areas in safari clothing. Pinning on medals, patting shoulders, talking to privates in a firm and fatherly manner stolen from a pile of used John Wayne scripts:

"Mr. President, this is your helicopter, sir."

"They're all my helicopters, son."

Ah, but now here is Johnson from beyond the grave. Speaking to adviser McGeorge Bundy in 1964, on the eve of widening American commitment:

Johnson: "I stayed awake all last night thinking of this thing . . . It looks to me like we're getting into another Korea . . . I don't think we can fight them 10,000 miles away from home . . . I don't think it's worth fighting for. And I don't think we can get out. It's just the biggest damned mess that I ever saw."

Bundy: "It's an awful mess."

Johnson: "What the hell is Vietnam worth to me? What's it worth to this country? Of course, if you start running from the communists, they may just chase you into your own kitchen."

Bundy: "And that's what the rest of the world is going to think if this thing comes apart on us."

Johnson: "But everybody I talk to that's got any sense says, 'Oh, my God, ple-ee-ease give this thought.' This is a terrible thing we're getting ready to do."

What ghostly, Halloween whisper is more chilling than the live voice of this dead man speaking to us from this dead year? The voice has broken all barriers of time and space to reach our ears. But we are helpless listeners. We can't batter our way back to that moment and elbow Bundy out of the room and endorse Johnson's misgivings and rip up the death warrant he feels compelled to sign with his bewitched pen.

Later, with his feet in the quicksand, Johnson calculates the effect of the war on his domestic politics. The "terrible thing" is under way. He asks adviser Larry O'Brien if carnage abroad will be helpful in a congressional vote on War on Poverty legislation.

Johnson: "What effect will bombing the hell out of the Vietnamese tonight have on this bill? I'd think Congress would be a little more reluctant to vote against the president."

O'Brien: "It certainly is not going to hurt us."

War, von Clausewitz said, is an extension of politics. Politics, Johnson knew, can be a beneficiary of war. Does he have enough votes for the poverty bill? Not now. But maybe tomorrow, after the B-52s do their work.

The Johnson tapes made a little blip on the nightly news and on the talk shows. We have grown used to the idea of Oval Office tapes. The news goes by us in a blur, and it is easy to put the Johnson tapes in the same category with 9-1-1 tapes and tapes pried loose from a black box after an airline disaster. Eerie footnotes to catastrophe. Nothing more.

But they are more. They are a warning to any generation that is sent, armed with rifles and pep talks, into far-off countries on errands not clearly defined. "What the hell is Vietnam worth to me?" the dead man whispers, in a voice that comes to us from beyond 55,000 graves.

—October 27, 1997

George Forbes vs. George Forbes

It's fun having George Forbes back in the news columns again, if only for a while. It gives us pundits a chance to dust off words like "outlandish" and "irrepressible" and "outrageous."

City Hall is a duller place since Forbes retired from the daily scrimmages of public life. He left a void of adjectives none of his followers has been able to fill.

Boring, bland, technocratic words often are used to describe hizzoner the mayor. Words like "micromanager" and "manic" and "meddlesome." The City Council president is sometimes labeled "conciliatory" and "sober" and "concerned."

But this is the vocabulary of a chess tournament. When Forbes was running council, the ambience was more that of a demolition derby. It was exciting to peek from the bleachers as Forbes hurled debris around—the occasional folding chair, for instance, or the occasional snooping reporter.

Then mellowness came to him as it does to most of us. And he retired from elective life to become president of the local chapter of the NAACP.

This statesmanlike work kept his talent for brass somewhat muted. But then, just when some were beginning to think that, like Sinatra, he may have given his last virtuoso performance, he burst from behind the curtains to wow the public again.

Word reached the NAACP that the Shell Oil Co. might be charging service-station owners more for gas on the East Side than it was on the West Side and suburbs. This has racial implications in our town, where the Cuyahoga carries more vivid symbolism than that little ol' trout stream in the movie A River Runs Through It.

So the NAACP decided to join in a class-action lawsuit against Shell. Or at least a news release was dutifully prepared to that effect by my old Cleveland Press pal, Powell Caesar, who acts as NAACP spokesman.

The NAACP's legal battle against Shell would, naturally, be led by that fearless, outspoken civil rights champion, George Forbes.

But who could possibly defend Shell against such a powerful opponent? Where would Shell find a defense attorney with enough stature, experience and ferocity to match George Forbes? It was time to face facts. Only one man had the credentials to take on George Forbes. And that man's name was George Forbes. So Shell quickly hired him.

Well! This set up the kind of contest that is normally possible only on a computer. You can rig a computer so that Babe Ruth the pitcher faces Babe Ruth the hitter. But rigging a lawsuit so that George Forbes complainant faces George Forbes for the defense? In the category of special effects, it seemed as sensational as Leonardo DeCaprio playing himself as twins in *The Man in the Iron Mask*.

It was outlandish! It was outrageous! But it was not irrepressible. At least not to Kweisi Mfume, national president of the NAACP. In fact, Mfume moved to repress it.

He suggested that Forbes should not represent both sides of the issue, that he ought to be on one side or the other side. This seems to me like a narrow view. Who says you have to be on one side or the other side?

After all, how many pockets does a pair of pants have?

Mfume isn't from around here, so he can be forgiven for selling Forbes short in the virtuosity department. If I were running a big oil company faced with a civil rights action, George Forbes is the first person I would want to hire to help me out of my jam. This is what is known as spreading oil on troubled waters.

After some swing and sway about its position, the local NAACP was deliberating whether to support the lawsuit. But it won't be too hard for the chapter to reach a decision it can live with.

After all, the letterhead says it's an organization dedicated to the advancement of people. And whatever happens, at least one person is going to advance. You know who, too.

—March 18, 1998

In our hearts, we know he told the truth

I woke up with a cold, but I would have walked through an ice storm to vote against Barry Goldwater in 1964. I was trying to save humanity.

The media portrayed Goldwater as a warmonger and a kook. "In your heart, you know he's right" was the Goldwater campaign slogan. "In your heart, you know he's nuts," snarled the bumper stickers of the opposition.

Many things made me nervous about Goldwater. But, for me, the presidential campaign turned on a very clear-cut issue. The issue was a war in Vietnam, a war I felt we had no business fighting. And Lyndon Johnson agreed with me.

It was Goldwater, at the angry Republican convention of 1964, who stood at the podium, glared down at the crowd and sternly said: "Don't try to sweep this under the rug. We are at war in Vietnam. And the secretary of defense refuses to say if our objective is victory."

How much more soothing it was to listen to Lyndon Johnson denounce that speech as a right-wing lie.

I heard him do it right here in Public Hall. He flew into town on Air Force One, then landed in a helicopter at Edgewater Park. A motorcade took him downtown through a cheering crowd of well-wishers.

The crowd pressed in so close that Norman Mlachak, who was driving the *Cleveland Press* car, ran over some guy's foot. Norman, a gentle man, felt terrible about it.

"It wasn't your fault," I told him. "Let's just hope the guy was a *Plain Dealer* subscriber."

Inside the hall, Johnson spoke loud and plain about his intentions in Southeast Asia.

"I will not send American boys to fight in Veet-nam," he said to wild applause.

So there you had it, a clear-cut choice. The warmonger rashly claiming we were already at war and had no plans to win. The peacemaker announcing that a ground war committing American troops was out of the question.

When it was over, we followed Johnson back to Edgewater and waited until his helicopter was just a winking light disappearing in the gathering dusk. The harsh journalistic rule was you always waited until the president was out of sight. Just in case something bad happened.

The only casualty that day was one man with an injured foot. But ahead of us all, over the horizon where we couldn't see, were hundreds of thousands of casualties-in-waiting. Fleets of twisted and shattered helicopters. And the wreckage of trust and innocence never regained.

Barry Goldwater died the other day and went to live on the opposite side of heaven from Lyndon Johnson. The great, lopsided election of 1964 is an old dance card pressed in the pages of history. But the problem it poses is as fresh as tomorrow morning's headlines.

What if the guy who seems so prickly and unsettling is bringing you the truth? What if the guy who seems so warm and caring is bringing you a lie? How are we supposed to gaze into the cracked crystal ball of the news media and sort it all out?

It is good form to speak well of the dead. So, when Goldwater died, politicians across the political spectrum paused to utter kind words about him.

If you distilled all the rhetoric down, what most of them said was that, right or wrong, he spoke the truth as he saw it.

There was a time when such a sentiment might have been considered faint praise. But in this era of spin and double-talk, evasion and illusion, political honesty seems like a gold-plated virtue. In fact, it seems like more. It seems like a quaint souvenir of a time hopelessly beyond recapture.

"If people only say one thing about you, what do you hope it will be?" an interviewer asked Goldwater some years ago.

"That I was honest," he replied.

And that's what they all remembered after he was gone. And thinking back, I remembered, too. I remembered choosing the man who comforted me with lies over the man who frightened me with truth.

I don't know that we've ever stopped doing that. Do you?

—June 3, 1998

Saving ourselves

In a battlefield cemetery, each marble cross marks an individual crucifixion. Someone—someone very young, usually—has died for somebody else's sins.

The movie *Saving Private Ryan* begins and ends in the military cemetery above Omaha Beach. By sundown of D-Day, 40,000 Americans had landed on that beach, and one in 19 had become a casualty.

The military brass purposely chose troops with no combat experience for the bulk of the assault force. The brass reasoned that an experienced infantryman is a terrified infantryman. The odds of dying in the early waves were so great that an informed soldier might be paralyzed with well-founded despair. But the young and idealistic might move forward into the lottery of death.

Director Steven Spielberg made *Saving Private Ryan* as a tribute to D-Day veterans. He wanted, reviewers say, to strip the glory away from war and show the '90s generation what it was really like.

The reviews have praised the first 30 minutes of the film and the special effects that graphically show the blood and horror of the D-Day landing. Unfortunately, American movie audiences have become jaded connoisseurs of special-effects gore. In the hands of the entertainment industry, violence has become just another pandering trick.

But Spielberg wasn't pandering. Shocked by and wary of his depiction, I bought a copy of Stephen Ambrose's book *D-Day*. The story of the Normandy invasion is a story of unimaginable slaughter. Worse than I ever knew, and I thought I knew something about it.

The young men who lived through those first waves are old men now. Many have asked themselves, every day for more than 50 years, why they survived. It is an unanswerable question. The air was full of buzzing death. When the ramps opened on many of the landing craft, all the men aboard were riddled with machine-gun bullets before they could step into the water.

Beyond this cauldron of cordite and carnage, half a world away, lay an America united in purpose like no citizen under 60 has ever seen. The war touched everyone. The entire starting lineup of the 1941 New York Yankees was in military uniform. Almost every family could hang a service flag in the window, with a star embroidered on it for each relative in uniform.

In the early hours of D-Day, with the outcome of the battle still in the balance, the nation prayed. Ambrose tells us that the *New York Daily News* threw out its lead stories and printed in their place the Lord's Prayer.

"I fought that war as a child," a historian on television said the other night. I knew what he meant. So did I. We all saved fat and flattened cans and grew victory gardens. But we did not all go to Omaha Beach. Or Saipan. Or Anzio. Only an anointed few did that.

The men of World War II are beginning to leave us now. In my family, six have gone and two are left. We have lost the uncle who was on Okinawa, the cousin who worked his way up the gauntlet of Italy and the cousin who brought the German helmet back from North Africa.

These men left us with a simple request. You can hear that request in *Saving Private Ryan*. I haven't read a review that has mentioned it, but it is what makes Spielberg's movie a masterpiece.

In the film, a squad of rangers is sent behind enemy lines to save a man whose three brothers have been killed in battle. Higher headquarters wants him shipped home to spare his mother the agony of having all her sons killed in combat.

So eight rangers risk their lives for one man. And when one of the rangers is mortally wounded, he asks Private Ryan to bend over so he can whisper to him.

"Earn this," he says.

And that is the request of all the young men who have died in all the wars—from Normandy to the Chosin Reservoir to Da Nang to the Gulf.

Earn this.

When the movie ended, the theater was silent except for some muffled sobs. But the tears that scalded my eyes were not just for the men who had died on the screen and in truth. Or for the men who had lived and grown old and were baffled about why they had been spared.

I walked out into the world of Howard Stern and Jerry Springer and *South Park*. Into the world of front-page coverage of Monica S. Lewinsky and the stain on her dress that might have been Oval Office semen.

"Earn this" was still ringing in my ears. And the tears in my eyes were tears of betrayal.

—August 5, 1998

....

An unrepentant sinner is unfit to lead us

Of course, the decent and principled thing to do is resign. But we know he won't do that.

He is a man who claims he feels our pain.

But he apparently lacks the empathetic sense of honor that would spare his nation and his family the pain of a sleazy public debate over the details of his reckless and childish genital urges.

He lied to us. And to make sure his lie would be a theatrical success, he imported a Hollywood producer to coach him on how to set his jaw and how to wag his finger.

It is not surprising that he did this. For he lives in a world of illusion in which truth is secondary to theatrics. His ethical notions ripened in an era of marketing and hype where image has a bigger payday than truth.

He came to us from a generation where principles are negotiable and standards of decency are merely cosmetic artifices of repression.

It took successive waves of congressmen to persuade him that he had shamed America. At last, his political instincts were aroused by their earnest petitions. So he followed their advice and stumped the countryside admitting sin.

Any earnest admission of sin includes an acceptance of sin's consequences. Confession is a humbling experience that reaches completion through penance.

But the great White House hope is to escape all penance. The idea is to get a pass. At the same time this president was confessing sin, he was urging his lawyers to fight on, exploiting hand-by-hand all legal loopholes, in an attempt to ratify his moral purity.

This was an act of ultimate crassness. If, at this moment of tardy truth, the president is unwilling to fire himself, the least he can do for America is fire his lawyer, David Kendall.

That would spare us the farce of listening to Kendall and his legalisms, which are an outrageous and cynical insult to our intelligence.

But the arrogance of this presidency and the legal profession is such that Kendall still insists his client told the truth when he denied a sexual relationship with Monica Lewinsky. Nobody in America believes that anymore.

Kendall is playing a silly and irrelevant lawyer's game. Everybody knows that.

So why doesn't the president, his soul presumably laid bare, fire Kendall? Or muzzle him?

The answer is obvious.

The goal of the White House is survival. Truth continues to be a sideline issue. We are governed by a man who has a history of telling lies and getting caught and talking his way out of trouble.

He has built a career on a series of half-baked admissions. He smoked pot but did not inhale. He wriggled out of the draft, but so did a lot of people. He had extramarital affairs, but a lot of people do. It's all a personal matter.

It is that idea, in the darkness that is descending, that gives the White House a glimmer of optimistic light. Will the American people be willing to excuse the president's behavior on the grounds that what he does with his zipper is personal and nobody's business but his?

The answer lies in the polling data. In other words, it lies with you.

Congress has no clear idea what to do about the president's zipper. You better believe that congressmen are lying back in the weeds, waiting for some sense of how you react to the Starr report to instruct them on how to proceed.

The question on America's mind is a tough question. An ironic one. We live in a sex-drenched society. Television programs are X-rated. Condoms are distributed after some concerts at Blossom Music Center. For many, sex is no big deal with no big rules.

Ultimately, the Clinton defense will be that sex with an avid young woman and the lies that followed it are not matters that affect the ship of state.

The congressmen will look to you for guidance. If they looked to me, I would tell them this: We can do better in America than to pick a president who is an embarrassment. And anybody who really felt our pain would quit.

—September 14, 1998

Failing a test of character

When I got into this business 35 years ago, there was a firm though unwritten rule about how we wrote about the extramural sex lives of public officials.

We didn't.

This rule had one exception. If we could draw a bright, straight line between an official's sex life and a betrayal of public trust, his rutting season was fair journalistic game.

If Senator Fraud, married with children, was fooling around with a young woman in the typing pool, we didn't write about it. But if Senator Fraud was reckless enough or dumb enough to put his mistress on the typing pool payroll even though she couldn't type, he was fair game for exposure.

That rule seemed sensible to me, and I followed it faithfully. Once upon a time, I was in Los Angeles covering a politician whose name was a household word. Early one evening he took off in a limo with a female entertainer whose name was also well known.

"This is where the coverage stops, fellas," he told two of us who were enviously watching him depart for his hotel suite. He figured we would probably use our liberated time to search for transient amours of our own. And he was right. It never crossed our minds that there was a story there that the public "had a right to know."

I thought the old rule was a pretty good rule. I still think so. I'd like to see it come back, though it never will, for a lot of bad reasons.

So my quarrel with William Jefferson Clinton is not that he engaged in adolescent, truck stop sex with his emotional clone, Monica Lewinsky.

By now we know more about this dysfunctional duo's hasty aerobics than we once knew about the mating habits of Timmy the gorilla. The report on their antics is a prosecutor's version of *Debbie Does Dallas.* But one piece of telling evidence is missing.

Nothing we have heard indicates that Clinton's quickies with Monica threw the ship of state off its course. No foreign prime minister was left fuming in an anteroom while the president was satisfying his shallow, tomcat imperatives. Life in America went on, unaltered.

Until last January, the president would have slipped past the old rule of the antique old-boy journalism network. Monica, according to the old rule, was overlookable. A person to be kidded about in the Monacle saloon on Capitol Hill. But not a person to be written about.

This opinion will come as a blow to some of my new friends on the voicemail. Twice I have said in this space that if the president had any honor, he would resign. Moralistic readers have called to thank me for taking a stand against adultery and fornication. Critics have phoned to chastise me for hard-heartedness and remind me that only he without sin should cast the first stone. Messages from these two ardent camps have made it impossible to clear the voice mail fast enough. I clear it at 1 a.m., the next morning at 10 it's full again.

I hope this column will reduce my phone traffic to a trickle. My feelings on this matter, if I'm lucky, will appeal to neither side of this increasingly polarized argument.

It's none of my business whom anybody has sex with. That includes the president of the United States and my plumber.

When the president was asked in the Paula Jones deposition whether he had had sex with Monica Lewinsky, his answer should have been "none of your business." If that answer had purchased a contempt-of-court citation, so be it.

The reason William Jefferson Clinton is unfit to be president is not because he sinned. We all sin. His supporters are right about that.

The real test of character is what you do when your sins have found you out. And what the president of the United States did was lie. And to us. And with plenty of time to think it over. And with the help of a drama coach. And worse, he lied dumb. Only an adolescent mind would have believed that his lie might work.

I have raised four kids. All of them, in adolescence, lied to me. Every parent has had that experience. The time always comes when the lie is discovered. Then you have to sit down with the kid and explain that lying only made matters worse.

I didn't mind doing that with my kids. I don't think I should have to do that with the president of my country. I think I have a right to expect my president to be an adult.

It is ghastly to think that a man with the fate of the world in his palm is not an adult. It is chilling to think that his advisers are dumb enough and immature enough to reason with the faulty logic of children.

He must resign. Not because he's too sinful to be president. Because he isn't old enough.

—September 18, 1998

A *new language of lies*

The small story is about non-sex sex and non-perjury perjury. The big story is about a nation gradually going insane.

There are already signs of madness all around us. And, as Al Jolson said in the first talking picture and Monica Lewinsky said in her first meeting with the president, "You ain't seen nothin' yet!"

We already have White House insanity. White House officials proclaimed Monday a good day for the president. In these nutty times, a good day means that the leader of the planet kept his cool during a worldwide discussion of his kinky non-sex sex habits, aired on a major religious holiday.

"It was not a setback for him," a White House source said. And that, crazily enough, is true. But it's a truth that could only be true in a context of dementia.

We have poll insanity. A CNN poll showed that the president's job approval rating went up after the broadcast of his grand jury testimony. Then the anchor lady added this advisory:

"We should stress that this poll is merely a snapshot," she said. "Six hundred adults were polled on their reaction to the broadcast. That number includes 300 people who didn't see the broadcast."

In a lucid world, that would be a bizarre admission. But we have broken the bonds of lucidity and are launched on a lunar mission of lunacy.

Media insanity, always reliable, is in full gallop. My favorite talking head is Dick Morris on Fox News. Morris, that sly old fox and former White House adviser, once held a telephone to a hooker's ear so she could hear the voice of the president. It got him canned. Now he probably wonders who might have been on the other end of the man who was on the other end of the phone.

Especially hurtful to old English majors like me is the linguistic insanity. The president's grand jury testimony was a bedlam of it.

An early victim was the old saying "it takes two to tango." This long-accepted truth, passed down from mothers to daughters, apparently does not apply if the president is on your dance card. According to his testimony, Monica did the tango and he merely got the tang.

As columnist Maureen Dowd put it, "the president claims that oral sex, (the second word of which is sex) isn't sex." Or at least, if I understood him, it isn't sex when it's done to him. If he were doing it, then it would be sex.

There were less spicy verbal casualties. When asked if he was ever alone with Monica, the president said "that depends on how you define 'alone.'" And he waved off one question that stymied him, saying that the answer depended on "what the definition of 'is' is."

The president is a poster boy for bilingual education. Though I don't know where you go to learn the kind of language he speaks. A good start is Yale Law School, I guess.

There is madness aplenty. The debate in the country is about who caused it.

We know we are being driven crazy, but who is the chauffeur? Is it Ken Starr or Bill Clinton? The two of them personify the issue that is carrying the country toward schizophrenia. If Congress moves on to long and horrible impeachment hearings, divisiveness will make the present insanity dangerous.

Last Saturday night I talked to a politician whose name you would know. He is a staunch supporter of Bill Clinton, even though he admits that he is one of the people Clinton lied to about his relationship with Monica Lewinsky.

It is his opinion that the country can't afford to lose Clinton. Not over this. There are, he says, grave international problems on the horizon. It is, he says, the wrong time for a change in leadership.

Is Clinton really that indispensable? In my lifetime, two sainted presidents have died in office. Each died while the world was in a state of white-knuckled uncertainty. But America went on. We did not all pile back in the Mayflower and retreat to England.

If Clinton was able to put his country ahead of his pride, he would step down. If he understood honor, he would step down. But honor is not his strong suit. We saw his special genius on display Monday. He is a master of deceit.

To save his skin, he will allow his country to break loose from the moorings of the rational. So far, he has seduced us into endorsing non-sex sex and non-perjury perjury. He is instructing us in the language of lies. And he is an excellent teacher.

The sentiment I keep hearing is that lies about sex aren't really lies.

See? The man has already got some of us speaking his language.

—September 23, 1998

Good Morning, Class

....

God-fearing teachers

When my old math teacher, Mrs. Kanarsky, caught a kid talking out of turn in class, she would wing an eraser at the offender. It was her view that no rowdy should be allowed to interfere with a child's right to learn.

Pity she's not still around. I would like to ship her a boxcar full of erasers to pepper the Ohio Federation of Teachers with. For that body went to court this week to sabotage the educational ideals it pretends to promote.

The timing was terrible, bordering on the obscene. Yesterday, the Ohio Department of Education released the results of the annual state ninth-grade proficiency test. This is always an occasion for Clevelanders to brace themselves for a spasm of stomach-churning despair. And the news this time was reliably awful.

Only 10 percent of Cleveland's public school ninth-graders passed the math portion of the test. Only a quarter of them passed the reading test. As a basis of comparison, 82 percent of Parma's public school students passed reading, and 61 percent passed math. The urban education crisis is alive and epidemic in the Comeback City.

America is scared to death about its growing dumbness. A Gallup poll taken this week shows that Americans now put education on the top of their list of concerns. Ahead of crime, Medicare and the whole laundry list of issues the politicians are fighting about in this bleak Washington winter.

One might assume that an organization called the Ohio Federation of Teachers would be calling for almost any new idea that might catch hold and grow little shoots of hope in this barren educational wilderness. Bad assumption.

The teachers organization went to court to block a pilot program that would allow Cleveland parents to use vouchers to send their children to schools of their choice. Any public voucher money that goes to parochial schools will violate constitutional separation of church and state, the patriots declared, staunchly.

It is certainly true that almost all of the private schools the state has agreed to give money to are church-affiliated. But it is also true that, statewide, 72 percent of private school ninth-graders managed to pass the latest proficiency test, compared to 48 percent of students in public schools.

Now let us consider Mrs. Jones, who lives in Cleveland and is worried about two things: getting her kid a decent education and protecting her constitutional guarantees of separation of church and state. Let's say that, in her mind, it's a tie. She just isn't sure which worry should worry her most.

So she looks at the public schools and she says, "Well, my kid can flunk math and reading in a God-free environment. Or he can go across the street and learn to read and add, but he may have to learn it from people who mention God once in a while."

I don't know what Patrick Henry would do with Patrick Henry Jr. But the odds are pretty good that Mrs. Jones is willing to put up with God so her kid can read his own diploma—which he eventually will be handed whether it's worth anything or not.

So far, 5,000 Cleveland parents have violated their own constitutional rights by applying for vouchers, which will be awarded by lottery. There is some precedent for this action. After World War II, the G.I. Bill allowed veterans to use public money to pay tuition at private colleges.

The war against dumbness hasn't been won. In fact, we're losing it. In Cleveland, where there are still pockets of resistance, it's just about lost. The old cliches haven't solved the problem. New ideas are needed and ought to be welcomed. And they are, by the victims of the educational disaster.

I think teaching is the noblest profession. The noblest. But when I hear from the education establishment, they rarely want to talk about the special nobility of their calling. They want to talk about dough and job security and the rest of the assembly-line issues of old-fashioned trade-unionism. If Mrs. Jones' kid is a defective product, that's all right. Just as long as nobody shuts down the line.

Opponents claim vouchers would do irreparable harm to the Cleveland school system. Somebody isn't paying attention. How much more harm can be done? How low do you have to go to know where up is? Where's Mrs. Kanarsky with that eraser?

—January 12, 1996

....

Truth in spending

"Good morning. Our guest today on *Face the City* is Mr. Whole Truth. Thank you for coming, Mr. Truth."

"Thank you for asking me. I rarely get invited anywhere."

"Oh? Why is that?"

"I depress people."

"Well, let's hope we can change your image this morning. Now, my first question for you, Mr. Truth, is . . ."

"Not Mr. Truth. Just Truth. Truth has no sex or age or color or race or ethnic origin. Truth is simply truth."

"I think we can all agree with you on that, Mr., er, Truth."

"You'd be surprised."

"Anyway, my first question is this. Shouldn't we take all the money we're planning to spend on a new football stadium and give it to the Cleveland schools?"

"No."

"But wouldn't you agree that spending millions for a football stadium while schools are closing down shows we don't have a sense of priorities?"

"No. It shows we do have a sense of priorities, and our sense of priorities is shallow, moronic, materialistic, delusional, uncivilized and ultimately self-defeating."

"Since you feel that way, Truth, why wouldn't you give the money to the schools?"

"Because we know how to build stadiums but we don't know

how to run schools. If we decided to give money to the schools, we wouldn't know who to give it to or what would happen to it. We'd never see it again and there's no reason to believe much good would come from it."

"But, Truth, don't you believe it takes a whole village to raise a single child?"

"No."

"You don't?"

"No. It takes a good parent, preferably two. Or at least a grandmother, or an aunt, or somebody who cares about the child. Children used to be raised way out in the middle of the wilderness without a village in sight. If you ask a village to raise a child, that's a cop-out. It takes a whole parent to raise a child."

"So schools can't educate children who haven't been raised properly at home? Is that what you're saying, Truth?"

"Of course that's what I'm saying. That ought to be obvious, for heaven's sake."

"What about children who come from families trapped in the cycle of poverty and despair?"

"The Depression was full of families trapped in the cycle of poverty and despair. But nobody ever used that as an excuse to be a rotten parent. Some of the best parents are poor parents, and some of the worst parents are rich parents."

"But don't the schools have an obligation to try to teach right from wrong?"

"No. The schools have an obligation to teach reading, writing, arithmetic, history, geography and science. Right and wrong is something they have an obligation to enforce. Schools should be a haven and sanctuary for the thousands of good children who come willing to learn."

"Well, you'd certainly concede that the Cleveland schools need money, wouldn't you? Wouldn't you agree that that's an obvious truth?"

"No."

"It isn't true?"

"It isn't obvious. If they want to make it obvious, they ought to stop busing entirely. Knock off the legal fees to fat lawyers. Sell that fancy building on East 6th Street to a hotel developer and move in to one of the schools they closed. Fire a lot of the consultants that are padding the payroll and issue a public audit. Until that happens, they'll be waiting on a levy like the folks who waited for the *Robert E. Lee*."

"But that sounds very harsh, Truth."

"What's the matter? Didn't you ever hear of a harsh truth?"

"I can see why people think you are depressing, Truth. You're really not very nice, are you?"

"No."

"Not very compassionate, are you?"

"No."

"I'm glad our time is up. Our guest today has been Mr. Whole Truth. I'm sorry you came and I hope you don't come back very soon. What do you say to that?"

"Next time invite my brother, Half. He's real popular."

—March 11, 1996

Teachers who don't know English

Now we know why kids can't speak good or write nice. English is a second language for members of the National Council of Teachers of English. Their primary language is gobbledegook.

The other day, the council released its report on national standards for teaching English. Some people thought the report would be controversial. But it is too dull and dumb to be controversial. Its convoluted sentences risk hernias straining to state the obvious, except in those cases where the obvious is rejected in favor of the indecipherable.

Here is a nine-ton example of the obvious:

"Students read a wide range of print and nonprint texts to build an understanding of texts, of themselves and of the cultures of the United States and the world; to acquire new information; to respond to the needs and demands of society and the workplace; and for personal fulfillment. Among these texts are fiction and nonfiction, classics and contemporary works."

According to my captured *Gobbledegook Code Book,* what this means is that reading is good for you. And you learn a lot by reading. And it helps you in your job. I haven't deciphered "non-print texts" yet. I guess it means computers. But who cares?

We paid tax dollars for this enlightenment, you understand. A committee has been working on it for four years. Now I am going to have to go back to my conservative friends and admit that I am a chump. They warned me that a government-sponsored group of extraterrestrials from the education establishment wouldn't be able to control themselves. That whatever they wasted taxpayer money to produce would be either meaningless or outrageous.

Try this:

"Students develop an understanding of and respect for diversity in language use, patterns and dialects across cultures, ethnic groups, geographic regions and social roles."

That's a tough one. I get: "Not everybody talks like you talk. That's swell. There is no right way or wrong way. But don't bank on that or you'll flunk the test. Then again, maybe not. We're not sure."

I have a soft spot in my heart for English teachers. The best teachers I ever had were English teachers. And when I went off to college, I majored in English—a fact I wisely hid from some of my associates.

In the summer, I worked on the docks unloading semitrailers. None of my co-workers had graduated from high school. I feared they might resent my academic pursuits. But when they found out I was in college, they were friendly and encouraging. They perceived college as a ticket out of sweat and backache toward a destination of ease and prosperity. They demanded to know what I was studying—how I was using the opportunity they never had.

"You look like a smart kid," one of them told me. "I bet you're gonna take up something like dentistry."

I did not deny this. From then on, our lunch-break

conversations expanded politely to include discussions of root canals and bridgework. Mouths were opened for my inspection. My wisdom tooth wisdom was solicited. I arbitrated debates on the merits of pulling whole mouthfuls of teeth at once as the cheapest way to acquire the inevitable dentures.

I yearned to escape this lie and return to my classes of fellow English majors. There were two kinds of us. There were slovenly boys with beards and girls who wore no makeup and dressed entirely in black clothing well-sprinkled with dandruff. These were the expectant novelists and poets. Then there were the neatly groomed, wholesome-looking students who hoped to become English teachers.

The novelists and poets seemed like revolutionaries. But they turned out to be tame. They eventually went to work for advertising agencies and became great seducers of mainstream society. It was some of those harmless-appearing English teachers who radically changed American culture.

They clambered up the ladder of the education establishment, dynamiting standards, sneering at classroom teachers, primping and posturing for each other. They eventually became itinerant superintendents or consultants, spouting meaningless jargon during job interviews as they moved from city to city. They smothered failing school systems in a smoke screen of gobbledegook. They became expert at drafting plans and reports full of empty, glowing phrases and hid their ineptitude behind the tortured syntax of their stilted studies and vacuous "visions."

My old English teachers and my friends on the loading dock would scorn them with a bitter contempt. As my summer on the dock ended, the guy who thought I was going to be a dentist found out the truth. He couldn't believe it.

"Why would you pay good money to study that?" he asked. "Everybody knows English."

It was an embarrassing question then, but not anymore. Not everybody knows English. Members of the National Council of Teachers of English don't know English. And if they don't, good luck to your kid.

—March 13, 1996

Education has become an elective

At Georgetown University, English majors no longer have to study Shakespeare. A course called "Women, Revolution, and the Media" can be elected as a substitute for the Immortal Dead White Male Bard.

Georgetown doesn't have a patent on such heresy. A study by the National Association of Scholars reveals that colleges all over America are chucking mandatory requirements. For example, 86 percent of the colleges surveyed required English composition courses in 1964. By 1993, only 36 percent required them. The only possible explanation for this is . . . duh?

The scholars association released its gloomy report yesterday while you and I were off playing democracy. The timing was especially apt, since our form of government, more than any other, relies, in theory, on voters willing to exercise their brains.

So it is chilling to learn that while 38 percent of the colleges surveyed required some history courses in 1964 (nothing to write home about, or even call collect) only 12 percent required history in 1993.

This probably explains why a young woman in a former newsroom once looked at me earnestly and inquired, "Which came first? World War II or Vietnam?" If Lincoln had written the "Gettysburg Address" for her, he would have had to begin it with "Once upon a time." But in this study-what-feels-good era, it doesn't matter. "Why do I need the 'Gettysburg Address'?" today's student might ask. "I'm not going to mail anything there."

Given what a college education costs these days, there ought to be a parents' revolution. But there won't be. The aim of a college degree is not education. It's the other way around. The aim of so-called "education" is a college degree. A little piece of paper to wave under the nose of an employer that will launch a graduate on his broken-field run down today's minefield of an employment path. Eight careers and then downsizing.

Once, we counted on the great universities to maintain the standards of what educated people ought to know. That idea got tossed out in the touchy-feely '60s. Since then, colleges have participated in the agenda-ridden dumbing-down of society. My father got a better education at East Tech High School than my sons got in college. Unless you count water-skiing, which they took and he didn't.

Rita Zurcher is the director of research for the National Association of Scholars. To accompany yesterday's report, she wrote an op-ed piece in *USA Today* mentioning the fact that Georgetown, which evicted Shakespeare, would die before it surrendered basketball. The question of which comes first, education or sports, is not unfamiliar to Clevelanders.

There was a time when we had both, but that time seems, like history, to have become history. Nowadays, if Shakespeare wants to stay viable, he'll have to compromise. A little tinkering here and there might make him relevant to today's basketball majors. For example, the line in *Macbeth* that goes:

"So foul and fair a day I have not seen."

Can be altered slightly to read:

"So fair a foul shot I have not seen."

Or, in the case of Chicago Bulls player Dennis Rodman, who head-butted a referee:

"So foul a foul I have not seen."

Rodman's action caused the NBA officials to wonder, Hamlet-like:

"To fine or not to fine, that is the question.

"Whether 'tis nobler for the game to suffer the slings and arrows of athletes paid outrageous fortunes,

"Or take arms against a sea of morons and by opposing, bench them. To fine: to bench; to play no more . . ."

There! Now, if we can just get that on a video, Shakespeare may become the comeback kid. On the journey through life, Shakespeare is a better traveling companion than a basketball, or even a pair of Nikes.

It's the duty of the colleges to teach that. If they've stopped, somebody ought to send in the fraud squad.

—March 20, 1996

We both fail

Have you ever noticed how one person can say something and nobody will mind? But then another person will say pretty much the same thing and everybody gets mad?

No? Well, I have.

A while back I wrote a column that got all the schoolteachers mad at me. And that made me pretty blue, because schoolteachers have been some of the most important people in my life.

Time after time, I have written lovingly in this space about all I owe to a few exquisite teachers. Especially the teachers at John Adams High School, which now sits derelict over on East 116th Street like a great ship driven on the rocks by a storm of educational chaos.

I like teachers. But a while back, I made a little bet. I made this bet at a time when the headlines were full of stories about how the Cleveland schools needed to get more money for per-pupil expenses.

My bet was that if you sent me 15 kids, I could teach them basic skills in my living room, throw in a bologna sandwich and a little touch football in the park, and still make a profit. If I had that column to write over again, I would have taken the day off instead.

The morning it ran, the dew was still on the grass and the newspaper was still in the petunia bed when my voice mail was full of angry teachers. My plan had stung them like a spitball. A posse of them wanted to march me off to detention hall.

I had insulted their ability to teach, they said. I had trivialized their professional dedication. I had hit them below the belt with my cockeyed scheme. I was, at best, an idiot. At worst, a crank.

And I believed them. Because back when I was going to school, if a teacher said you were wrong, that was the end of the matter. Now, of course, it's usually just the beginning of the matter.

Well, a couple of months passed, and I found myself, for no good reason, standing way up in the peanut gallery of the

Chicago Bulls' arena watching the president of the United States make a speech.

Some eons into this address, he began rattling off his plans for the future. And he said words to this effect:

"I envision an army of volunteers who will go out into the community and teach children to read. So that, because of this volunteer effort, every child in America will know how to read by the third grade."

"Oh boy," I said to a newsperson next to me. "He's in for it now." Because the audience he was speaking to was crammed full of members of the teachers union.

But they all cheered when they heard this plan. They didn't treat it like a spitball at all. They treated it like an apple. And ever since, I've been trying to figure out why.

After all, what the president seemed to be saying was:

"Look, you teachers can no longer teach kids to read. You know it and I know it. The question is, what are we going to do about it? My idea is that we get somebody who is not a teacher and has never been in a classroom. And we ask that person to teach kids how to read. And, by golly, I bet that will work."

This didn't seem a whole lot less insulting than my idea. It certainly didn't seem any less fanciful. But nobody called the president a mean, old so-and-so for suggesting it. In fact, he was greeted with tears of joy. And the ground was already soggy with the overflow from a week of pipe dreams.

There were, of course, some differences between the president's idea and mine. I had expected pay for my efforts. And, under my plan, I would replace a teacher. The president's army of tutors would work for nothing. Educational payrolls would remain untouched. Free reading teachers would teach reading, while paid reading teachers cheered them on.

When the president got through talking about his idea, thousands of balloons fell from the ceiling and hundreds of people hugged each other. When I got through writing about my idea, I took the phone off the hook and lay down with a cold rag on my head.

Yet, both the president and I were saying the same thing. Both of us were admitting that the present educational system isn't working. And that it won't fix itself. And that money isn't enough. Otherwise, why have an army of reading donors? Why not just an army of cash donors?

But when it comes to a solution, I think the president and I are both full of beans. Neither of us has the answer to the education crisis, because there isn't one answer.

One answer won't address rotten parents. And truancy. And eroding standards of behavior and academics. And drugs. And power plays by unions, politicians or administrators.

Rather than hack our way through this thicket of horrors, we pretend we can sail over it with a combination of magic and money. With make-believe bridges to the future or nostalgic bridges to the past.

But here in the present, high school roofs let in the rain. Hired bodyguards are ready to bivouac in classrooms in case of a strike. Politicians posture; union leaders bluff; the administration stonewalls. And what used to be America's pride is now a national disgrace.

What we used to say about education was: "Just do it!" Now we whine and say, "How?" And shove another season of children into the thicket to bleed on the thorns.

—September 11, 1996

Not in front of the children

As mentioned here before, it is the angel Gabriel's duty to break the bad news to God. Most of the bad news comes from Earth, the one planet in the universe that can't seem to make up its mind.

This indecision tries God's patience. So Gabriel does his best to be diplomatic.

"The papers just arrived from Earth," he said to God the other day. "I have some good news and some bad news for You."

God uttered a small sigh, which caused a 60-mph wind to knock out service to CEI customers in Willoughby.

"Give me the good news first," said God.

"Well," said Gabriel, "You may remember that the court banned prayer in Cleveland school board meetings. Do You recall that?"

"Of course I recall that," said God. "I recall everything. Who do you think I am? Some witness at a congressional hearing?"

"Well," said Gabriel triumphantly. "The good news is, a higher court ruled that the school board can start praying again."

God smiled so brightly that the sun shone in Cleveland, a sight rarely seen between October and May. But then God stopped smiling abruptly and the sun in Cleveland immediately vanished again, to the surprise of no one who lived there.

"What's the bad news?" God said.

"The bad news is the reason the court gave for permitting prayer," said Gabriel. "I'm afraid the court said prayer is all right at a school board meeting because children rarely attend school board meetings. Prayer is all right, providing children aren't forced to listen to it."

"You've got to be kidding," God said. "You mean the courts down there gave Me a TV-M rating? They think I'm for mature audiences only? Like *Baywatch?*"

"Gee," said Gabriel. "How do You know about *Baywatch?*"

"I KNOW ABOUT EVERYTHING!!!" thundered God, setting off seven earthly seismographs for reasons the Associated Press later reported were "under investigation."

Gabriel was afraid to speak. He waited to see what would happen next.

"Let's not get excited," God said. "Let's pull Ourselves together. Let's not lose Our tempers."

"No, Sir," said Gabriel.

"What's that you're holding behind your back?" God asked.

"It's only my horn, Sir."

"Well, why are you hiding it like that?"

"It's just that I hate to let You see it, Sir. Whenever I bring news from Earth, it always upsets You. And I'm afraid You'll lose patience one day and order me to blow it. And I'd hate to blow it, Sir, because I've gotten rather fond of Earth."

"You have? How odd."

"Well, it's just that they're so . . . so . . . disarmingly hopeless, Sir. Most of the time they mean well, but they really haven't got a clue. Even when they do something right, it's usually for the wrong reasons. Like this prayer thing, Sir. They've convinced themselves that prayer is for adults only. But they're still arguing about whether TV violence is for adults only. They're so . . ."

"I know," said God. "That's why I keep them around. It fascinates Me to guess how they will all turn out. Of course, I have the ability to know how they will all turn out. But I don't use it. It's more fun not to peek."

"Yes, Sir," said Gabriel, who was beginning to relax a bit.

"It's Christmas down there, Gabriel," God said, kindly. "At least they don't forget that. This year they seem to be making a great fuss over St. Elmo. Nice chap, Elmo. Glad to see he's getting a little attention. Usually only sailors think of him when they get a little glow of St. Elmo's Fire around their masts. Don't quite know how he's gotten to be such a celebrity, but it tickles Me."

Gabriel made a slight noise that he hoped sounded like a cough.

"We won't be too hard on them this week, Gabriel," said God. "All children are naturally holy. It is adults who need prayer, especially school board adults. Have they prayed for anything yet?"

"Yes, Sir!" said Gabriel. "They have prayed for deliverance."

"Good," said God. "Deliverance from greed and division and stupidity and stubbornness, I presume."

"Not exactly," said Gabriel. "They're asking deliverance from a man named Mike White."

"What on earth for?" asked God.

Gabriel sighed.

"Sir," he said. "I've got some good news and some bad news for You . . ."

—December 23, 1996

Stealing an education

Judy Kincaid was caught stealing an education for her son. They arrested her and made her give it back. Then they threw her in jail for five days. The education she was trying to steal belonged to the city of Euclid.

Taxpayers there bought it and they own it. If I lived in Euclid, I would not want mothers like Ms. Kincaid pilfering my belongings. Let one get away with it and pretty soon others will try it.

So you can't blame the city of Euclid for Ms. Kincaid's problems, and nobody does. There is a sentiment that her punishment of five days in jail was perhaps a bit harsh. But, on the other hand, the publicity about her sentence sent a stern message to others who might be tempted to steal Euclid's education to nourish their children. The message is: Read the headlines and think twice.

Still, we can't help feeling a little sorry for Judy Kincaid. There is something in her story that seems right out of *Les Miserables*. It has echoes of the penniless mother who was jailed for stealing a loaf of bread to feed her starving child. The idea of punishing such a woman and depriving her child makes us squirm.

And since we're squirming already, let's increase our squirm count and squirm some more. Because Judy Kincaid's story isn't just sad. It is also seasoned with the unmistakable taste of irony, which, like garlic, lingers as other flavors fade.

The state's most recent estimate of the cost of a public school education in Euclid is $6,584 per pupil per year. So that's the price tag on the education Judy Kincaid tried to steal for her son, Quenten, who is 5 years old.

If the schooling she so desperately wanted had been for sale, Ms. Kincaid might have been able to buy it. She would have walked into the education market a little light of funds. But hardly penniless.

In Cleveland, where she lives, the annual per-pupil expenditure is $6,197. So, had she been able to take the money earmarked for Quenten and spend it on a day's worth of school in Euclid, she would have been less than $400 short.

But she would have gotten a lot better deal. And she knew it.

For example, in Euclid, 49 percent of ninth-graders pass the ninth-grade proficiency test. Those may not be numbers worthy of hiring a brass band. But Euclid's achievement looks like a Mensa awards banquet from the vantage point of Cleveland, where 8 percent of ninth-graders pass the test.

If Ms. Kincaid had been given a voucher for $6,197, she likely would not have cashed it in the Cleveland public school system. But, of course, she wasn't given a voucher. The education establishment claims that vouchers will ruin public education. A view most easily held if you are not a parent.

When I went to the Cleveland public schools, one of the great things was we didn't feel short-changed. Forty years after my graduation, I still don't feel short-changed. With all due respect to Euclid, the idea of my mother smuggling me into the Euclid school system would have seemed, at best, a pointless lateral move.

Of course, society has gone to hell since then. And the Cleveland schools went with it. But it's small wonder that that explanation doesn't satisfy Judy Kincaid. Society isn't her problem. Quenten is.

Ms. Kincaid broke the law. But she isn't the penniless mother caught stealing bread for her child. She is a mother with the price of bread locked away in a vault where she can't get at it. Forced to feed her child sawdust.

If Ms. Kincaid has been paying as much attention as I have, she has heard 15 years' worth of school superintendents arrive in Cleveland to announce that a whole generation of children has been lost. This is the kind of speech that is apt to make a mother desperate when it is time to offer her son to the sleight-of-hand artists who make kids vanish.

So she did a bad thing. She defrauded Euclid and served her time for it. Now she and Quenten will return to Cleveland, where educational fraud is an established custom. And there, she will no longer be news.

—December 11, 1996

Lawyers are eating the schools

The Cleveland school system isn't dead yet. The lawyers are still sucking on it.

Lawyers will do almost anything and call it the Lord's work. But they draw the line at necrophagy, which my trusty Webster's informs me is "the eating of dead bodies. Especially the practice of feeding on carrion."

It's a pretty repulsive word. We associate it with creatures who aren't very nice. Vultures. Hyenas. Worms. Anything that makes a gourmet meal out of roadkill.

School system lawyers do not fall into that category. Their presence in the sick room means there are small signs of life in the body. Their attendance indicates a pulse is still faintly beating. Necrophagia is beneath them. Their habits are more fastidious. They are parasites. But they are parasites with an alibi.

A generation ago, the Cleveland school system was found guilty of deliberate segregation. The remedy for this called for mandatory busing and an improvement in the test scores and the quality of education of minority students who had been wronged.

The remedy failed. It nearly killed the patient. There aren't enough white kids left in the system to make busing practical. Test scores have dropped. The quality of education has become more dismal.

In the same period of time, lawyers anointed to supervise the "remedy" have been paid $10 million. For nothing.

Ten million dollars is a lot to pay for nothing. Basically, it was conscience money. At this writing, nobody holds the slightest hope of "integrating" the Cleveland school system. Nobody knows how to get test scores up. Nobody has a practical plan to improve the educational results in the schools. Nobody is sure it can be done.

But as long as there is a federal judge on the case and as long as checks are being written to "civil rights attorneys" and school administration attorneys, a little transparent fiction can be maintained that something is happening to benefit minority children. Just don't ask what.

The stricken and tortured parents of Cleveland don't believe this fiction. Last November they uttered a deathbed prayer in the form of a big levy. They voted to part with money they could ill afford to give up because their children's lives were at stake. Nobody expected the levy to pass. On election night, some of its supporters wept because they were so moved by the fragile hope and the vulnerable faith symbolized by the vote.

It was obscene that night to be a cynic. The people in the neighborhoods had done what they could do. It remained to be seen whether their trust would be trampled and their gesture mocked. This week, we found out.

U.S. District Judge George White agreed to raise the fees for the "desegregation lawyers" back to rates of as much as $340 an hour. And, at the same time, the head of the teachers' union indicated a desire to reopen the union contract because the levy had passed.

The teachers' union gambit will probably come to nothing. But the lawyers are already counting their pay raise. The cynics won a victory after all. Hope and sanity lost again.

My kids are out of school. And I don't live in Cleveland. And I'm white. So maybe I just don't understand why a civil rights lawyer who lives in New York and a U.S. District judge should be cutting deals on how to spend money squeezed from the poor and desperate who are struggling to educate their children.

The voters gave the stricken school system a transfusion of blood money. And the lawyers were first in line, looking to tap a vein. They will hang around as long as any vital signs remain. But they have demonstrated that they are not part of the cure.

The conscience money has been paid in full. After $10 million worth of patent medicine, it's time for the quacks to leave the room.

—January 10, 1997

Remember responsibility?

The other day, on Page 1, a woman shared with us the plight of her 14-year-old son. He is in trouble in school for not doing what he's supposed to do. His mother said she had been told he is a victim of oppositional defiance disorder.

I had nothing to do with this story. It was written by our man in Mentor, Kevin Harter. My phone, however, rang off the hook all day. Scores of people felt compelled to call and to reveal that they think oppositional defiance disorder is spinach.

The tone of the calls can be summed up by one man's frustration. "I have managed to somehow hang on through all kinds of [expletive]," he said. "But oppositional defiance disorder is the last straw."

This caller obviously felt that he, too, was a victim of oppositional defiance disorder. The alleged ailment (which merrily abbreviates to ODD) had victimized his common sense.

It used to be said that America was a country in which anybody could grow up to be president. That may still be true. But the presidency isn't considered such a great Cracker Jack prize anymore. People such as Mario Cuomo and Colin Powell, who might have won it, didn't want it.

The great promise of today's America is that anybody who tries real hard can grow up to be some kind of victim. Ours is one nation, increasingly divisible, with excuses and victimhood for all. Even those of us who can't win victim status on our own are not left out. We get to be victims of the victims.

One of the things the boy with ODD did, according to school officials, was extort 50 cents for a can of pop from another student. This allegation filled me with nostalgia. Extortion by big boys was a rampant crime in my old junior high school.

Back then, I regarded myself as the victim. I regarded the extorter as a juvenile delinquent. The only question was whether to rat on him to a teacher. The down side of this was that the next time he saw me, he might beat the whey out of me.

In those days, we did not have teams of psychiatrists roaming the halls, armed with syndrome handbooks. We did not have "grief counselors" either, ready to swoop down and smother us with cliches when tragedy struck one of our number, thus making us victims of grief.

We were left to pretty much tough things out on our own. Naturally, we became callous and unfeeling. When victimized by big boys, we said things (well out of their hearing) like: "He's a punk." Or, "He's a creep." Or worse. It was never explained that the person victimizing us was a fellow victim—just like us, only 50 cents richer.

In the story the other day, a child psychiatrist gave us the lowdown on ODD. "It's exactly what it sounds like," he said. "It takes a pattern of behavior a period of time, six months to a year, to be diagnosed. Frequently, a kid does just the opposite of what he's told to do or expected to do."

This ODD breakthrough came too late for me. I had a hand in raising four kids and, looking back on it, they all had ODD. That is to say, they all went through periods of time when they did just the opposite of what they were told to do or were expected to do.

But I didn't know it was ODD. In fact, I thought it was normal. Not pleasant, but normal. Sometimes I called it back-talk and sometimes I called it smart-mouth and sometimes I called it acting like a brat. Sometimes I called it hell. But most of the time, I simply called it adolescence.

Today, I will get more calls. These will come from psychiatrists bawling me out for not taking ODD seriously enough. How do I know this? Let's just say I am psychic.

I have no defense. If somebody had paid me $100 an hour to diagnose ODD, I might have diagnosed it. But, as a parent, I was working for free. So I treated it as best I could.

My manner of treatment consisted of a few swats here, a little grounding there, and a lot of yelling way over there. A combination of what would be called, in today's parlance, verbal, emotional and physical abuse. Back then, we just called it "raising your kid." But what did we know? Nothing! And our parents knew less.

"Own up," our parents told us. "Face responsibility. Don't make excuses. When you're wrong, take your medicine." We passed these poisonous thoughts on to our children. So that when they did something wrong, they felt bad about themselves. And if they didn't, we made them feel bad about themselves. God, what barbarism! I burn with shame remembering it.

But my kids somehow survived me. The way I know is, none of them has turned up on *Oprah* or *Jerry Springer*. Now I am a grandfather and I get to watch my kids trying to cope with their kids. This is what is called Grandparents' Revenge.

My granddaughter will be raised in an ODD world. A world short on cures and long on alibis. Short on heroes and overpopulated with victims. Some night, when nobody's looking, I will whisper to her that life isn't fair, but you live it anyway. An old drill sergeant gave me the three-word secret of life.

"Suck it up!" he said. I've never met the shrink who can improve on that.

—February 14, 1997

Psychiatric science fiction

Well, gang, you broke your previous record for most telephone calls after a single column. More than 300 of you dialed in to say you thought "oppositional defiance disorder" is junk. And you're still calling. But I've stopped counting.

This deluge of sentiment followed last Friday's piece about a local woman whose son got in trouble at school for not behaving himself. She revealed he had been diagnosed with the above ailment, which abbreviates to "ODD."

If I boiled your sentiments down to three simple sentences, they would probably be these: You are fed up with alibis for bad behavior. You are tired of people excusing their wrongdoing by hiding behind some sort of victim status. You are worried about a country that seems to have lost its ability to tell rights from wrong.

The largest block of callers were schoolteachers. Some of them taught in the city, but most of them taught in the suburbs. All of them said that classroom disruption was a major problem. And that the problem is made worse by policies requiring unruly students to be treated with kid gloves, and teachers to function as psychiatric social workers, dispensing therapy instead of discipline.

One of you sent me out to the newsstand for the February issue of *Harper's* magazine. It features an article by L. J. Davis titled "The Encyclopedia of Insanity—A Psychiatric Handbook Lists a Madness for Everyone."

This is a scathing book review of the new, 886-page *Manual of Mental Disorders* released by the American Psychiatric Association. Of the manual, Davis writes:

"[Its] customers are the therapists and this may be the only manual in the world that actually makes its customers money. Each disorder, no matter how trivial, is accompanied by a billing code, enabling the therapist to fill out the relevant insurance form and receive an agreed upon reward."

Included among the "mental disorders" listed are "bad writing, poor handwriting, coffee nerves, inability to sleep after drinking too much coffee, jet lag, snobbery and playing video games."

Our chief suspect, oppositional defiance disorder, is in there too, along with "conduct disorder" and "disruptive behavior disorder." Davis includes the symptoms of these. If you've ever been around a teenager (or been one), they may seem familiar to you:

"Failure to listen when spoken to. Talking back. Annoying other people. Claiming that somebody else did it. And (among a lot of other stuff) failure to clean up one's room."

Davis enters the homestretch of his article on this whimsical note:

"The book's authors seem to have overlooked a few real money-makers. A number of people believe they have been abducted by [aliens] and subjected to fiendish experiments. But because the [manual] never describes this condition, there is nothing wrong with such people. A person who snores . . . is ready for the booby hatch, but a person who claims to have been kidnapped by a flying saucer is perfectly sane."

When I wrote about ODD, I predicted a half-dozen calls from psychiatrists angrily denouncing me. I couldn't have been more wrong. Eight psychiatrists called to say they thought ODD was bunk. One added that its only purpose, as far as he could tell, was as a useful category when billing an insurance company.

In fact, of the 300-plus calls I got, only three callers were upset by the column. One was the mother of the boy in trouble at school. Another was a mother whose son had been diagnosed with ODD. And the third was a psychiatric hospital administrator who said I was trivializing childhood emotional disturbance.

But that is exactly what I am not doing. The horrible suicide rate among young people and the increasingly youthful age of child murderers, muggers and mothers suggest that something is terribly wrong.

I've had friends with emotionally disturbed children. Friends who did all they could to help their kids and faced the searing heartache that it wasn't enough. Didn't come close.

It is these people and their pain who are being trivialized by the psychobabble of the *Shrink's Guide to Billable Syndromes*.

The irresponsible and agenda-based use of grim words like "sexual harassment," "homelessness" and a menu of assorted "isms" makes the words almost meaningless and dilutes our ability or interest in solving the very real problems they represent.

So does confusing syndromes with plain, old-fashioned sinning. There's a difference. Knowing the difference is what parents are for. Teaching the difference is the great and thankless gift of parental love.

—February 19, 1997

Mark Twain's classic should be left alone

Howard Stern's movie opens to cheerful reviews, and a local school considers evicting *The Adventures of Huckleberry Finn* from its reading list. Has America finally arrived in cultural hell?

Let us marshal our optimism and strain to think wishfully. Stern's movie may be a thud at the box office. It probably won't, but it may. I say a little prayer of thanksgiving every time I notice that *The People vs. Larry Flynt* continues to play to relatively sparse audiences, despite the critics' admiring endorsement of it.

Huckleberry Finn got its biggest plug from Ernest Hemingway. Like most writers, Hemingway was a mixture of ego and paranoia. You will notice that when writers nominate other writers for praise, they are usually careful to pick dead ones. Writing is a jealous and competitive craft. Once, somebody asked John Updike if he ever mentored younger writers. "Did you ever hear of an actress mentoring a younger actress?" he replied.

But there are some writers whose worth is undeniable. In *Green Hills of Africa*, Hemingway said this:

"All modern American literature comes from one book by Mark Twain called *Huckleberry Finn*."

If this is true, the English faculty at Brush High School has a sticky problem on its hands. Sometime this month, a committee will decide whether to remove *Huckleberry Finn* from a mandatory reading list. The problem is that the n-word is used more than 100 times in the book's pages.

The n-word is not as proscribed as we like to pretend it is. It falls from the lips of stand-up comics. It punches out of the fierce lyrics of popular music, sometimes hidden behind a peek-a-boo bleep. It profanes playgrounds in various parts of town. But it is a stranger in a formal setting like a classroom.

A black student at Brush complained that some of her fellow students snickered and giggled as the word was read aloud from *Huck Finn*. I'm sure that is true. I can close my eyes and hear them. An 11th-grade English class is a great venue for snickering and giggling. My own class snickered and giggled its way through *Hamlet*. And that was back in the days before Beavis and Butt-head and a flock of drive-time shock jocks made snickering and giggling a pop art form.

But we did not read *Huckleberry Finn* in high school. I read the book first when I was 14 and thought it was a great children's adventure story. I next encountered it in a college classroom, where a professor praised its ride down the river as a metaphor for life. Then, in my 40s, on my third reading, I finally got it.

Out there on the river, with Jim, the runaway slave, Huck is in no doubt about the "right" thing to do. The right thing to do is to turn Jim over to the slave catchers. Huck has been taught that Jim is a piece of property. And he believes it. It is a fact of his society.

But all along the river, smug white society reveals itself as absurd and evil. Jim, the piece of property, is more of a man—more of a human being—than any of the scalawags and scoundrels on display. So Huck does the "wrong" thing. He shields Jim. He ignores the signals from what he mistakenly believes to be his conscience. He heeds, instead, the whispers from his soul. In doing that, he is convinced he will be damned to hell. And he is puzzled that his act of "treachery" makes him feel better.

Written 112 years ago, *Huckleberry Finn* was an almost revolutionary unmasking of racism. It is more than that, but it certainly is that. Taking the n-word out of it dilutes the racism Twain was arguing against. Mark Twain is not Mark Fuhrman, on trial for the inappropriate use of epithets.

The question is, are 11th-graders ready to handle a frank and open exploration of racism and what it is and is not? I doubt it. How can they be, when adults of all colors are not yet ready to handle such an exploration?

Great books are often painful to experience. Here's Hemingway again:

"All good books are alike in that they are truer than if they had really happened. And after you are finished reading one, you will feel that all that happened to you, and afterwards it all belongs to you: the good and the bad, the ecstasy, the remorse and sorrow, the people and places and how the weather was. If you can get so that you can give that to people, then you are a writer."

If the Brush faculty retires *Huckleberry Finn* from the mandatory reading list, some people will proclaim victory and others will cry travesty. But, really, nothing will have been won or lost.

The greatest American novel, which explores the greatest American evil, will remain on the library shelf. Waiting, as it has for a century, for America to grow up.

—March 10, 1997

....

Busing's inevitable crash

I was talking to a Cleveland cop last night who remembered what it was like when busing started.

"We put on riot gear and rehearsed for it," he said. "They showed us movies of the riots in Boston when busing began there. They told us the law was the law, and we were damn well going to enforce it. But, as it turned out, there were no real problems."

We were proud of how we behaved in Cleveland. We knew there were blameless children in the center of this drama. We didn't want to do anything to hurt them. We owed them restraint. And we gave it to them.

So the buses rolled. And many Clevelanders went home to pack. The ones who could manage it pried a down payment loose from their savings accounts and moved to the suburbs, where they could send their children to school in their own neighborhoods. Others, if they could afford it, transferred their kids to parochial schools.

Busing was supposed to be an educational remedy for a deliberately segregated school system. The remedy was swallowed and the patient died. This week, Cleveland NAACP President George Forbes told a reporter why.

"Busing hasn't worked," he said. "It's not because it's the fault of blacks or the NAACP. Whites did not comply with court-ordered busing. Busing resulted in white flight, and black kids paid the price."

For a Forbes statement, this isn't bad. Almost half of it is true. Then it turns into mild race-baiting. But hey, everybody's got to make a living.

When he says "whites did not comply with court-ordered busing," I assume he means whites who moved away or transferred their children to private schools. But he makes no mention of blacks who moved away or transferred their children to private schools. Certainly he knows plenty who did. I do.

When he says "black kids paid the price," he is ignoring part of the bill. Every student in the Cleveland system, white, black or other, has paid the price for the toxic prescription written by the federal court pharmacy.

Since there are more black kids in the system than white kids, it is true that more black kids have been poisoned by the nostrum that was peddled as a cure-all. But when the system caved in, it fell on everybody who had the misfortune to be trapped.

Economics is what trapped them. This isn't a free country. It costs money to move to Shaker or to Lakewood, even more to move to Beachwood or Westlake. The economic reality of Cleveland is that more poor black people live there than poor white people. So it was pretty obvious from the beginning that black people were going to have a harder time escaping a school system that was inferior.

"Busing hasn't worked, but that's not the fault of the NAACP," Forbes said. He's right. It's not. It's the fault of white flight and black flight from the illogical notion that shipping a diminishing number of black kids across town to sit next to a diminishing number of white kids (or vice versa) would somehow have a beneficial effect on test scores and homework.

It didn't work. And what I want to know is, who ever really thought it would?

I never thought it would. But, of course, I didn't say so at first. In those days, quarreling with busing automatically branded you a racist. And who needed that? Not me. Why, I was living way out in Aurora then. My kids weren't involved. Besides, it was like the cop said. The law was the law. Why stick your neck out?

Then, little by little, I began to find out that plenty of civic frontmen were in the same boat as I was. Newspaper editors, television people, leading businessmen, even the consultants who were brought into town to craft the busing plan—they lived in the suburbs, too. Their kids weren't going to participate in this dubious course of treatment either.

I didn't talk to anybody who thought it would work, because the seeds of its destruction were obvious right from the start. But it was just something we were apparently going to have to go through. Not a solution to the tragedy of racial division. Just another chapter—just another plot twist.

This had to be obvious to the NAACP, too. It had to be. These are smart and sophisticated people. They had to know that the answer to inferior education is superior education. That the answer to mediocre teachers is first-rate teachers. That the worst buildings are remedied with the best. That educational malnutrition calls for an extra helping for the starving.

But it was show time. And the show went on and had a long and lucrative run for the lawyers and the administrators and all the pied pipers who led the city's children on their dizzying dance.

Last night, the cop remembered the trouble they had warned him about when busing began. "Thank God, it went off quietly," he said.

And it did. Why, it was as easy as robbing the cradle.

—June 27, 1997

....

Tests are unfair to dummies

In North Carolina, 14 students flunked a grade-school proficiency test. But they refused to give in to defeat. So guess what they did?

They hired a lawyer and sued the school system.

This is being called a "first" in educational circles. Those of us already dizzy from going around in educational circles will find that ominous. By now, we have grasped the fact that every new first is worse than the last first.

What seems to make this case a first is that the students aren't claiming the test discriminated against them because of race or sex or some other complaint that we've all gotten used to.

These students—some white, some Hispanic, some black— charged that the test discriminated against them merely because they weren't smart enough to pass it.

And the evidence is on their side. About 90 percent of the students who took the test did pass it. Only those not able to pass it failed it. How could discrimination get any more blatant than that?

It is time to admit that for years we've known that tests are rewarding only to those who pass them. Only a fool would argue otherwise. That's why tests are called tests and not gift certificates.

But there is, apparently, a growing feeling that schools are no place for tests. So reporters cornered the Johnston County, N.C., school superintendent and demanded to know what proficiency tests were doing in the middle of his school system.

"They are used to give us information about students and about schools and how they are meeting the curriculum," he said.

In response to this seemingly innocuous utterance, great cries of derision rose from many throats. Lawyers predicted that, very soon, more suits would be filed by more flunkees against more school systems. And if the lawyers say so, it will happen. That is what is known as a self-fulfilling prophecy.

So before it happens, perhaps we should revisit why proficiency tests got into school systems in the first place. Do you remember why? I do.

They got there because America discovered that kids were graduating from school without knowing much. In fact, some kids were being handed diplomas they couldn't even read.

"How is this possible?" America asked its educators. "Why would a kid get promoted to the 12th grade if he can't read?"

"That's called social promotion," the experts responded. "It's good for the kid's self-esteem. It is very important that a kid feel good about himself. Most of the evil of society comes from people who feel bad about themselves."

"These kids don't seem to be able to do math, either," America said. "You ought to see them try to make change when they're clerking in a store."

"Oh, well," the experts said. "It is old-fashioned to make a kid memorize things like the multiplication tables."

"Is that why they don't know when the first World War was fought or what century Abraham Lincoln lived in?" America wanted to know.

"Yes indeed," the experts said. "There is a lot more to history than merely memorizing dreary lists of dates."

"But if a kid memorized a dreary list of dates, at least he'd know something," America said.

"Ah," said the experts. "But at what human cost?"

Well, this illumination left America uneasy. And that's why America demanded proficiency tests. America wanted information about students and schools and how they were meeting the curriculum. Just like the North Carolina superintendent (hereafter referred to as "the defendant") said.

This seemed reasonable, since America was being billed for educational proficiency. But it just trampled all over the rights of test victims. So, in North Carolina, a new category of victimhood was invented just for them. And it's heading this way.

To save court costs, it might be easier if kids just started bringing lawyers to class with them. That way, if the teacher asked Johnny to name the capital of North Dakota, Johnny's lawyer could leap to his feet and say:

"Objection! I object to that question! It violates my client's right to privacy and against self-incrimination! Here's a list of answers he knows! If your questions don't fit, you must acquit!"

That scheme would guarantee a lot more "A's." Especially in an age when "A" often stands for alibi.

—August 8, 1997

Basics? Why bother?

A new casualty report is in from the front lines of the War on Dumbness.

Kids from 23 countries, including America, took a test in basic math. There's good news and bad news. The polls show you like good news, so let's look at the good news first.

We beat the heck out of Cyprus and South Africa! Aw-rright! (. . . Nobody else though.)

Well, it wasn't a fair test. Who cares about "basic" math? We don't waste our time on "basics" here. We dream great dreams and envision great visions. We look ahead to the 21st century, which, as any American math student knows, is probably only 40 years from now . . . or whatever.

I mean, what's the point of getting a doctorate in Educational Jargon and Sociological Babble if all you're going to do is teach a kid how to balance a checkbook?

So what if when an American kid buys something, he's not certain he got the right change? Let him go shopping in Cyprus or South Africa. That way, he can be sure he didn't.

Like, whoa! This is a multicultural, multiethnic, multiracial, multilingual society. There's no such thing as "basic" anymore. Nobody has a right to tell anybody else what's basic. "Basic" is a concept invented by dead white European males to perpetuate their reign of terror and oppression.

They know that in Coeur d' Alene, Idaho, a town whose very name shrieks of diversity. Know why? It's French, which is not as diverse as Hispanic but which is better than nothing.

The school board there wants to get rid of courses that clutter up the school curriculum. They said their kids would be better educated if world geography, world history, reading and computers were dropped from the requirements needed to get a diploma.

Here's what the curriculum director said about it:

"It's not that we don't value these things. It's just that if we keep adding everything back in, we are back to where we've always been: a very prescribed course of study that doesn't give students any flexibility if they are going into a particular field."

They got themselves one smart cookie of a curriculum director. I mean, when you think about it, almost every kid is probably planning to "go into a particular field," right?

Although maybe the Idaho kids better stay away from fields that are particular about whether somebody can read. Or whether somebody can point at his own country on a map of the world. But maybe the world maps of the future will be like the directories in malls. Maybe they will have little signs on them that say "You Are Here."

They asked a high school class president in Coeur d' Alene what he thought of the idea of overthrowing the tyranny of basic requirements. He liked it.

"Why take history when you could take painting or pottery?" he said.

There's a lad with vision! The world needs more pots and paint. There's entirely too much vinyl siding around. Why take history when you can wait for the movie to come out? Oliver Stone and Steven Spielberg will teach you all the history you need. And it will be funner. And what they leave out, you can pick up from rock lyrics on MTV.

There's only one flaw in the Idaho plan. But it's a huge flaw. Idaho wants to get rid of computers. That's treason. No, it's worse. It's heresy.

In Texas, there's a plan to junk textbooks and buy 4 million computers. In a low-income area of New York, each school kid gets his own $1,500 laptop computer to take home with him.

Computers are our secret weapon in the War on Dumbness. We are counting on them the way Hitler counted on the V-2 rocket and Saddam counts on anthrax. They will preserve our intellectual dominance of Cyprus and South Africa. And keep us securely third from the bottom on the list of the world's dumbest nations, hovering just below Russia, Lithuania and the Czechs.

Who cares if our kids are dumb, as long as their computers are smart? All they have to do is go around with computers chained to their necks. That's an advantage we didn't have when we were young. The only thing we had tied around our necks was our mittens.

Back then, the best computer for basic math was your mother doing the dishes while you sat in the kitchen and recited the multiplication tables.

It was a very low-tech concept. But you know what? We could make change for a dollar without asking a Lithuanian.

—February 27, 1998

....

Johnny is differently knowledged

Back in 1768, a colonist named John Dickinson coined a phrase when he wrote:

"Then join hand in hand, brave Americans all!

"By uniting we stand, by dividing we fall."

But, hey! What did he know? That was then. This is now!

Listen instead to a fellow named Steve Phillips talking about what's the matter with the San Francisco school curriculum:

"Students read a lot about George Washington and Columbus, but little attention is paid to the traditions and culture of African-Americans or Latinos. They're fed up with it."

Phillips and his fellow school board member, Keith Jackson, want to change the school system's reading list to make sure that 40 percent of the books are written by "authors of color."

They say this is only fair since a mere 13 percent of San Francisco students are white. Or, to use the term an irate caller once pinned on me, "persons of non-color."

Naturally, *Huckleberry Finn* is on the hit list. Among authors of non-color, Mark Twain always shows up as the diversity patrol's least-wanted man. The San Francisco scholars want to replace him with a book by Toni Morrison or Alice Walker.

Phillips and Jackson say they don't like *Huckleberry Finn* because of its depiction of blacks. No matter that it was one of the earliest and most powerful anti-slavery novels ever written. There are too many "n-words" in it. Almost as many as you hear on a rap CD.

Shakespeare gets to stay, though. And so do *The Canterbury Tales*. Their preservation is a little mysterious. Way back in my own school days, even students of non-color acted fed up when forced to stumble through a reading of "The Nun's Priest's Tale."

But back then, nobody cared if we were fed up or not. We were not encouraged to assert our ethnic rights. I, for example, was a German-American student of non-color. Yet I, too, had George Washington and Columbus rammed down my throat.

"Who cares about Columbus?" I might have said, if enlightened. "I'm fed up with him! Wasn't he some kind of Italian or something? Let's hear less about him and more about Bismarck!"

Even the fact that Columbus got his financing from the Queen of Spain cuts no ice, apparently, with San Francisco's Latino students. They are fed up with him anyway. The Queen of Spain was no Latino! She was about as Latino as Wayne Newton. Like students of non-color, today's students of color are mainly interested in studying the one subject they find most fascinating—themselves, their lives and times. There is nothing like an exercise in self-esteem to cut through the distractions of attention deficit disorder.

If the world had turned out to be flat, Columbus would have been in trouble. If diversity turns out to be a fancy name for division, America will come apart at the seams. Critics of the San Francisco school plan think the school board is sailing perilously close to the edge of reason.

"What will happen when San Francisco students have to compete against other students whose education was grounded in the classics of Western literature?" one critic asked.

Ah, but that's an easy one. You just change the rules of competition. Students are only expected to know the things they want to know. Each ethnic group gets its own test. Nobody will be smarter than anybody else. People will just be differently-knowledged.

Can't you already hear that term tripping off the tongue of

some crusader for educational inclusiveness? "It is unfair to flunk Johnny in history because he doesn't know much about George Washington. George Washington is diversitorally insignificant. Johnny is differently-knowleged."

Academia is obviously cuckoo enough to allow this to happen. The problem comes in when Johnny gets out into the real world. The real world isn't as real as it used to be, but it's still real enough to expect an American kid to come out of an American classroom having learned something about American culture.

If you want to learn about the traditions of your own ethnic culture, the best thing to do is to ask your grandmother. And get your high school diploma someplace where the school song isn't "I Left My Smarts in San Francisco."

—March 13, 1998

....

Free speech is wasted on the young

Stories about kids' rights fascinate me. When I was a kid, kids didn't have rights. Or, if we did, a conspiracy of adult silence kept us from knowing about it.

We had heard of rights. But we thought they were something that came along when you got older, like wedding rings and false teeth.

While I was in the middle of being a kid, everybody's father and uncle and cousin went marching off to war to defend the Constitution and preserve justice and freedom in the world. But when they all came marching home again, we kids STILL didn't have rights.

So it was with some envy that I read about the great human-rights victory won by Sean O'Brien, 16, a junior at Westlake High School. He won the right to post a notice on the World Wide Web saying that his band teacher "sucks."

"Raymondsucks.org" was the name of Sean's Web site, created to enumerate the perceived shortcomings of teacher

Raymond Walczuk. When school officials found it there, they suspended Sean for 10 days, threatened him with expulsion and even gave him an "F" in band.

But federal Judge John Manos decreed the punishment must be held off until after a court hearing next month.

This is considered a landmark victory in the age-old struggle for free speech. That's why the story was on the front page of yesterday's newspaper. And that's why Master O'Brien's two attorneys cranked out a news release heralding their triumph.

"The case is a national legal 'first,'" Sean's co-counsels, Avery Friedman and Ken Myers, informed the media, "testing a student's non-threatening, non-obscene use of the Internet."

This is stirring stuff. Perhaps the words "Raymondsucks.org" will take their place in the history books next to such legendary battle cries as "Remember the Maine!," "Remember the Alamo!" and "Your mother wears combat boots!"

But great victories are not won without cost. So Sean's lawyers are suing the school for $550,000 as first aid for the damaging wounds their young client suffered during his historic skirmish for justice.

If his teacher, the now legendary "Raymondsucks," was bruised at all in the fray, he will presumably have to pay for his own bandages. I don't know. So far, he has issued no news releases.

Given the age we live in, it is probably true that the phrase "Raymondsucks" is not an obscenity. Though it used to be, kind of. These days, about the only phrase left that is generally considered obscene is the phrase "Mind if I smoke?"

Even so, I had a sort of post-traumatic shock experience when I read it. I imagined what might have happened in the old, precyberspace days, if I had taken a can of paint and written "Pettys-ks" someplace where my shop teacher, Mr. Petty, might have seen it.

He certainly would have smacked my rear end with a paddle. That's a given. He often did that kind of thing with no great provocation. He kept busy in wood shop making paddles while the rest of us were busy sanding our plant stands.

And when word of my First Amendment exercise reached my father, even the Founding Fathers wouldn't have saved me from what, at the very least, would have been called "a good talking-to." Which I would have had to endure alone—without the opportunity to have two lawyers present.

I have no wish to be hard on young Mr. O'Brien. He seems like a smart and articulate kid, based on the snippets I caught of him on the city's television stations. And I think the school's threatened punishment seems a bit harsh. A good talking-to might have been best, although in our era, a teacher who gives a kid a good talking-to may wind up in a paddy wagon.

But it's going to take me a while to think of Master O'Brien as another Patrick Henry or another John Peter Zenger.

It seems to me that saying your teacher s–ks on the World Wide Web is . . . well . . . at least unwise.

But that's just my opinion. An opinion of an aging man scarred by a childhood when kids didn't have rights. And it's an unenforceable opinion. Words like "unwise" and "wrong" and (here's an oldie) "naughty" don't mean anything anymore. The bottom line is legal or illegal. Nothing else counts.

Besides, Sean's freedom fight isn't going to seem very unwise if he gets to keep whatever portion of $550,000 his lawyers leave him. I'll look pretty silly then. And he'll look like a young man who kept his eyes on the prize.

Still, there's something about this whole landmark episode that . . . what's the word . . . help me here . . .

"Sucks." There, I said it. Don't we all feel righteous now? No? Well, give it a minute.

—March 20, 1998

....

A *principal's failure*

Seventeen years ago, Terry Butler forged a prescription for a painkiller.

Yesterday, the pain came back.

In those 17 years, Butler had become one of the few bright

stars in the dismal, nerve-wracked gloom of the Cleveland school system.

He worked his way up the ladder from science teacher to assistant principal to principal of East Technical High School. Insiders sang his praises. He was optimistic and energetic—the kind of guy who can turn things around, they said.

Then, yesterday morning's paper gave him a wider reputation.

"Cleveland schools suspend 22 who committed crimes," said the front-page headline. Next to it was a picture of Butler hugging a student. Over his right shoulder, another student gazed at him, a prescription for misery written on her face.

It was the kind of look that pleads "Say it ain't so." But Butler kept saying it was so. He acknowledged his crime before the East Tech student body. And then to a stream of reporters who visited him.

Five times, by his count, he lied on a state renewal certificate that asks teachers if they have ever been convicted of a crime.

"I figured it was a case of damned if you do and damned if you don't," he said.

The prescription he forged was for drugs.

He knew something about drugs. When he was a kid, he worked summers at Sack's Drug Store at East 142nd Street and Kinsman Road. He went on to college but kept working there part-time. He was interested in the sciences.

Back then, in the 1960s, drugs were not the plague they have since become. That was before the biggest pharmacy in town was out on the streets and pharmacy interns were 11-year-old lookouts.

As children in the neighborhood began to wither and life on the streets grew meaner, Butler decided he wanted to do something to help kids find their futures. That's when he switched to education and became a science teacher.

He worked as a substitute at first. He taught at Nathan Hale, then went on to FDR, both middle schools. When I first met him, he was an assistant principal at John Adams. I visited my old high school and watched him dispense the medicine of hope to children anemic from its lack.

I didn't know he had a guilty secret. I didn't know about his conviction 17 years ago. I didn't know about the forgery and the

five lies. Yesterday, Butler said that, as the years passed, he began
to think his secret would remain safe. But his past caught up
with him in the end, just like in an old-fashioned movie.

Here are the details of his crime as he tells them:

"I had a toothache back around 1981," he said. "And since I
knew something about pharmacy, I wrote a prescription for Per-
cocet and another for [an antibiotic.] Since I wasn't a doctor, I
forged a doctor's name. I did it one time.

"The pharmacist caught on and they arrested me and I
pleaded guilty and was given probation. I didn't put it on the
state form. I figured it might jeopardize my career."

That, he says, is it. The whole crime spree.

The drugs he prescribed himself are the same drugs my dentist gives me. They would draw few customers to a drug house.
One is for pain. The other is for infection.

No one has invented a drug to take the chronic pain away
from the Cleveland school system. Nothing can seem to fight
the virulent infection that drains its energy away.

But, after sitting by the bedside for 20 years, I think maybe it
is the crushing irony that hurts the most. A merciless, stabbing
irony that takes no pity on the maimed.

Fred Holliday, perhaps the most promising school superintendent the system ever had, shot himself in a school stairwell so
that children would find his body. Terry Butler, a principal people got excited about, got his name in the paper along with the
names of 21 other system employees who had lied about con-
victions for drugs, theft and fraud.

He is guilty of lying and cover-up—offenses judged more
harshly in a high school than in a White House. But he did what
he did, and he will face the music.

But it must be said that, in a week when greedy lawyers are
trying to loot the school system for a few last millions, there is
some irony in Butler's downfall. His deception seems so much
smaller. And, unlike the lawyers, he will be missed.

—April 22, 1998

A *teacher's revenge*

Here is a story with a happy ending to end your week. I take great delight in bringing it to you. Almost perverse delight, in fact. It proves the old adage that it's always darkest just before dawn.

Or, to mix a metaphor, a few weeks ago, Raymond Walczuk was drowning in April showers without an umbrella. And now, everything is coming up May flowers.

You've heard of Walczuk. Half the state has. In distant Atlanta, CNN heard of him and tried to put him on national television. But he declined. He is, understandably, no red-hot fan of the media.

Walczuk may be better known to you by his cyberbabble nickname. During the peak of his notoriety, he was introduced to the front pages as "www.raymondsucks.org." He is the Westlake High School band director ridiculed on the World Wide Web by one of his students.

"Raymond is an overweight, middle-aged man who doesn't like to get haircuts," the student, Sean O'Brien, 17, wrote on his Web site. Then he added Walczuk's home address and phone number.

"Naturally, the phone rang off the hook," Walczuk says. "Some of the calls were cranks. But there was an overwhelming amount of support from students and teachers who thought this was terrible."

Walczuk has been a teacher for 18 years. His wife, Tina, also is a teacher. In their combined careers, they had seen a lot. But they had never seen anything like this. And it was just beginning.

After Westlake High School suspended Sean for his naughtiness, his father rented him a couple of civil rights lawyers. The result was a lawsuit that ended when Sean got an apology from the school and $30,000 to split with his attorneys.

He also got a couple of victory laps around the city's TV talk-show circuit. Show biz was clamoring for Walczuk too, but he had enough dignity, taste and awareness of the piranhalike feeding habits of the legal profession to refuse.

"CNN called and wanted me to appear on a show with Sean," he said. "Now, why would I do that?

"One evening, my wife and I took our two kids to Applebee's for dinner. When we got back home, our neighbors told us a TV crew had been standing on our front lawn. That night, our house was on the news with a reporter standing there claiming I wouldn't come to the door."

Many of you got plenty stirred up about the Internet case and its resolution. Hundreds of people called my voice mail, overwhelmingly supporting Walczuk. Many of the calls were from his band students.

"Mr. Walczuk is tough but he's fair," most of them said. "He expects a lot from us and that brings out the best in us."

Walczuk's name (and his foul-mouthed nickname) faded from the news. At the end of April, he took the Westlake High symphonic and concert bands to a state competition. For the first time ever, two bands from Westlake shared honors, along with bands from North Royalton High School, as the best in Ohio.

Then, last weekend, the Westlake bands and orchestra were awarded the "Sweepstakes" trophy at an international band competition in Montreal. Walczuk had the best band in a couple of lands.

This was great stuff. Since the media was so hot to hear from him, Walczuk decided to send news releases to the TV stations announcing his kids' achievement. But, as of yesterday, only one station had shown any interest. CNN hasn't called either.

I'd been itching to talk to Walczuk for weeks. I figured this might be a good time to catch him in a mellow mood. How did he feel about the apology and the $30,000 going to Sean and his lawyers? Was it ironic? Outrageous? Demeaning?

"It was wrong," he said, simply.

I reviewed the content of Walczuk's unsolicited Web profile, which described him as "an overweight, middle-aged man who doesn't like to get haircuts." For the record, Walczuk is 39 years old. He stands 5 feet 10 and wears a size 42 regular suit. And his hair is as short as his patience is long.

"Teaching has changed a lot since I got into it," he said sadly. "Most of the kids are still great. But, because of the band activity, I talk to teachers from a lot of schools around the country.

"They all have seen a growing lack of respect for teachers. It used to be if a teacher walked down the hall, kids kind of quieted down. Now they just ignore you. If they're talking bad language, and they often are, the bad language continues. A lot of teachers are nervous about disciplining the kids because of repercussions. Maybe we'll have to start teaching with lawyers in the classroom."

Gloomy thought. And I promised you a happy ending. And you've waited long enough.

In fall, there will be a band banquet at Westlake High to celebrate a year of triumph in which Ray Walczuk got the best out of his kids. Well, most of them, anyway.

Medals will be awarded. And, since Sean O'Brien is a band member (baritone horn, second-last chair) he will, if he attends, receive a medal from his old pal "www.raymondsucks.org." I'd like to be there to see that. It appeals to my disreputable taste for perfect, subtle revenge.

But pin it gently, Ray. Pin it gently.

—May 8, 1998

The Verdict is In

Things suddenly got more complicated

We didn't think they'd arrest a Tim, did we? We thought they would arrest an Ali. Or an Ahmed. And, thinking that, we began to plot our revenge.

The first thing to do would be to find out what terrorist group Ali and Ahmed were working for. And where they came from. And what foreign country looked the other way while they met to plan attacks against our government. And to plot the murder of babies.

Once we had found out these things, we would act. There was no doubt about that. We would put the friends of Ali and Ahmed on an enemies list. Possibly even a hit list. Any government that offered them shelter or sponsorship would have to change its policies immediately or suffer punishment. In fact, immediately might not be soon enough. And there would be no appeal from such punishment. This we swore on the bodies of dead children buried in the rubble. This we pledged in the name of our own children, whose lives suddenly were more precious and more vulnerable.

We began to coalesce. Fear and anger unified us. We shoved political differences to the background. By Friday morning, we wet a finger and lifted it into the air and saw, with some satisfaction, that the national wind was blowing away from panic and toward grim resolve.

And then they arrested Tim. Not Ali. Not Ahmed. They arrested Tim, with his crew cut and his white skin. Tim, who grew up near Buffalo and served in the Gulf War. Whose father worked at the General Motors plant and who liked basketball and who went to Mass on Sunday morning and who put on little Halloween shows in his basement and charged the other kids admission.

As they led him out of jail and toward a waiting police car, a deputy dropped back a step and we saw Tim's face. We had met the enemy and he was us.

And what did we feel in that moment? A sudden stillness as the winds of resolve stopped blowing. Some embarrassment and shame because now the world would know and shake its head and remind itself that the greatest threat to the American way of life is the Americans who live it.

We were like an audience that suddenly finds itself watching the wrong movie. Somebody had switched reels on the projector and now aircraft carriers were out of the picture along with thunderous calls for U.N. sanctions and stern ultimatums to the heads of foreign states. No point making crank calls to the Arab grocer and whispering ugliness into his wife's ear. Because the greatest act of terrorism in the history of the country had been, allegedly, committed by Tim. Our Tim. Who wasn't "different" in any useful way. It was Tim's most triumphant Halloween show of all—popping out of that jail dressed up like the kid next door. He stopped the Pentagon and the State Department cold in their tracks. And now, somebody would have to explain things to the dead.

The dead lay invisible in a curved amphitheater of rubble carved by the ferocity of the fertilizer bomb. They will never see Tim's face or learn his country of origin. They were not in the audience when the reel changed. Nothing about them is any different than it was before. They are still infants and mothers and fathers and grandpas and grandmas. The wind blows over them and rain falls on the rubble and trickles down toward them. Search dogs sniff around them. They are the same dead we swore to avenge last Friday morning.

Let us imagine the small figure of an American citizen, you or I, walking into that silent but well-populated amphitheater and looking way up at the tiers of invisible dead and breaking the news that things have become a little more complicated than they seemed at first.

I guess we'd say something like this:

It wasn't an Ali or Ahmed who did this to you. It looks like it may have been Tim.

The country Tim comes from is America. Your country.

So if Tim really did this, America was the country that looked the other way while he was planning his attack against the government and plotting to murder babies.

Which terrorist group he might have been working for is a little unclear at the moment because all of a sudden it turns out there may be a whole lot of hate groups out there. But most of the people who belong to those groups are Americans too and they have certain immunities that Ali or Ahmed do not have. They have the right to hate and to talk about hating. There's not much we can do about that in a free society. You do understand that, don't you?

I will take your silence as an indication that you do.

So we're not sure at this point just what we're going to be able to do for you. Or rather, about you. Because now people with breath to speak will want to speak in your name.

Anti-gun people will speak in your name and say that Tim always kept guns. Pro-gun people will speak in your name and point out that the murder weapon was fertilizer and fuel oil, and guns had nothing to do with you. The left will claim you were killed by the hatred of the right. The right will say you were the victims of men driven mad by the ATF's actions at Waco and perceived anti-constitutional policies of the left.

Many will claim to speak in your name. None of them will say anything new. And, little by little, as the rubble comes down and the Masses are said and your graves are closed, we may even pretend you are a tragic catastrophe of freedom rather than an unnatural catastrophe of hate.

We hope you don't think we're going back on our word. If only it had been Ali or Ahmed, you would not have died in vain. But, if it was Tim, we'll have to get back to you. Ok? . . . Ok? . . . Ok, then.

—April 24, 1995

Casualties of noise

I plan to use this weekend to pry my mind away from that rubble in Oklahoma City. Good luck to me. I wanted to write about Ginger Rogers. I can't write about Ginger Rogers. I don't feel like dancing, thank you. I should have taken the day off.

A man on the voice mail says: "Sure it was terrible what happened to all those kids in the bombing. But what about all the kids who are killed every year in abortion clinics?"

That's called, I guess, keeping your priorities straight.

I don't want to fight with anybody while those bodies are still in there. I just want everybody to shut up. I want to shut up, too. Until they get them out.

A man on the voice mail says: "Tell me how come those police did such a good job arresting those bombers but when it comes to O. J., the police screwed everything up. Tell me that wasn't deliberate."

A week to the minute after the bomb went off, they observed a couple of moments of silence in Oklahoma City. It sounded good on television, that silence. It was a small eye in the storm of national yammering. It reminded you how nice silence is. The silence came down like a healing gift. It brought back an old Sunday school lesson. "Be still," it says somewhere in the Bible. "Be still and know that I am God."

But we are not a nation that values stillness.

The caller on the voice mail says: "Clinton has to bear his share of the blame. He has set the rich against the poor in America. He has us at each other's throats."

I thought about poverty. There are several kinds, but most of us only talk about one. I guess I have never been poor. Once, about 10 years ago, I was flat broke, though. All my possessions were gone. I had no bank account. I am not claiming this was a tragedy. I had a job and a small apartment. But I had no stuff. I was in my 40s and I had spent a lot of time and money accumulating stuff. Now it was gone.

I was forced to ask myself what my irreducible minimums

were. What did I really need to provide a quality of life in which I could flourish and grow? I decided I needed two things. A library card and a stereo. The library card would give me access to the world's great wisdom, literature and art. The stereo would connect me to the world's great music, written by composers who know what to do with silence—how to break it in a way that is ennobling, with music stolen from the thunder and the wind and the rain and birdsong. Music full of the hopelessness and hope that are the terrible and wonderful themes behind the mystery of living.

Then I started collecting stuff again. I have more now than I ever had before. According to the American version of poverty, I am free of it. But I listen to music less. I read less than I used to. I watch a lot of TV, hip-hopping between the news channels. I read three newspapers a day. I am angrier now than I was when I had nothing. I have developed quite a long list of people who make me angry because of what they think and say. I've never been within 100 miles of most of them. But I am steeped in their anger and mine three or four hours a day.

And yet I can't think, at the moment, of anybody I know personally who I am angry at. I know black people and white people, Republicans and Democrats, gay people and straight people. The people I know as people are nice people.

It is only when I plug into the noise and become part of the noise that lines are drawn and tribes are formed and people stop being people and become threats. Then it is exciting to find other threatened people to talk with. People eager to share abstract bitterness. People anxious to form little duets and trios of righteousness.

Technology has broadened the communion of hate. There is the much-vaunted Internet, which a month ago was furnishing to anyone the recipe for a bomb made from fuel oil and fertilizer. Just five days ago, the Internet asked: "Are you interested in receiving information detailing the components and materials needed to construct a bomb identical to the one in Oklahoma? Complete details of the bomb and how it was used and could have been better . . . ?"

Five days and already the technology of doom has taken a

step forward. A duet or a quartet or a small chorus of haters, their heads full of noise, can kill another piece of the government they hate. The noise has turned them into things and, to them, the government is a thing. Library cards, music—just things. Their heads are full of the sound of the noise roaring at them and they have lost the blessing of silence. The noise has robbed them of reality.

The noise has been very loud all week. It sounds like this: rights Waco Constitution talk show host First Amendment FBI rights freedom of speech Randy Weaver Second Amendment Congress political advantage repression government rights . . . etc. . . . etc. . . .

What chance do the silent dead have against this noise? *The Daily Oklahoman* published a page of obits. Little lost lives of people taken from the rubble.

A woman who told her co-workers she had just planted 79 gladiola bulbs. A young wife of seven weeks. A man who, last Christmas, bought tickets and took two poor kids to see *The Nutcracker* because he believed that every kid should see it at least once. These are small and gentle stories. They are the true stories of American lives. But the noise overpowers truth, then masquerades as truth.

They are casualties of noise, all of the dead. And I, who make noise for a living, feel complicit in their deaths. Maybe I shouldn't. I'm going to tell myself I shouldn't. But it's going to be a quiet weekend here.

—April 28, 1995

The verdict is in, justice is out

The jury blew it.

Robin Kasper, the jury said, was annihilated by accident. The man who robbed her at gunpoint didn't mean to shoot her. Farthest thing from his mind.

The gun was just a fashion accessory. A little business card robbers carry so their victims don't mistake them for census takers. And what good is a gun if you don't point it? And where are you going to point it? At the ground? That's unreasonable and unbusinesslike.

But then the gun "went off." This is a phenomenon that reliably occurs when a finger pulls the trigger. A 5-year-old knows that. But when 30-year-old Vincent Wright's finger pulled the trigger, his brain was astonished by the sound of gunfire. Or so the jury believed.

It was all a big misunderstanding between Vincent Wright's finger and his brain. After all, if he had really intended to murder Robin Kasper, would he have shot her in the shoulder? The bullet entered her shoulder, but then mischievously passed through her lung and cut her aorta, and she bled to death there on the seat of her car while her little daughter watched and screamed.

This regrettable turn of events was quite a surprise to Vincent Wright, the jury decided. But what was done was done, so he reached in through the car window and scooped up the Christmas money Robin Kasper had just withdrawn from an ATM. And then he and an accomplice drove out of the bank parking lot in a hurry. Just in case somebody who witnessed it all might jump to the conclusion that a murder had taken place.

You can't blame him. The cops thought it was murder, and so did the prosecutor's office. And so did the members of Robin Kasper's family. They came to the courtroom thinking that Justice was on their side.

They thought of Justice as an understanding friend. Justice could not bring Robin Kasper back to life or mend their shattered lives or erase whatever horrible, bloody imprint had scalded a little girl's memory forever.

Justice could do only one thing. Justice could set up its scales and give measure for measure. On one of the scales, Justice would place their agony and loss. And on the other scale, Justice would display the murderer. And call him a murderer. And call his deed murder. Innocence on the right, guilt on the left. A balance of righteousness. A solemn exercise of the precious equilibrium that keeps civilization from collapsing into chaos.

But a courtroom is a theater and Robin Kasper's death robbed her of a speaking part. It is the job of defense lawyers in our system to produce chaos, not eliminate it. Confusion is their friend. It is their duty to complicate the obvious, until a jury's brain is numb. To make a jury lose focus and overtheorize. They are masters of illusion and the art of misdirection.

Vincent Wright's lawyers put on a magic show and it worked. And when the show was over, the jury rewarded the magicians by deciding that Robin Kasper hadn't been murdered at all. She had gone to the bank and died there. And while Vincent Wright had played a part in her demise, his part had been involuntary. He had committed an act of involuntary manslaughter—a kind of felonious whoops.

In the hours after the verdict was announced, WWWE AM/1100 provided a therapeutic sounding board for the stunned and outraged Clevelanders who called to protest the outcome. One of Wright's attorneys called in, expressed his condolences to the Kasper family but declared that the system had worked.

"Robin Kasper was just at the wrong place at the wrong time," he said, sadly.

If that is true, where, anymore, is the right place? What time, anymore, is the right time? Where is the righteous balance when murder isn't murder and guns fire against the wishes of the robbers who hold them?

Vincent Wright will go to jail for a long while. But that isn't the point. The Kaspers were denied the gift of balance and sanity. Justice had a thumb on the scale. If anybody was in the wrong place at the wrong time, it was the Vincent Wright jury.

—May 17, 1996

Kia cried, "Where's Daddy?"

This is a Father's Day message for Kia Taylor's father.

Your daughter is dead. She starved to death.

That's not the kind of greeting American Greetings peddles. So this piece of newsprint will have to do.

Forgive the omission of those little drawings of sailing ships and fishing rods that usually adorn Father's Day cards. They don't fit the message.

The sentiment here was best illustrated by a dial on the scale in the morgue. Your daughter, sir, weighed 18 pounds when she died. Half as much as she should have.

She didn't die in a hurry, because you don't starve to death in a hurry. She died a week at a time. She didn't know what was happening to her because she was only 4 years old. Her death was a result of the life she was living—she died of the world you brought her into.

Your sister is in jail, by the way. Joann Givens has been charged with murder in your daughter's death. The department in charge of the county's children lists Joann Givens as a paternal aunt. There's not much mention of you or your own paternity.

The news accounts of your daughter's death are well populated with women. We know all about Kia's mother, Marlene Taylor. She had problems with drugs but no problem bearing children. She delivered eight of them. The county placed five in your sister's house on Cedar Avenue. The older three were placed elsewhere.

But where are the men in this story? Where are you?

Judith Goodhand, the county director of children's services, has no idea where you are. Neither do the lawyers representing Joann Givens. Nobody, so far, has heard from you.

Maybe you're dead. If you're dead, excuse me for bothering you. Then again, maybe you're not dead. Maybe you're reading the newspaper every day, following this complicated story of needles and crack and starvation and welfare and kids who are born and handed from woman to woman, a strange, ugly, lethal story with no men in it.

If you're reading this, you ought to know that the county is planning your daughter's funeral. You brought her into the world and the county is sending her out. TV will probably cover it. The news will care about her for a day and then she'll vanish. Another little girl who never had a chance.

You know, Pop, they had a big, pro-children rally in Washington a week or so ago. Thousands of people rode there on buses and they put up a big rostrum and professional singers sang stirring songs. And many bold phrases ascended toward the heavens, floating up like soap bubbles from the mouths of the noisily compassionate.

Everybody at the rally agreed that America had to do something about children. Everybody agreed that not enough was being done. And that more should be done. And, then, having unburdened themselves of such sanctimony, the people at the rally rode back home.

But you know what, Dad? Without you, such rallies are a farce. All the while the stirring songs were being sung and the pretty phrases were being launched, your little girl was starving to death in a house on Cedar. And that little girl wasn't America's responsibility or Judith Goodhand's responsibility. She was your responsibility. Yours.

It isn't the children we should be doing something about. It's the parents we should be doing something about. But what? What?

When they hauled your daughter's small body out of the house, a doctor looked at her and at the other kids and said:

"They looked like children from a Third World country. You could count their ribs, and their bellies were swollen."

Well, we're not a Third World country. We've got welfare, dad. And we've got social workers. And we've got Medicaid and school lunches. And lots of paperwork.

But if we had twice as much of all this stuff as we have, it wouldn't have saved your daughter. Because she didn't have you.

When they're 4 years old, they have to be coaxed, Pop. And,

if she'd had you, this might have been the year somebody said, "Be a big girl, Kia, and tell Daddy what you want to tell him."

And she might have smiled and said: "Happy Father's Day." But she can't. And forgive me if I don't.

—June 14, 1996

Jewell's days of infamy will pay off

Crazy people go crazy a little bit at a time. So their friends are likely to overlook it.

"Do you think Joe is acting weird lately?" Joe's friend might say. "No weirder than usual," another friend might say. And then they forget about Joe until he combs his hair in bangs and curses his defeat at Waterloo.

The same is true with nations. Every day our national news is full of insanity. Most of this insanity is reported with a straight face. So we get used to it. And then something happens—often a small thing—that briefly opens our eyes.

"You gotta be kidding," we say to America. But America ain't kidding. America is seriously bonkers.

Such a small thing happened last week in the saga of Richard Jewell, who has been dropping in on the media like a one-man collection agency to claim the money the press owes him for branding him the mad Olympic bomber.

Sooner or later, it was obvious, Richard Jewell's victory lap would take him to the offices of CNN. A CNN announcer was among the first to tell the world that Jewell was the No. 1 bombing suspect. I watched the announcer do it, and he was pretty nervous about it.

He was so nervous that he made it clear he was reading a story from the Atlanta newspaper. Probably he thought this would get him off the hook. But it didn't work. After all, Atlanta newspapers don't get delivered to grape-stompers living outside Paris.

CNN made Richard Jewell's name a nasty household word in several languages.

So, after leaving NBC with about $500,000 in damages, Jewell and his lawyer visited CNN. And there, a conversation took place which, based on news accounts, apparently went something like this:

Jewell: "I was living a nice, quiet life, minding my own business, until you CNN guys came along. Then you destroyed my privacy, blackened my good name and made me infamous all over the world."

CNN: "That's true. We're real sorry about it."

Jewell: "So I figure you owe me a lot of money. Here's a piece of paper with a number on it. That's what I figure you owe me."

CNN: "Fair enough."

Jewell: "Well, thanks. I'll be going now. I got a couple more stops to make."

CNN: "Wait a minute."

Jewell: "Huh?"

CNN: "Just to show there's no hard feelings, how would you like to write a book?"

Jewell: "What kind of a book?"

CNN: "We were thinking about a book that tells how you were living a nice quiet life, minding your own business until guys like us came along, destroyed your privacy, blackened your good name and made you infamous all over the world."

Jewell: "Who'd publish such a book?"

CNN: "We would."

Jewell: "But why would you publish a book that told how your irresponsible actions gave me a rotten reputation?"

CNN: "Because that way we could get back some of the money we just gave you. After all, you just got through saying that nobody had ever heard of you until we gave you a bad name all over the world, right?"

Jewell: "Right."

CNN: "And if nobody had ever heard of you, nobody would want to buy your book, right?"

Jewell: "I guess not."

CNN: "So if you owe your worldwide rotten reputation to us,

isn't it only fair that we get a share of the book sales? After all, what did Random House ever do for you? Did they imply you were a murderer and put a panel of experts on television to say that you had the personality of a lone, crazed bomber?"

Jewell: "No."

CNN: "So it seems to us it would be damned ungrateful of you to let somebody who hadn't made you infamous publish your book. Here's a piece of paper with a number on it. That's what we figure our share ought to be."

That's apparently where things stand. Negotiations are still under way. Jewell's lawyer, Lin Wood, says he isn't sure yet what Jewell will do about the offer.

"They brought it up," Wood said. "How can you say no to that?"

And how can you? It seems crazy all right. But in a country where insanity is the norm, how could Jewell turn the offer down?

His friends would say he's nuts.

—February 3, 1997

....

He deserves to die

"We are not here to seek vengeance on Timothy McVeigh," the judge told the jury. "Try not to overreact."

Earlier, a cop had told them:

"I held her warm hand sticking out of the rubble. I could hear muffled moans behind some concrete.

"I felt she was drowning because I thought I could hear running water. I was told it was not running water. It was blood.

"In three minutes, her hand turned very cold. I checked for a pulse and found none."

Put yourself on the jury. Multiply that story by 168. Consider the dead baby whose face was gone. Consider the implication of the victims found with gravel in their lungs. Then define "over-reaction."

Maybe it means, "Don't kill him because you're mad at him. Kill him because you think it's the right thing to do."

Except that leads nowhere. If we weren't mad at him, it couldn't possibly be the right thing to do. The "overreaction" part is just words. Just something pretty the judge thought he had to say.

"We are not here to seek vengeance on Timothy McVeigh," the judge said. Well, of course we are. He did something to Americans and now Americans are going to do something back. It's just a question of what. Are we jurors going to turn our tear-streaked cheeks and tell him to go and sin no more? No. We are going to punish him, all right. Vengeance is very much on the agenda. If we take our time and think it over and follow the rules, we get to call it justice.

Very soon, a lawyer is bound to stand up and say:

"Will killing Timothy McVeigh bring 168 people back?"

No. Next question.

"If you kill Timothy McVeigh, aren't you just as bad as he is?"

No. Nice try. Next question.

"Isn't a whole life spent in prison as severe a punishment as death?"

Ask the woman whose pulse grew faint and stopped. Ask the victims with gravel in their lungs. Don't ask the baby with no face. He is too young and maimed to answer.

Ask them if they think life in prison is as bad as death beneath the rubble.

Suppose you said to them: "Here's a proposition to consider as your life runs down like a clock. Instead of dying right now, we'll take you to a cell someplace. You'll have barbells and cable TV, and you'll get to read magazines and walk in a small yard and complain about the food.

"Your relatives can visit you regularly. So you'll be able to watch your children grow up and see how they turn out. Journalists will drop by every couple of years to update the world on how you're doing. Maybe you'll even get your own Web site like Charlie Manson has.

"But you'll never get out. You'll die in prison 10 or 20 or 40 years from now. So what do you think? Which is the better deal? Living like that or dying now?"

Ask those who died frantically trying to live if they think living is the same as dying. You know the answer. What's next, counselor?

"Even though you've found him guilty, suppose McVeigh is innocent. Do you want to risk killing an innocent man?"

An innocent man would jump into the witness chair and shout his innocence until the rafters rang.

"But you can't infer his guilt just because he didn't testify."

We know. But we did it anyway. Sorry. Next question.

"If you kill him, you make him a martyr."

If we lock him up, we make him a martyr, too. What else?

"He may have important information to give us."

Right. And he may turn into the *Encyclopedia Britannica* with a death sentence hanging over his head. Next?

"What it really all boils down to is that the death penalty is wrong. Uncivilized. Inhuman."

Maybe.

"At last you agree."

Maybe. The death penalty comes and goes like a fashion statement. But here's the trouble, counselor. Right now, it's in fashion. They killed two murderers in Texas the other night and called it a doubleheader. In Florida, they're shoving them into the chair so fast they don't have time to fix the wiring.

If McVeigh doesn't deserve the death penalty, nobody does. He's white, educated and sane. He came from a decent family and he had a couple of bucks in his pocket. And he killed 168 people. What do you suppose happens if we let him live and they try to execute some minority guy from a rotten home with no education who kills a convenience store clerk?

"But it is absolutely wrong for you to take that into consideration."

Easy for you to say. Get real. Next?

"I have nothing further. I rest."

We envy you.

—June 6, 1997

Dead drunk with power

Quick! Rush a breath analyzer over to the office of the American Civil Liberties Union. The inmates are drunk on their own self-righteousness. And this time they've gone too far.

They are mean drunks, too, those ACLU rowdies. Give them a couple of belts of self-righteousness and they stagger off to pick a fight with God.

"Get that baby in the cradle off the City Hall steps!" they roar every Christmas time. "Get that menorah out of that public park!" They cause a little scene each December like somebody's tipsy uncle who gets on everybody's nerves and steps on the toys and makes the children cry.

But this is the slow season for God-bashing. Nothing much for the ACLU to do but prowl around checking logos on suburban police cars for any sign of a cross lurking in a city seal. Or hope a tipster will phone to report that the Ten Commandments have been sighted violating a public wall.

So, with nobody else to pick on, the ACLU has gone after Alcoholics Anonymous, an organization that was sitting over in the corner, sipping its ginger ale, minding its own business and causing no trouble for anybody.

This made front-page news in this newspaper, and no wonder. Alcoholics Anonymous, without taking a dime from the public purse, has probably done more good, salvaged more lives and healed more families than any human welfare program since the dawn of time.

Every first-class substance abuse center in the country, including the expensive and prestigious Betty Ford Clinic, bases its treatment program on the 12 steps of Alcoholics Anonymous. And these steps have been borrowed and modified by therapists who treat disorders such as compulsive gambling and eating.

Alcoholism is lethal. Not just to the alcoholic but to his family members and to innocent strangers he chances to encounter. The most recent statistics show that in 1995, 22,716 traffic deaths were alcohol-related. That doesn't count homicides and assaults, battered wives and children, lost jobs and families drowned by a pattern of behavior that resembles outright insanity.

For many years, judges, frustrated by the ravages of alcoholism, have sentenced DUI offenders to attend Alcoholics Anonymous meetings. This is not a sure-fire answer. It is an immutable fact of all welfare programs that, to be helped, the recipient has to want to help himself. That's one of those unfortunate truths that some social engineers do headstands to try to avoid.

But given the stakes—and the track record of AA—many judges feel that drug abusers might benefit from hanging around other drug abusers who are successfully staying clean and sober. If one in 10 drunks sentenced to an AA meeting manages to grab the brass ring, that's one less drunk who might swerve across the curb and wipe out somebody's little girl.

Now comes Joan Englund, legal director for the Ohio ACLU, to threaten such judges with a lawsuit. She has just discovered that a couple of the steps in the 60-year-old AA program mention some kind of God. Immediately, general quarters were sounded on the ACLU poop deck and the God SWAT team rushed to battle stations and things were as exciting as Christmas in June.

And what is this spiritual threat to the rights of good, solid, American citizen-lushes convicted of vehicular menacing? It is step 3 of the 12-step program, which says:

"We made a decision to turn our will and our lives over to the care of God as we understand him."

Lots of room for flexibility there, wouldn't you say? And they mean it, too. You get to supply your own God. It can be a he, a she or an it. It can be the spirit of the group or the spirit of '76 or the awesome power of the sunrise. As long as it's a little bigger than you are.

But even that much God is too much for the ACLU, which takes a kind of Linda Blair, *Exorcist*, mention-God-to-me-and-I'll-throw-up-all-over-you view of spirituality.

So Ms. Englund has vowed to monitor judges who send drunks to AA meetings. She's willing to sue, she says, but she hopes the issue can be resolved amicably.

Well I sure hope it can't. Neither, I am delighted to say, does Judge Thomas J. Pokorny, who called the ACLU's position "outrageous."

And it is. It is also ridiculous, pitiful and somewhat revolting. It's a power binge, using the Constitution as a breath mint.

The ACLU ought to step outside itself and breathe some reality and get its head on straight. Otherwise it can go and take a 12-step walk off a six-step pier.

—June 25, 1997

....

Leonard Hughes' luck held

Once, they made a four-star movie called *Twelve Angry Men*. Henry Fonda was the hero. He was the only man on a murder jury who thought there was a chance the kid on trial didn't do it.

Little by little, in a tense hour and a half of movie time, he persuaded the other jurors to change their minds. He asked them to search their souls and the evidence, which they reluctantly did. And at the end of the movie, they all switched to Fonda's side. Justice triumphed. An innocent youth was spared an unjust punishment.

Why don't they make movies like that anymore? Maybe it's because they don't make juries like that anymore—a conclusion that might reasonably be reached by reading the daily news.

The angst of the Leonard Hughes murder jury would make a pretty strange movie. You certainly couldn't call it *Twelve Angry Men II*. In the first place, the Leonard Hughes jury had some women on it. They were among the ones who wept as they returned a verdict that reportedly violated their consciences, their logic and their understanding of truth.

Eleven of them believed that Leonard Hughes intentionally shot and killed Patrolman Hilary Cudnik. But they told the judge they believed the opposite. Eleven of them believed

Hughes should face the death penalty for what he had done. But they told the judge he shouldn't.

Only one juror blocked a conviction for aggravated murder. He is the leading man in this story, which will never reach the big screen. But his part had little scope to it. He didn't convince the other 11 jurors that he was right. They thought he was wrong, but they voted his way anyhow. We can call it justice, but it won't win any four-star ratings.

Hilary Cudnik died because Leonard Hughes shot him. So everybody was able to agree that Leonard Hughes murdered Hilary Cudnik. The matter at stake was whether Hughes acted intentionally. Or whether murdering Patrolman Cudnik was just bad luck.

The trial revealed that Hughes is a lucky man. He has a police bullet in his head, but he's still alive. The bullet even did him a favor. His lawyers claimed it gave him amnesia on all memory of shooting Patrolman Cudnik but left intact the useful recollection that Hughes' goal was merely to run away.

Hughes is 37. He knows the streets. What would make him think that leaping from a car and pointing an assault rifle would be an efficient way of avoiding contact with police? Bulletnesia wiped that answer away.

What was he doing with the rifle in the first place? Well, he had a little custom of shooting a rifle in the air on New Year's Eve. What about his alleged vow to his drug-dealing crony that if the cops ever stopped him, there'd be a shootout? Bulletnesia again.

Eight people testified they saw Hughes gun down Patrolman Cudnik. Then Hughes got on the stand. Asked if he'd done it, he consulted a portion of his memory that was conveniently intact. He didn't shoot anybody, he said.

Equipped with such pieces of the puzzle, the jury retired to put it together. Eleven jurors, black and white, formed a clear picture of Hughes' intent. The one holdout didn't see it that way. So, to avoid a hung jury, 11 jurors decided to compromise their best judgment and save Hughes from a death sentence. Leonard Hughes' luck held. Hilary Cudnik never had any.

As justice, this is hard to swallow. The sporting thing to do is to accept the verdict and pay homage to the justice system. But the jurors haven't helped. Within hours of their verdict, they were explaining to the media that they had taken the best settlement they could get. They sounded like labor negotiators giving the bad news about a flawed contract to a dismayed membership. Justice wasn't really done, so said they all-but-one. It was more like a bad episode of *Let's Make a Deal*.

I heard a juror trying to explain it all on WTAM radio. After he was through, host Bob Becker opened the lines to phone calls.

The calls poured in from the random and unofficial jury of listeners, men and women, black and white. All were upset. Some of the callers were upset with the verdict, and others were upset by the people who were upset.

Several policemen called in to say they felt betrayed. Other people called to state that police regularly betray the community and that police evidence can't be trusted in cases against blacks. The anger broadened out until Hilary Cudnik and exactly what had happened to him and why became a lesser issue. A lightning rod, attracting charges and counter-charges, frustration and bitterness from the atmosphere.

This mixture of sentiments was absolutely predictable. It is a mixture we have all come to expect. What we call a jury pool is no pool at all. It is a sea of troubled waters—the boiling confluence of many separate streams.

Justice tosses on its surface like a chip and is sometimes pulled under. And below, beneath everything, is the anger of not just 12, but multitudes.

—August 22, 1997

....

The issue here is bigger than bosoms

The road to gender equality has many twists and turns, not to mention a few bumps and grinds and jiggles.

Most recent of these is a $3.75 million out-of-court settlement that gave men the right to work at Hooters, a restaurant chain so named because its bosomy waitresses proudly showcase the upper stories of their anatomical attributes.

This milestone caused much discussion in my chapter of the Clarence Thomas Male Awareness Group, Lodge No. 41. Bob spoke first.

"God didn't mean for men to work in a bosom bar," he said. "They're not up to it physically. It's women's work."

We all booed loudly.

"I'm surprised at you, Bob," said Frank. "That's old-fashioned, sexist, stereotyped thinking. A person's gender should have nothing to do with what that person can or cannot do. Each person should get an equal chance to show what he or she's got."

"That's my whole point," Bob said. "Nobody goes to bosom bars to see what he's got. They go to see what she's got. Give he and she an equal shot and it's no contest."

"You just don't get it," said Frank. "The issue here is bigger than bosoms. The issue here is discrimination. And we all know that discrimination in any form is just flat wrong."

"Now wait a minute," said Bob. "Suppose the bunch of us here decided to open a bar designed to showcase our physical attributes. What would we call it?"

We all looked around the table.

"Stomachs," somebody said.

"OK," said Bob. "We call it 'Stomachs.' The whole idea of the place is that everybody who works there has got a big stomach, right? Are you saying that some skinny guy can apply for a job and sue us for discrimination if we don't hire him?"

"Yes," said Frank. "We'd have to give him some job that didn't require him to use his stomach."

"Like the chef in this joint," said Sam, who was trying to get a fork in his quiche.

Frank looked at his newspaper. "According to the Hooters settlement, Hooters had to agree to hire men as greeters at the door or to clear tables and bring salt and pepper shakers," he read.

"What's the point of going to a place called Hooters if the person bending over your table to put down a pepper shaker is some hairy-chested guy smelling of Mennen?" said Bob.

"Lemme see that newspaper," Sam said. He took it and read for a while in silence.

"It quotes a spokesman from Hooters named Mike McNeil," Sam said. "He says, 'Hooters doesn't sell food, it sells sex appeal. To have female sex appeal, you have to be female.'"

"Absolutely right," said Bob.

"I don't know about that," said Frank. "That's the kind of thing I might have said myself some years ago. But now, when I hear a statement like that, all my warning flags go up."

"Your warning flags go up when you hear somebody say that to have female sex appeal, you have to be female?" said Bob. "Why? Mine don't."

"It's just the kind of flat, general statement that the movement has been struggling against," said Frank. "I just hear something wrong in it. It seems to lack inclusiveness. It makes no allowance for diversity. It suggests we ought to turn the clock back."

"In your case, it's a cuckoo clock," said Bob.

"Well," said Sam. "This article settles it. It says that Hooters agreed to pay the male victims of bosom discrimination $2 million. That's a big win. And you know that old saying, 'To the victims go the spoils.'"

"I thought the settlement was for $3.75 million," somebody said.

"It was," said Sam. "The lawyers who filed the suit got the other $1.75 million. That's not bad for a bosom suit. As usual, their cup runneth over."

"If all the lawyers in America went on vacation for a month, the national victimization rate would drop like a rock," said Bob. "If I was a lawyer, I'd stay out of Hooters unless I wanted to sit there all night staring at the salt and pepper."

"Lawyers don't go to Hooters," said Sam. "They've got their own special place with a special brand of exciting appeal aimed right at them."

"What's it called?" somebody asked.

"Looters," Bob said.

—October 6, 1997

Tucker's true life and crimes

No great American hero ever died amid the pomp and ceremony that surrounded the passing of Karla Faye Tucker, murderess.

She was solemnly launched into eternity live on CNN, with the network's chief anchor counting down the minutes. There is no archived script for such an event. So it was staged like the combination of a death watch and space shot.

It was gripping television. But then, Tucker was a made-for-TV murderess—telegenic, articulate and as perky as a game-show host.

In the last months of her life, we got to know her, in that surface way we "get to know" TV celebrities. We took note of her hair and her smile. We learned that her last meal had been a prudent salad.

The pope spoke on her behalf and so did Jerry Falwell, who helped out with the play-by-play of her demise. Many people who perish pulling kids out of burning buildings die with less prestigious endorsements and more indifferent reviews.

In a manner of speaking, we haven't seen the last of her. *The Karla Faye Tucker Story* is bound to pop up as a TV movie (unless it already has and I missed it). When her exploits are fully examined, there will be more on the menu than salad and repentance.

According to her biographer, Beverly Lowry, writing in this week's *New Yorker*, Tucker was smoking marijuana at age 8, shooting heroin at 10 and sleeping with rock musicians at 13. At 20, she followed in her mother's professional footsteps and became a prostitute.

She was the leader of her own gang. She became acquainted with a biker named Jerry Dean. They didn't get along very well. Dean parked his Harley on Tucker's living-room rug, soiling it. And once, in a fit of pique, he stabbed some photos of her mother and she punched him out. She was proud of her punch.

The night Tucker put the pickax through Jerry Dean, she was

high on speed. She went to Dean's apartment to steal motorcy-cle parts. Tucker's colleague, Danny Garrett, a bartender at a swingers' bar, went along.

Garrett hit Dean in the head with a hammer and broke his neck. But Dean was still alive and making gurgling sounds. So Tucker took the ax from the wall and began to chop away at Dean until he grew quiet.

That's when Tucker discovered someone else in the room. A married mother of two named Deborah Thornton had met Dean that day at a party and gone home with him for sex. Thornton was hiding under a sheet, shaking. Tucker hit her with the ax but it did not penetrate. Her friend, Garrett, helped her finish off Thornton.

We heard none of this the other night on CNN. That's good. Karla Faye Tucker died pretty close to mealtime. The details of her crime might have diminished our appetite, both for supper and societal guilt.

For the death of Tucker is said to have left us with a grave moral question. She is said to have "put a face" on capital pun-ishment and forced us to reconsider its barbarity.

I am no great fan of capital punishment. We had it in my youth. Then it went away. Then it came back again. We often hear that ours is a nation where laws rule men. But live long enough and you discover that trends rule laws.

My own opinion is that capital punishment came back because people were understandably sick of hearing about mur-derers paroled after seven years. Tucker, herself, would have been eligible for parole in 2003, after serving 20 years for two murders.

But if capital punishment is a flawed answer, it's much worse if applied unevenly. Suppose the face Tucker put on it had been a different color, or had a bad complexion, or had been a man's face? Suppose she had found Allah instead of Jesus? Would we have shared a last meal with her and Bernard Shaw the other night?

Tucker's death, some say, should remind us of the moral lessons of repentance and forgiveness. OK. But it also should remind us of another moral lesson that's a lot easier to grasp.

It's a lesson so basic that I only mention it because nobody has and somebody really should. It's simply this:

If you shoot heroin and become a prostitute . . . or if you park your Harley on the wrong living-room rug . . . or if you are a married woman and you park your shoes under the wrong guy's bed . . . you're liable to wind up dead.

And, in the end, they all did.

—February 6, 1998

....

For unto us a suit is brought

And it came to pass, in the city of Lorain, which was in the county of Lorain, that a decree went out from City Hall that a manger scene should be placed across the street in Veterans Park, which is public.

But upon hearing of this decree, some of the elders of the city of Lorain took counsel with each other, saying:

"If it comes to pass that we put a manger scene in a public park, what will surely come to pass next is that lawyers from the ACLU will show up and sue us."

And verily, the director of the Ohio ACLU heard of the plan. And he commanded his servant, saying:

"Go forth into the ranks of the ACLU and find a wise man with great common sense and bring him hither."

But the servant spake unto him, saying:

"Master, of wise men with great common sense we have none. All we have are lawyers."

So a lawyer was brought unto the director of the Ohio ACLU. And he said unto him:

"Go hence into the city of Lorain in the county of Lorain and there, in a park which is public, ye shall find a manger scene. That's a no-no. Slap a writ on it."

So he went forth. But when he was still a long way off, news of his coming was brought to the elders of the city of Lorain. And many were sore afraid. And others were just sore.

But there was among them a wise elder with great common sense and some street smarts, too. And he spake unto the rest of them, saying:

"Fear not and neither be ye sore. Let us be as wise as serpents and as harmless as doves. For if we can't outwit one ACLU lawyer, we don't deserve to be elders. We ought to be home watching MTV. Send for the janitor!"

Then the janitor, who was called a maintenance engineer, was brought before them. And the elder said unto him:

"Depart hence with your crew and go to the shed where we store the manger, and there ye will find a couple of reindeer made from pipe cleaners and a few mechanical toy soldiers.

"And when ye have found them, take them from the storage shed and carry them to the park which is public. And when ye arrive thence, ye shall place them like this:

"The pipe cleaner reindeer ye shall place about 10 feet from the manger. But farther than 15 feet from the manger, ye shall not place them.

"As to the mechanical toy soldiers, ye shall place them no farther than 15 feet from the manger. But closer than 10 feet, ye shall not place them.

"And when ye have done all of these things, take the rest of the day off."

Then the maintenance engineer did thus. Which is to say he placed the pipe cleaner reindeer about 10 feet from the manger. But farther than 15 feet he did not place them. And he placed the mechanical toy soldiers no farther than 15 feet from the manger scene. But closer than 10 feet he did not place them.

And behold, when he was through, he had finished.

And lo, he finished just in the nick of time. For along came the ACLU lawyer, bearing writs and frankly incensed. And, seeing the elder, he spake sharply unto him, saying:

"You have placed a manger scene in a park which is public. This gives great offense to the reliably offended."

But the elder spake right back to him, saying:

"Manger scene? What manger scene? I see a holiday scene. For behold, there are pipe cleaner reindeer placed about 10 feet from the manger. But farther than 15 feet, they are not placed. And there are . . ."

Then the ACLU lawyer interrupted him, saying, "OK, OK. You don't have to go through all that again. I guess this year I can't sue you. But I'll be back next year."

And he departed from thence and went thither, from whence he had come.

And so it came to pass that the city of Lorain, which is in the county of Lorain, was able to celebrate the season. And proclaim sentiments of peace and good will in Veterans Park, which is public. All because of a loophole.

For, it is sometimes said that, when a good lawyer dies, he is put to work in heaven finding loopholes. The loopholes from heaven are called blessings. And all the lawyers in heaven are called angels. All five of them.

—December 8, 1997

The Iacona dilemma

Beneath the tears, the anger and the prayer vigils surrounding the Audrey Iacona case is a troubling legal and moral paradox.

Ms. Iacona, 17, was sentenced to eight years in prison for the involuntary manslaughter of her baby, born after a 32-week pregnancy.

Regarding the jury's verdict, Judge James L. Kimbler said:

"I agreed with the jury that the baby was alive and, but for the actions of Ms. Iacona, would still be."

But had Ms. Iacona managed to find a doctor willing to perform a legal, near-term abortion, she would have escaped prosecution. Even though her actions would have ended the baby's life.

Finding such a doctor isn't easy.

"Not in Cleveland," an abortion consultant told me. "Even

though the procedure is legal, I don't know of a doctor around here who would be willing to do it.

"But there are names of such doctors available to women who come in for counseling. It is the procedure called a 'partial birth abortion.' But the correct medical term for it is 'near-term abortion.'"

Such near-term abortions are rare. The consultant estimated that only 600 of them are performed nationally. Ninety percent of abortions in area clinics are performed in the first 12 weeks of pregnancy, she said.

But rare or not, near-term abortions from a consenting doctor are legal any time during the duration of a pregnancy, the consultant said.

The fact of their legality injects another troubling element into the whirlwind of discussion surrounding the Iacona case.

Since the verdict was announced, the phone lines of local news organizations have been swamped with callers emotionally debating the outcome of the trial.

Some callers feel that the punishment was too severe. But most argue that Ms. Iacona received a just sentence and that media coverage has portrayed her, inaccurately, as a martyr.

The abortion consultant I spoke with agreed that Ms. Iacona deserved punishment because of her actions after her baby was born.

"If the baby was born alive, she could have run upstairs and asked her mother for help," the consultant said. "That way, the baby's life might have been saved.

"If the baby was born dead, she still should have immediately told someone. What she's guilty of is irresponsibility."

But to the question of whether Ms. Iacona had the right to take actions that would end her baby's life, the answer seems to be that she did have that right, provided that she had exercised it 24 hours earlier, with medical assistance.

It is easy to see the legal, medical and emotional distinctions between what Ms. Iacona did and what she might have done. But the moral distinction is harder to evaluate. And it is the moral distinction that has kept the abortion debate volatile and bitter through two decades.

Many supporters of abortion rights feel that virtually no restrictions or obstacles should be placed in a woman's path, regardless of her age, if she decides she wants an abortion.

Anti-abortion activists think that abortion is little more than legalized murder. And that a climate in which abortions are freely permitted leads to an attitude of indifference about the sanctity and value of human life.

It was Audrey Iacona's apparent attitude of indifference that seemed most damning during her trial. A girlfriend testified that Ms. Iacona told her the baby had been born dead and then said, "Now we can go bikini shopping."

It should unsettle both sides of the debate that, had Ms. Iacona hooked up with the right doctor late in her pregnancy, the law would have protected her attitude of indifference.

Her child would have ended up in somebody else's legally sanctioned refuse can. And her comment about shopping would never have made the newspaper.

—February 18, 1998

Not guilty — or innocent

In the old days, we used to cover big murder trials working breathlessly against tyrannical deadlines. So, back in the composing room, two headlines would be set in type.

"BLOTZ GUILTY, JURY SAYS," one headline would shriek.

"JURY SAYS BLOTZ INNOCENT," the other one would scream.

The second headline was legally inaccurate and we knew it. Blotz was either going to be found "guilty" or "not guilty." Juries don't find murder defendants "innocent." Innocence is a flat statement that means "Blotz didn't do it." Not guilty is hardly the same as innocent, as any O. J. scholar will quickly agree.

But we were afraid that, in the rush to get the verdict in print, somebody might snatch up the wrong headline. If you're in a hurry, "Blotz Guilty" looks an awful lot like "Blotz Not Guilty." It was safer to give the harried typesetter a choice between guilty and innocent.

Attorney Terry Gilbert, who knows better, made the same choice in front of a lot of cameras last week.

The results had just come back from a DNA test of blood traces found in the home of Dr. Sam Sheppard 44 years ago. The tests indicated that the blood belonged neither to Dr. Sam nor to his murdered wife, Marilyn.

But the stains matched the DNA profile of Richard Eberling, a convicted murderer, who was a handyman on the Sheppard property about the time of Mrs. Sheppard's murder.

"We now have conclusive evidence that Dr. Sheppard did not kill his wife," Gilbert announced.

But he doesn't. What he has is evidence that somebody else bled in the Sheppard home, perhaps on the night of the murder.

In his second trial in 1965, Dr. Sam was acquitted of his wife's murder. A jury decided there was not sufficient evidence to find him guilty.

I covered a little bit of that trial for the old *Cleveland Press*. The verdict seemed reasonable to me. I never thought there was enough evidence to convict Dr. Sam beyond a reasonable doubt. But I was stingy about dispensing this attitude around the city room, where it was greeted with considerable scorn by all the reporters who covered the Sheppard case.

Agreeing that Sheppard should have been found "not guilty" of his wife's death is not the same as saying he is innocent of it. As an op-ed piece in yesterday's paper pointed out.

James E. Starrs, George Washington University professor of forensic science, advanced the theory that Dr. Sheppard might have contracted with somebody, perhaps Eberling, to murder Marilyn. If that happened, even DNA evidence pointing to Eberling would not absolve Dr. Sam of complicity in the crime.

Naturally, this is the kind of speculation that makes passengers on the Sheppard-is-innocent bandwagon hit the roof. To them, it probably shows that Dr. Sam's enemies will go to any length and create any fiction just to tarnish him with guilt.

But what it actually shows is that the crusade to have a dead man judged "innocent" of a 44-year-old crime is almost a mission impossible.

Even if Eberling, at this point in time and after all this hubbub, confessed to the murder, there are many who might regard his confession as suspect. Just as surely as the pro-Sam side would scoff at any claim Eberling might make that Dr. Sam instigated the crime.

That is why, try as I might, I can't ignite my emotions about the latest twists and turns in the Sheppard murder case. Warm passions alone can't heat a cold trail.

Even in the middle of one of his blistering editorials fingering Dr. Sam as the murderer, *Press* editor Louie Seltzer wrote these lines:

"The murder of Marilyn Sheppard is a baffling crime.

"Thus far, it appears to have stumped everybody.

"It may never be solved.

"But this community can never have a clear conscience until every possible method is applied to its solution."

There are forensic methods available now, such as DNA testing, that were unheard of in 1954. But the Sheppard case remains a puzzle.

Goaded by the *Press*, the community found Dr. Sam guilty at his first murder trial. Perhaps the community cleared its conscience with a "not guilty" finding at the second one.

But "innocent?" That's a headline I don't expect to read.

—March 11, 1998

....

God and the Boy Scouts

I have forgotten how to tie one of those knots where the rabbit comes out of his hole, goes around the tree, then back in his hole again. But I still remember the Boy Scout oath, which says:

"On my honor I will do my best to do my duty to God and my country and obey the Scout Law; to help other people at all times; to keep myself physically strong, mentally awake and morally straight."

Probably nobody in the history of Scouting has ever been as mentally awake as the Randall twins of California. At the tenderfoot age of 9 years old, the Randall twins already had minds that were sensitive, hair-trigger mechanisms capable of sounding an alarm at the first sign of theological incursion.

At least that's what their father says:

In 1990, the Randall twins decided to become Cub Scouts. But then, down in somebody's mom's basement, the twins were asked to recite the Cub Scout oath. In the middle of the first clause, the word "God" suddenly loomed up at them.

"My sons were agnostics who were still working out their religious beliefs," James Randall told the *New York Times.*

In dictionary terms that means that, at 9, the Randall twins had already endorsed Thomas Henry Huxley's view that the human mind cannot know whether there is a God or an ultimate cause or anything beyond material phenomena.

So, having reached this philosophical plateau simultaneously (twins, after all, do everything together) the Randall moppets were faced with a harsh decision.

Should they go on munching their Oreos and slurping their Kool-Aid and listening to somebody's mom invoke God and imitate wolf calls? Or should they sue the Cub Scouts for anti-agnostic discrimination and take their case all the way to the California Supreme Court?

Well, what does the streetwise old owl say? "Sue, sue, sue," he says. And that's what the Randall twins' father said, too. He, by the way, happens to be a lawyer.

Now, of course, you would have to be as silly as Oscar the Otter and as nuts as Sammy the Squirrel to believe it really happened that way. Anybody with any sense can figure out that it was Daddy who was the motivating force behind the whole thing.

And Monday, when after eight years of legal wrangling the California Supreme Court ruled that God could stay in the Boy

Scout oath, it was Daddy who, according to newspaper accounts, had to choke back the tears at the news.

One can understand his distress. It is a shattering blow in today's America when organizations refuse to cave in their principles in the face of an alleged victim waving a lawsuit.

In addition to the Boy Scout oath, a lot of us remember the Boy Scout Law, which says, in part:

"A Scout is friendly. He seeks to understand others. . . . He respects those with ideas and customs other than his own."

But there's a limit to how friendly anybody can expect even a Scout to be. Respecting somebody else's ideas doesn't mean you have to scrap your own. For instance, you don't have to say, "Goodbye, God. You'll have to leave now. Here come the Randall twins."

In an accompanying ruling, the California high court said the Boy Scouts acted legally when they removed a teenage assistant scoutmaster from one troop after learning he was gay.

If I had to use one careful word to describe this action, the word I would choose would be "prudent." I predict I will shortly discover that choice wasn't careful enough. Besides, these days, the word "prudent" counts for nothing, even in an organization whose motto is "Be prepared."

So the gay would-be scoutmaster followed the precociously anti-theological Randall twins to court. There he was told, in essence, that his right to be gay does not supersede the Boy Scouts' right to resist appointing young gay men as scoutmasters. This contradicted a similar decision reached by the New Jersey Supreme Court the other day.

"This is [not] the end of the line on this question nationally," vowed a spokesman for the Lambda Legal Defense and Education Fund, a gay rights group.

And I'm sure he's right. Nationally, the Boy Scouts aren't out of the woods yet. But, in California anyway, they still have their compass.

—March 25, 1998

Lessons from gender school

"Sex Harassment Seems to Puzzle Supreme Court," the *New York Times* front-page headline said.

Oh great. Where's that supposed to leave the rest of us?

And wait until you hear about the sexual harassment case that seems to have the Supreme Court puzzled.

The court-baffling saga involves Kimberly Ellerth, who quit her job at Burlington Industries after a year in which her boss "made near-constant remarks about her appearance," told her to "loosen up" and said, "You know, Kim, I could make your life very hard or very easy at Burlington."

Furthermore, a Reuters account says Ms. Ellerth's boss patted her on the rear end at a company party and told her that her job would become a lot easier if she wore short skirts.

Ms. Ellerth did not succumb to this lyrical seduction. She got promoted anyway. Then she quit her job and sued the company for sexual harassment. The question is, has she got a case?

My hand is in the air. "Call on me! Call on me!" I cry. As a graduate of a mandatory "show up or you're fired" sexual harassment seminar, I know the right answer to that one.

"Pay her what she wants," I say. "And get rid of her boss. He's toast."

And I should know what I'm talking about. I got straight A's in sexual harassment. The company paid big bucks for a traveling sexual harassment evangelist to come in and scare the itch out of any male with a drop of lasciviousness in his DNA.

No more pin-up calendars in the tool crib. Even if the women never go in there. Such obscenities create an invisible cloud of sexism that seeps around corners and pollutes the workplace with lawsuit particles.

No dirty jokes, either. Not if a passing female can overhear one. Even if she's some distance away, she may have the ears of a beagle. So go into the men's room and turn on the water faucet. Or stand outside with the smokers. And even that's risky.

We graduates of the mandatory "be there or else" seminar

learned our lessons well. Instantly, conversation in the workplace took on the unmistakable accent of heightened awareness.

"Excuse me, Ms. Thompson. Would you mind if I made a nonthreatening remark about your attire? I warn you in advance that it is somewhat subjective."

"You may proceed with caution, Mr. Smith."

"Very well then. That dress. It's nice."

"In what way is it nice, Mr. Smith? Be careful now."

"It seems to fit very well. It enhances certain unspecified characteristics of your corporeal person."

"Thank you, Mr. Smith. You'd best not further amplify your evaluation."

Enlightenment blazed everywhere. The anti-sexual harassment crusade was on a roll. Consciences were raised to dizzying and rarified altitudes. The seminar business was booming. Lawyers were getting richer. Public service announcements on the radio lectured against harassment. And leading the parade was the women's movement, always ready to aid victims like Anita Hill and denounce sinners like Clarence Thomas and champion allegations, proven or unproven.

Then along came Jones. Paula, that is.

And suddenly the great crusade made a U-turn.

On the same day the Supreme Court justices were announcing their startling confusion about whether fanny-patting was sexual harassment, the National Organization for Women announced it wasn't interested in Ms. Jones' sexual harassment complaint against the president.

NOW President Patricia Ireland said Ms. Jones' case was flawed because she could not prove her career had been damaged by her alleged encounter with an unzipped governor in a hotel room.

And, on the other side of Washington, Supreme Court Justice Antonin Scalia was pointing out that the indignities Ms. Ellerth had suffered did not seem to have hurt her career.

"How did all this come up?" Justice Ruth Bader Ginsburg asked at one point, referring to the complexities of the sexual harassment law.

My gosh, if she doesn't know, how are we supposed to know?

And what good did it do me to go to sexual harassment school? I could have told you that fanny-patting and crude come-ons were sexual harassment 10 years ago.

The Supreme Court is clueless. And Ms. Ireland seems to be saying, "If we like the guy, it ain't harassment," a sentiment that would have gotten me expelled from awareness college.

Quick, somebody think of something! Or the next thing you know, the guys in the tool crib are going to want their *Penthouse* back.

—April 27, 1998

Pesho's killers are textbooks of evil

Justice has done its inadequate best for Mary Jo Pesho.

Her murderers got life sentences. But so did her family, sentenced to a lifetime of nightmarish memories.

The punks who killed Mrs. Pesho will have their freedom restricted.

But how free are the Peshos to walk through a shopping mall or a parking lot without numbing waves of recurring trauma?

The gruesome trial testimony about the way Mary Jo Pesho died sickened our city.

How the Pesho family members managed to endure it and keep their sanity is impossible to imagine.

As the details of Mrs. Pesho's last agonies became public, we talked about the murder and the murderers in the low, murmured tones we use to greet news of a fatal disease.

For that is what Mark DiMarco and Shannon Kidd are. They are cancer. They are plague. They are AIDS, confounding the immune system of civilized society.

Just locking them away in a cell is no justice and no cure.

It is neither justice nor cure to allow DiMarco and Kidd to pay for their atrocity in the conventional way. To idle away the years lifting weights and improving their tattoos and watching *Beavis and Butthead* on prison television.

DiMarco, the head butcher, will be theoretically eligible for parole in 33 years. He could be a free man at age 53, with a piece of paper marked "one torture and murder—paid in full."

But in 33 years, the surviving members of the Pesho family will still be serving their sentences. Still tortured with remembering. Still awakened at 3 a.m. by the dreams that murder sleep.

Justice, in her clumsy way, calls 33 years a life sentence. But it isn't, not for a man. The lifespan of some creatures is 33 years. But men live longer. Even creatures disguised as men live longer.

If the creature called Mark DiMarco is freed at 53, he will have a lot of life ahead of him. If Shannon Kidd is paroled at 45, he will be a year younger than the woman he helped kill—free to celebrate all the birthdays he robbed from her.

Is this really the best that justice can do for Mary Jo Pesho? Or for the rest of us in the state of Ohio, in whose name justice labors?

Some think the death penalty would have been much better.

But there, I reluctantly disagree.

DiMarco and Kidd are germs. Kill them and we lose our laboratory sample.

They are too valuable to flush away. Or to merely lock away and ignore with the rest of the germs brooding in the prison culture of Lucasville.

DiMarco and Kidd are prisoners of war. Hostages from a murky and demonic world. We have captured them and now we should make them useful to us. We should use them to broaden our education.

They need to be studied like alien life forms, the toxic waste dumps of their natures analyzed, all the moments of their mutant lives prodded, dissected and examined like a frog on a laboratory table.

Their parents, their teachers, their friends should be deeply questioned. We should trace and track their gradual evolution from infants to monsters, taking note of any signals along the way that they were gradually losing their humanity, or rejecting it.

They should earn their continued existence by becoming textbooks of evil. They should pay for their crime with answers. And we should pray that there are answers to find.

—June 12, 1998

Chocolate and nuts

The Supreme Court has ruled that you and I don't have to pay for Karen Finley to smear her unclad body with chocolate.

Ms. Finley doesn't do this for kicks. According to the *New York Times*, she "uses her body, sometimes appearing nude and covered only with chocolate, to make a statement about the abuse of women."

The sticky part is, the medium overwhelms the message.

So, by an 8-1 decision, the court said that decency may be considered when passing out tax money to artistes. This includes Ms. Finley, whose art is like an O Henry! bar—mostly chocolate and nuts.

Ms. Finley was not sweet-tempered about the ruling. Here is a little Whitman's Sampler of some of her views when she watched her handout melt in her hand.

"It's a major tragedy," she told the press. "No matter what you do, you're still a victim. I think it's very sexist. The witch hunt can happen anywhere."

Her colleague, artist Tim Miller, added this lamentation: "The court decision is a further nail in the coffin of freedom of ideas and expression in this country. One hundred years from now, the decision will seem as absurd as the Dred Scott decision."

See? That's why you can't write satire in America anymore. The ludicrous has become the norm. Delirium passes for logic.

I would be willing to contribute tax money to buy two dictionaries—one for Ms. Finley and one for Miller. With little Post-It notes on the pages that define "victim" and "freedom."

In future dictionaries, the word "victim" will probably spawn a definition that covers 30 pages. America's whining production line produces a new and exotic classification of victim each month. They just keep rolling off like Ford trucks.

Now Ms. Finley has contributed a new species. She has been victimized by not being paid by the U.S. treasury for lunacy. Or lunacy in my opinion anyway. But my opinion counts because she expects me to pay the bill.

Artiste Miller's complaint frustrates me even more because it is so common and so unquestionably illogical. He thinks "freedom of expression" means you are entitled to get paid for it.

I don't quite understand where this notion came from. But it has a firm grip on the brain cells of many of the Finley-Miller persuasion. And even the Supreme Court justices, who are the entitlement gurus of the country, can't dislodge it.

Suppose I decide to pour chocolate over my bare self to make some kind of statement. Well, no, that would be plagiarism. Let's make it maple syrup.

Yukkk.

Then suppose I call the government and say: "Hi, there. I'm a performance artist and I make serious statements about pancakes and waffles. But I'm a little short of money because not many people want to see me, even though I've been working out with my ab roller."

"So what?" the government says.

"So I wonder if you can ship me some tax money to keep my freedom of expression alive. I figure my freedom of expression will cost you about 50k."

"Nope," the government says.

"Nope! Nope? What do you mean, 'Nope'?" I say, hotly. "This is a major tragedy. This is the worst thing since the Dred Scott decision. This is a further nail in the coffin of freedom of ideas and expression in this country.

And not only that, this is a long-distance call."

"Goodbye then," the government says.

Isn't that what you would want the government to do? That's what I would want the government to do.

Freedom of expression means you are free to express yourself. It doesn't mean you are paid to express yourself.

I happen to be paid to express myself. But if the editor decided enough of you didn't like my expressions, I would be gone, Jack, and you would be looking at an underwear ad.

My freedom of expression would still be intact. What would be missing is an audience and a paycheck. I would have to go someplace else to look for those.

And so, now, will chocolate-covered Ms. Finley. I wish her nothing but luck. Paid freedom of expression is a tough racket. But somewhere, there's got to be a chocoholics convention just waiting . . .

—June 29, 1998

As I was Saying . . .

Child molesting, then and now

I was sexually molested once when I was a kid. It's the kind of thing you don't forget, but it never really bothered me until last week. Then I read about Michael Jackson and now I'm having post-traumatic stress syndrome.

Maybe I'll feel better if I share. Like they do on the daytime talk shows.

One Saturday when I was about 12, I went to the old Shaker Theater to see *Treasure Island*. I went alone. This was back in the days when 12-year-old kids could wander around loose as long as they steered clear of traffic and polio. Or so our mothers thought, anyway.

None of my friends wanted to see *Treasure Island* because it was a movie made out of some book. And not just any book. A book our teachers told us we ought to read. In my circle, when a teacher recommended a book or a movie, that was the kiss of death.

So I went alone. And about a third of the way through the movie, some guy sat down next to me. And the next thing I knew, he had his hand in my lap.

This was such a startling development that I had no idea what to do about it. So I sat, frozen, like a surprised chipmunk. Which, of course, suited him fine.

Out of the corner of my eye, I tried to get some sense of him. It was too dark to see him plainly, but he seemed old. Looking back on it now, I would guess he was 19 or 20. That was old then. A kid tends to think that somebody old has some valid, if puzzling, reason for anything he does. I processed this thought. And, while I was processing it, he reached for my zipper and began to talk to me in low, soothing tones.

But I wasn't soothed. Far from it. I didn't have any idea why the guy was doing what he was doing but I concluded, more from a sense of queasiness than from reason, that I shouldn't be sitting there letting him do it.

"I'm gonna get some popcorn," I said.

I figured I'd better say something plausible and innocuous until I got out from under that hand. Without looking at him, I got up and marched up the aisle, zipping my fly in the dark. And then, because I had paid a whole dime to see this movie, I sat down in the back of the theater. But I couldn't concentrate on young Jim Hawkins and the menace of Long John Silver and the mystery of *Treasure Island*. There was something far more menacing and mysterious 15 rows in front of me. So I left and went home.

I didn't say anything at home right away. My instinct told me that recounting my adventure might have a negative effect on future movie-going. But the event nagged at me. It seemed to be the kind of thing I ought to tell. So I told my mother about it. And it turned out, as I had suspected, to be a really big deal.

My parents combined fright, anger and relief all in one emotional explosion. I was given a small, emphatic lecture about the characteristics of sexual deviance, most of which was beyond me. There was talk of calling the police, which was abandoned because of my inability to describe my groper. To my great relief, I wasn't banned from the movies. But I was told that, if anything remotely like that ever happened again, I was to yell and call an usher.

An usher, you notice. Not a lawyer.

That's all there is to the story. I have lived with it now for more than 40 years. If it has warped me, well, so many things have warped me that it's impossible to blame the eccentricities of my personality on any one event. But it certainly never bothered me until I read about the Michael Jackson settlement.

Michael Jackson, as the world knows, settled a sexual molestation suit out of court by giving the kid he is alleged to have molested "untold millions of dollars."

Jackson could still be charged with child molesting, but the kid will have to press charges and the smart guys say the "untold millions of dollars" may make further prosecution seem unmannerly and ungrateful.

USA Today, which, when in doubt, turns to polls like others turn to prayer, took one and declared that the people in USA-Land aren't sure what judgment to render in this matter. Neither am I.

On the one hand, I think a parent is crazy to let his kid go over and play with a person like Michael Jackson. When I was a kid, there were no people like Michael Jackson. The science of plastic surgery was not sufficiently advanced to manufacture them. And if there had been somebody like Michael Jackson, he wouldn't have made a nickel anywhere but on a midway. Whether he could walk without lifting his feet or not.

The very smallest risk you run letting your kid play with Michael Jackson is that the kid will adopt Michael Jackson as a role model. And want to commence alterations on himself. And start experimenting with the Clorox and the scissors and the sewing machine. And stretch his skin so tight his tearducts move up to his hairline and you can't tell whether he's crying or sweating.

But if you did let your kid play with Michael Jackson and your kid said that Michael Jackson molested him, what then?

I know what my parents would have done. They would have called the cops and moved heaven and earth to see Michael Jackson locked up someplace where they'd have issued him a new set of gloves for breaking rocks.

No matter how much money Michael Jackson had offered, it wouldn't have been enough. My parents would have said I was worth more. And that, if Michael Jackson had used me for prey, "untold millions" wouldn't have squared things.

On the other hand, if there had been a person like Michael Jackson back then and if he'd been innocent, he wouldn't have paid a nickel. He would have demanded to go to court to prove his innocence. Because the stigma of being a child molestor would have, and should have, killed him professionally. He wouldn't get a booking at an Elk's Club smoker.

But times have changed. Money squares anything today. All questions seem to have become one question. What's the payoff? What's the bottom line? Settlements have replaced moral judgments. We don't look to the clergy to tell us about sin and penance. We call a lawyer and he hangs a price tag on it.

Maybe my parents and I should have tried to find that guy in the movie theater. He may not have had "untold millions," but we might have shaken him down for his house or his car. That's what's causing me my pain this week. Why was I unlucky enough to grow up when there were some things money couldn't buy?

—January 31, 1994

As a species, operators are a vanishing breed

As has been noted here with irritation, telephone operators are disappearing. Every morning when we wake up, more are missing. They are an endangered species, heading for extinction while the Environmental Protection Agency is busy keeping an eye on tree squirrels and bats.

Just last week, I called my insurance company and, for the first time, was greeted by a robot. This robot handed me off to a second robot. The second robot lied to me:

"All our operators are busy now," this robot, a female, said. "You have a waiting time of approximately six minutes."

"I don't believe all your operators are busy," I said. "I think you've done away with them. If you are telling me the truth, put an operator on the line and let her tell me that she's all right. Let her explain that she's busy."

The lying female robot was caught off balance by this on-target accusation. She ignored me. Rattled, she turned on a record player and I had to listen for six minutes to canned, disco-style music beating on my eardrum. If they are going to make you wait six minutes, they ought to at least play one of those records of surf beating on the Maine coast or a rain shower in a verdant forest. But what do they care? They have no human feelings.

We've talked about the disappearance of telephone operators before, you and I. But now it has been made semiofficial. A new magazine called *P.O.V.* has come out with a list of jobs that are vanishing. And a companion list of jobs that are increasing. It is hard to say which list makes the future seem more gloomy.

The worst job to have if you want to keep it long is the job of bank teller. Bank tellers are being replaced by those drive-by ATM machines that spit money at you. Next on the hit list is telephone operator. Then comes factory worker. Factory workers also are an endangered species if they dwell in the First World. Which I think is still us, isn't it?

This list of vanishing jobs is dismaying but not particularly surprising. The list of expanding jobs, on the other hand, is not what I would have guessed it was.

For example, if you had asked me to guess the biggest growth industry in today's America, I would have guessed illegal Latin American nannies. Virtually everybody the president tries to shove into his Cabinet has an illegal Latin American nanny lurking at home. And since the president is breaking his neck to concoct a Cabinet of diversity, one assumes that illegal Latin American nannies, arriving by the boatload, are toiling all over the multicultural landscape. Snapped up as soon as they learn to say "koochie-koo" in English.

But, in fact, illegal Latin American nannies do not even make the top 10 list of fertile career opportunities. Nor do kibitzing TV lawyers, hard as that is for O. J. addicts to believe. The hottest job in the market right now is multimedia software designer. The second-hottest job is management consultant.

This last piece of information is ominous. I have had occasional encounters with management consultants, and these have always filled me with ignoble envy. The job of management consultant is, in my opinion, the slickest scam on earth. It's safer than running an illegal crap game and more lucrative than selling Manhattan tourists the Brooklyn Bridge.

It used to be that, if you ran a company, you were responsible for deciding how to run it. They paid you a fat salary and gave you an office with your own bathroom in it so you could give your employees the impression you never needed to use one. In exchange for these perks, the buck stopped with you. If you made a series of bad decisions, you could expect to be fired and you would have to join the men's room line with the rest of the hoi polloi.

But this left too much to chance. So the presidents of companies began hiring management consultants who flew in and, after a tour of the city and a $50 lunch, gave the presidents advice on what decisions to make. Then a junior executive drove the consultant back through rush-hour traffic and got brownie points if the guru made his plane to Des Moines.

The management consultant (often himself a refugee from a failed business) did a little dance with the company president that was as graceful to watch as the tango routine of Ramon and Yolanda. If the company had a bad year, the president would blame his misfortunes on advice from the consultant. And the consultant would claim the advice was good, but its implementation was flawed. That way, nobody was responsible for nuttin'—an enviable state which is fast becoming the New American Dream. Unless you're a welfare mother.

It does not bode well for us that the job of management consultant has risen to No. 2 on the "best jobs" list. No. 3 is something called an "interactive advertising executive." No. 6 is an "Internet surfer." No. 10 is a "cyber detective." America, which used to manufacture hard things you could bang on, is going into the business of . . . well, you know what I'd like to say. Bull-etc.

It was probably a management consultant who told a company president he could save a lot of money by doing away with telephone operators. All he would need to replace them was a software designer to cue the robots and the disco music and an interactive advertising executive to write the lie about the operators being busy.

But the public, which stands for a lot, will be pushed only so far. If executives don't start showing some consideration for their customers, management consultants won't save them. Their careers will be left in the hands of No. 7 on the good-jobs list: that perennial best seller, funeral director.

—April 3, 1995

Speaking English

Bob Dole did it again. He said something that makes good sense and caught hell for it. Such is the price you pay for releasing sanity into the atmosphere of the national loony bin. It stirs up the inmates and they get cranky.

A while back, Dole made a speech chastising big record companies for releasing records that demeaned women and celebrated violence. He did not call for legal efforts to censor such records. He just told the millionaires who cash in on them that they ought to be ashamed of themselves. Instantly, the record moguls, rights groups and professional victims' marching-and-chowder societies turned on Dole. They misquoted his speech and implied he was some kind of Kansas Nazi.

Then, when the predictable yawping died down, a couple of record company officials were quietly fired. That's because most of America agreed with Dole. The polls showed it. Most Americans still know that there is a difference between right and wrong. But it's the ones who don't who hog the microphones.

The other day, Dole endorsed the idea of making English the "official" language in America. And, as fast as you could say *"Schnell! Schnell!"* he was attacked for pandering to the voters, oppressing minorities and (in the words of one editorial) "supplying a feel-good answer to a largely imaginary problem."

Whoever wrote that line has never taken a taxi in New York. In a big-city taxicab, the language problem is far from imaginary.

You enter and discover the driver, a recent immigrant from some corner of the Third World, burning incense and paging through what looks to be a pornographic belly-dancing magazine. On the cab radio, strange music is wailing, sucked out of the ether from its source in a remote time zone.

"Hi," you say, nervously.

"Ramamizi dalonga?" he replies, good-naturedly.

"TAKE . . . ME . . . TO . . . THE . . . HILTON!" you say, loudly and slowly.

"Wango Sixth grmfery disco?" he inquires.

This question hangs in the air between you, unanswered. You

have the feeling that something important may have been asked, but there's nothing either of you can do about it. So he slams down his flag and you launch toward your hoped-for target uncertainly, like a Scud missile.

Once, in Atlanta, I hailed a cab to go 12 blocks to a hotel and the driver whizzed me, at 60 mph, far into the suburbs to a shopping mall. During the entire ride, we de-conversed—he remaining calm; my half of our dis-communication growing increasingly frantic. He finally returned me to the city, where I broke through the language barrier by not tipping him. He shook his fist at me and hollered something indecipherable. "Phooey on Bob Dole," perhaps.

In Cleveland, we are lucky. All our cab drivers speak English. All seven of them. But, according to my voice mail, there is a growing problem with doctors and assistant college professors who have not quite mastered our mother tongue (if I may call it that without being branded a sexist, anti-diversity fascist).

In the old days, everybody expected to learn English when they got here. In the late '50s, Hungarians fleeing persecution arrived in droves to settle on Buckeye Road. We shook their hands and welcomed them and wished them luck. We did not change the street signs to Hungarian or print ballots and driver's license applications in the language of the land they had fled. They were here now, and they were supposed to learn English as our ancestors had learned it. Or suffer the consequences.

But now we live in a consequence-free America, where house rules are considered repression and new rights are discovered every day in the absurd laboratories of anticultural multiculturalism. We've cut most of what used to hold us together, and language is one last, slender thread.

A newly arrived American of Hispanic descent named Ernesto Ortiz was quoted in the paper the other day as saying this: "My children learn Spanish in school so they can grow up to be busboys and waiters. I teach them English at home so they can grow up to be doctors and lawyers."

Dole and Ortiz make sense. Anybody who doesn't know that is a boob in any language.

—September 11, 1995

A *resolution tossed like empty cookie bag*

Notice how the stories about what to eat have disappeared from the TV shows and news columns? That's because we're halfway through January and most of us fat people have blown our New Year's resolutions. We couldn't take it off, and the media, which strives to be our friend, won't rub it in.

Pretty soon, we'll start to read those stories about how we ought to accept our fatness. The pop shrinks will croon preposterously that we ought to love our excess baggage and regard it as part of ourselves. If not most of ourselves.

A couple of weeks ago, when hope and resolve were still high, the government issued a new set of fatness guidelines. The government is concerned because the nation keeps getting fatter. The new fatness guidelines greatly resembled the old fatness guidelines, which can be fairly summarized as follows: If you like it, don't eat it. If you don't like it, eat a lot of it.

Along with the fatness guidelines, the government released a new formula we could use to tell if we were fat. Presumably, this service was for the mirrorless and for those who never try to button their pants. Naturally, because the government had devised it, the formula was as convoluted as a tax form. It needed an accountant from H&R Bulk.

My own formula is much simpler. If you can't see the zipper on your fly without taking your pants off, you are fat. If the easiest way for you to put on your socks is to lie on your back, you are fat. If, when you tip the shoeshine person, he tells you he hasn't started yet, you are fat.

This formula is rather gender-specific. I asked my female adviser to furnish some guidelines for women, but she let me down. The best she could do was this: If your high-heeled shoes nail you into the ground, you are fat. I suspect she made that up.

Her problem is, she isn't fat. From time to time, she thinks she's fat, the way all women do, but that doesn't count. I have had enough of sitting around tables listening to women who are not fat gabbing to each other about how fat they are. Then, if a woman who really is fat sits down with them, they all fall over themselves to assure her she isn't fat. This foolishness is for amateurs. We veteran fatties have no time for it.

There are two reasons why my female adviser isn't fat. The first is that nobody in her family was fat. This was a bequest from her genes to her jeans. The second reason is weird. She likes lettuce.

It took me years to believe this. How can you like lettuce? Lettuce is a decoration. It is a little tablecloth they put under salad, which isn't so hot either. Whenever my adviser ate lettuce, I figured she was showing off or trying to be some kind of role model. But over time, having seen her eat lettuce when she thought she was not observed, I have concluded, to my astonishment, that she likes it.

Now, no fat person likes lettuce. You can turn that rule inside out. Show me a guy who likes lettuce and I'll show you a guy who can see his underwear without a periscope. Such are my findings, and they're correct and they won't cost the taxpayers a cent.

By the way, speaking of correctness, you may have noticed that I have used the word "fat" several times in this column. Let's go back and count. I make it 23 times. How about you? There is a movement afoot to ban "fat" from the language as overly harsh. So I want to use it while I can.

I have socialized, in my time, with a lot of guys who are lushes. My experience is that a lush is happy to agree that he has a "drinking problem." There is a martyred dignity in the phrase that soothes him. But it is only when he thinks of himself as a lush that self-help is possible.

There are some people with weight problems that do not come from eating. Then, there are fat people, and they know that they are, and why.

I am fat because I love sugar. I am a sugar freak whose main delivery system is cookies. I regularly get up at 3 a.m. and eat cookies, a stash of which is usually at hand. If I stopped eating cookies, I would be thinner. That's a fact—but it's a fact almost impossible for me to face. What? A life without cookies? Impossible.

My friend the glutton feels the same way. He calls himself a glutton because that is what he is and he knows it. He will eat anything, as long as there's a lot of it. Except, of course, lettuce.

The glutton and I have already broken our New Year's resolutions to reform. This is not the government's fault. We don't need any guidance from the government about how to reform. We don't need to accept our fatness, either. But we do need to totally accept the fact that we won't get where we want to go without taking the pain.

It seems to me that that's what all America has to accept. To get something, you have to give something up. There's no easier way, and if we keep looking for one, a whole year goes by and the mirror is still an enemy. Once, we knew that here. It's no coincidence that, when we did, we were a thinner nation.

—January 15, 1996

Signs of spring

Now is the winter of our discontent, no matter what the calendar says.

In Lyndhurst a while back, Marlene Kellers found a letter in her mailbox from the Piccirilli Snowplowing Co., which shovels her driveway. The text of the letter tells you all you need to know about the kind of winter it has been. It reads, in part:

"Dear Valued Customer,

"Thank you so much for calling me endlessly last week to tell me it was snowing. I had not noticed. Just kidding.

"This is not directed at any one person, but as you read, please make your own decision as to which part of this letter applies to you.

"For those of you who did not know it already, I live in the snow belt. So, if you have snow, I have snow. There is no reason to call me and tell me you have snow in your driveway because, nine out of 10 times, you are looking out the window and have no clue as to how much snow is in your driveway. In most cases, I find far less than 2 inches and I am sick of people crying wolf. I have a life and cannot be parked outside your house and be waiting to brush off your car or wave to you as you go on about your business.

"For some STUPID reason, I chose snowplowing as a vocation. My contract clearly states 2 inches of snow before you get plowed. Two inches means 2 inches, not 1.5, not 1³½₂. Be assured I am capable of making a judgment call on what 2 inches of snow looks like . . .

"My repeat customers know I will show come hell or high snowdrift. New customers are a pain in the behind. I do not need idle threats. I do not care where you are going or where you have been or what time you're supposed to be there. You know I am doing my best for you. If you want to be on time, pray to God, if you have one, so that it may not snow.

"Last week we had two trucks go down at the same time. One lost its clutch, the other lost an alternator. No one knows we were at all-night repair shops paying some fat guy $75 an hour to tell us he could not figure out what the problem was. Nor does anyone care.

"I will treat you with respect and expect the same in return, and go out of my way to do my best for you, but, as the French say, '[expletive] happens.' Nothing is 100 percent. If you don't want these problems, move to Florida. No one does a better job than I do at clearing snow. We scrape our drives while others only backdrag.

"FINALLY, MANY OF YOU OWE ME LARGE SUMS OF MONEY. You people have some serious guts calling to complain when you owe me $500, $600 and in a few cases even more than that. I am owed tens of thousands of dollars and I WANT IT NOW!!! Write me a check for what you owe me. No amount is too small.

"Wishing you and yours a joyous New Year!!!!!!

"Very Sincerely, Cesare."

Ms. Kellers sent me this letter, saying she hoped I would find it interesting. I did. I phoned Cesare at the Piccirilli Snowplowing Co. to ask what customer reaction had been.

"Mixed," he said.

* * *

Now is the winter of our discontent, but there are warm spots. Last week, Marie Moatz, a 78-year-old widow who lives on the West Side, struggled out into the bleak, snowy darkness to clear a path to her door.

A police car prowled down her street, slowed, turned around and parked on the opposite side. A policewoman got out and slammed the door. "What now?" Mrs. Moatz thought.

"You shouldn't be doing that," the policewoman said. And she took the shovel away from Mrs. Moatz and finished the walk. Then she salted it. Then she said that if Mrs. Moatz ever needed anything to be sure to call her at the station. Then she drove away.

Mrs. Moatz went inside and fixed herself some coffee. She couldn't tell her husband, Claude, about it because he has been dead for 20 years. So she told me. She wouldn't give me the policewoman's name, though. She was afraid the officer might get in trouble for doing a good turn. And you know, it is that kind of world. The wind-chill factor of the human race is higher than it used to be.

But spring, though delayed, is a certainty. The Piccirilli Snowplowing Co. is also the Castle Landscaping Co., and that's the way Cesare wanted to be identified. For soon green grass will appear and the world will smell of spring.

The bleakness of this winter will be thoroughly forgotten and its snows will be a memory. Then birds will sing we-told-you-so and Cesare will acquire a tan, and Mrs. Moatz will awake one morning to the wonder of her 79th season of tulips.

—March 25, 1996

Catch this, Albert

Dear Albert,

There's an old rule in baseball that if a guy throws at one of your teammates, you throw back. That's OK by me.

The other day you threw a baseball at a photographer named Tony Tomsic. You hit him on the hand and drew blood. If he hadn't seen the ball coming, it might have driven the camera into his eye.

Tony and I were teammates at the old *Cleveland Press* for a couple of decades. In that time, Tony won a bushel basket of awards and came in second for a Pulitzer. The picture that edged him out that year was the photo of Ruby shooting Oswald.

The first time I worked with Tony was during a riot. Some citizens around Murray Hill went on a rampage over a matter of school integration. In the course of the day, blacks who made the mistake of trying to drive down Mayfield Road were dragged from their cars and beaten.

Tony was out there shooting pictures, but the participating militants did not want their faces preserved for posterity. A crowd of them chased us down the street and trapped us against a brick wall. "Get the cameraman!" they screamed. "Get the cameraman!"

I turned my back to the mob, blocked Tony with my body and started yelling "Get the cameraman!" along with them. This creative strategy was designed to confuse our attackers and it worked brilliantly for about three full seconds. Then the assailants tossed me aside, mugged Tony and grabbed his camera. Later that day the cops returned it, smashed. We took it back to the *Press* and pried it open with a crowbar. The film was OK and we printed the pictures.

This happened before you were born, Albert. It is probably a piece of history that doesn't interest you. My impression, perhaps erroneous, is that very little interests you but you. I mention it only because Tony, whose career has been longer than yours, has had worse moments than the one you gave him. Your little tantrum with the baseball is just a footnote on his resume. But such tantrums are becoming a major part of yours.

As a very young man, Tony happened to be in Cuba when Castro marched into Havana. He began snapping pictures, but the bearded Fidelniks didn't like that. He was arrested and brought before a magistrate who was a dead ringer for the late Ernie Kovacs. Except this cat wasn't playing for a laugh.

Tony was tossed into prison. Somehow, *Press* editor Louie Seltzer got a phone call through to him. His captors put Tony on the next plane out of Havana. He was lucky because back in those days, when the Cubans got you, they usually hung on to you until they could swap you for an American tractor. There's more to history, Albert, than they put in the *Baseball Encyclopedia*.

So, Albert, Tony has, as they say, been around. He's spent hours and hours on football fields and baseball diamonds shooting pictures for newspapers and *Sports Illustrated*. Football players have, in the intense momentum of a play, unintentionally knocked him silly. Line drives have narrowly missed him. He has recorded the feats of ballplayers since the days of the great Luke Easter. But he never looked through a viewfinder at anybody quite like you.

The unchallenged version of what happened the other day was that Tony was quite properly on the field shooting close-up pictures of you and the other players warming up. You didn't like that, Albert. Bad hair day or something. So you shook your finger at Tony and said, "No, no, no." And he backed off.

Then, a little later, he committed the crime of shooting you throwing the ball around. Which, after all, Albert, is what you do for money. And that's when you threw at him. And hollered, "I told you not to take my picture." And then you called him an unprintable word for idiot.

Now you've got yourself in the headlines again. You're on the front page of *USA Today.* "League Looks into Another Albert Belle Incident," it says. Little kids want to love you, Albert, but you're building an incident scrapbook that belongs in a plain brown wrapper.

Tony is a pro. Real pros have class to go along with their

numbers. Tony filed no complaint about what you did to him. He doesn't want to cause a problem that might kick the team in the teeth. This is a viewpoint you might consider adopting before it's too late. And it's pretty late now.

"Life goes on," Tony told me. "I'm just going to keep my eye on his hands."

But when you throw at somebody in baseball, even a photographer, you can expect something back. The ball you threw at Tony hit him. But the name you threw missed and sailed right back to you like a boomerang. Get the picture?

—April 24, 1996

....

What are Journalistic Ethics, anyway?

Not long ago, a big-shot editor from the *Washington Post* came to town to give a luncheon talk about journalistic ethics. I went because I heard the food was good. I figured I'd eat my steak and duck out before the ethics were served. When editors are paid money to talk about ethics, I always get heartburn.

But I was sitting up front and couldn't get away. Pretty soon, the editor launched into his views on journalistic objectivity. I popped a Tums just in the nick of time.

"When I became an editor, I decided I could no longer vote," the editor said. "I felt that if I made a personal choice in a presidential campaign, my bias might get into the news stories. I wish everybody who worked for me would decide not to vote. But I can't make them because voting is their right."

I could tell by the rustling and coughing behind me that this pious revelation had made the audience a little squirmy. The nobility of the editor's self-disenfranchisement was lost on them. And no wonder.

Most of them were non-journalists. But they were consumers of journalism. They knew that the *Washington Post* is a predictably liberal newspaper. So what if this editor didn't vote?

Suppose the editor of *Playboy* took a vow of chastity? What difference would it make as long as Miss July stayed Miss July?

It's no accident that most discussions of journalistic ethics are conducted by panels of journalists for audiences of journalists. If the lay public threw a seminar on journalistic ethics, the program would be so short there wouldn't be time to serve a fruit cup.

"Quit sticking your microphones in the faces of grieving widows," the public would say. "Quit sensationalizing the news with promos like 'Sex causes cancer, story at 11.' Be honest, fair and accurate. And now, let's adjourn so those of us with real jobs can get back to them."

What worries journalists about journalism isn't what worries the public about journalism. And I'll bet I can prove it. If I lose, you can put this column under your canary. If I win, put it under your parakeet so I get quoted.

For a whole week now, the journalists in Washington have been worried about an ethical sin they claim was committed by a *Newsweek* writer named Joe Klein. Klein wrote a harsh satire of the Clintons called *Primary Colors*. He wrote the book anonymously, and when reporters asked him if he was the author, he denied it.

The book took off and hit the best-seller lists and made Klein a lot of money. But he still denied he had written it. Finally, though, some magazine did some kind of computer analysis of Klein's style, and the computer fingered him as the author. Then, under a barrage of media interrogation, Klein finally broke down and admitted that he had written *Primary Colors* and lied about it.

Well!!! That threw the East Coast media into ethical meltdown. A reporter lying to other reporters??!!

This called for an exorcism. The reporters on the blab shows examined and re-examined this ethical atrocity, and Klein anguished and laid his soul bare on *Larry King* and *Charlie Rose* and in a whole variety of less exalted talk-show confessionals. It has been the big journalistic ethical agony of the summer. It hasn't died down yet.

You still there? Well, wake up. Here's one you will care about. Last Tuesday, a *New York Post* reporter named Tonice

Sgrignoli, 43, was arrested by the New York cops after she had: (1) Fraudulently obtained an identity badge; (2) Used it to sneak into the hotel where the families of victims of TWA Flight 800 were staying; (3) Posed as the cousin of a family member; (4) Stayed in the hotel for nearly three days, eavesdropping on the private conversations of people unhinged by grief to get a scoop for her newspaper; and (5) Got caught and kicked out.

I know you're not in the journalistic fraternity, but don't be shy. Which bothers you more? What Joe Klein did or what Tonice Sgrignoli did? Speak right up. Then go tune up the parakeet.

But while gaggles of journalists have fretted for weeks about what Joe Klein did, what Tonice Sgrignoli did was carried briefly on the wire service for one day and then dropped. As far as I know, nobody heaved a mild sigh over it. Except, perhaps, Sgrignoli, who, if fate is kind, will be looking for her next scoop in a horse barn.

This is why I duck discussions about journalistic ethics. Ethics are ethics, whether practiced by a journalist or a plumber. If I were a journalist, I wouldn't admit that. But I'm just a columnist with no place to hide.

—July 29, 1996

....

Buying a gift for your wife is tough

"How were your holidays?" I asked my friend. He is in enough trouble already, so I won't mention his name.

"Very instructional," he said. "I learned something."

"What?"

"Never give your wife a microwave oven for Christmas," he said. "Or, to be more accurate, never give my wife a microwave oven for Christmas if you're me."

"She didn't like it, huh?"

"It's already back at the store where I bought it," he said. "And

I'm still hearing about it. It was a real nice one, too. It had all these settings on it. You could do just about anything with it."

"Except warm her heart," I said, rather pleased with the remark.

"Well, it was a big mistake," he said, sourly.

"If you think that's bad," I said, "I'll tell you something I once did that was worse. Then you can go home and tell your wife about it and you'll both feel better."

"What did you do?" he asked.

"Well," I said. "Let's start by agreeing that women are hard to shop for. I'm a lot older than you are and it's taken me all my life to figure out how to buy presents for a woman."

"It's hard," he agreed.

"It is," I said. "When I was a young man, I went through my Victoria's Secret, Frederick's of Hollywood stage. I bought all that black, flimsy, see-through stuff. The kind of outfit a girl might wear to a funeral at the Crazy Horse Saloon. Intimate stuff. You know."

"Sure," he said.

"But it was so intimate that, after she opened the box and took it out, I never saw it again. No wonder they call it 'Victoria's Secret.' I don't know where any of it went, but if my suspicions are correct, she made some contributions to charity that brought a whole new meaning to the word 'Goodwill.'"

"Tsk-tsk," said my friend.

"In my mid-30s, I outgrew the black and flimsy stage," I said. "I entered the jewelry stage, but I didn't stay there long. Good jewelry costs a fortune. You can spend a couple hundred dollars on a piece of jewelry and then find out that she flips out over a $4.98 lapel pin with a ceramic cat on it."

"True," said my friend.

"So I took a flier on perfume," I said. "You can buy pretty expensive perfume without a home equity loan. And I was raised in the days when the ads said, 'Promise her anything, but give her Arpege.' Of course, that was a long time ago."

"Yeah," said my friend. "These days the saying is, 'Promise her anything, but make her vice president in charge of human resources.'"

"But the perfume bottles just stayed on the dresser gathering dust," I said. "It became apparent to me that the women I was drawn to preferred the smell of soap. Any old soap. Cascade, for Pete's sake. The women I was drawn to were too chilly all the time to sleep in flimsy little cobwebby things. They wanted to sleep in sacks. They got cold after 10 p.m. and wanted to lounge around in Army surplus arctic sleeping bags."

"A lot of women are like that," said my friend.

"I have concluded that there are about five women in America who aren't," I said. "So I changed my tactics. I went for cute. And that brings me to the story that ought to make you feel better about your microwave."

"Tell me," said my friend.

"One Valentine's Day I was going home from work when it hit me that I hadn't bought a gift," I said. "I had no idea what to get. And then, in a little store in the Arcade, I spotted something in the window. 'If I were a woman,' I said to myself, 'I would think that was real cute.' So I bought it."

"What was it?" asked my friend.

"It was a musical dustpan," I said.

"A what?"

"It was a dustpan with a little crank in the side," I said. "When you wound it up, it played 'Whistle While You Work.'"

"Cool," said my friend.

"Of course it was cool," I said. "And I regarded it as an astonishing piece of good luck. Why, if I'd set out to look for such a thing, I could have spent days hunting and never found one. But there it was, right when I needed it. So I had it gift-wrapped and took it home. I gave her a little kiss and handed it to her and said, 'Happy Valentine's Day.'"

"And . . . ?" said my friend.

"The reaction I got was thermonuclear compared to the reaction you got with your microwave," I said.

There was a silence. We were both deep in our own reveries.

"I feel better now," said my friend. "Thank you."

"You're welcome," I said.

"The only thing is," he said, "how do you shop for them?"

"You give them what they want no matter how ridiculous it

seems," I said. "That's the secret. The mistake we make is we think they are as sentimental as we are."

"I know," he said. "You should have seen the microwave."

"You should have seen the dustpan," I said. "Why it played for 10 whole minutes!"

—January 6, 1997

Looking for love with all the wrong notions

I got so wrapped up in the psychobabble of oppositional defiance disorder Friday I forgot to send you a valentine.

After 25 years of inexcusable verbosity, I regularly get requests for reprints of merely two of my columns. One is a Christmas column that the editor has formed the flattering habit of rerunning each Christmas Day. The other is a column about love. This the editor politely dismisses, having correctly appraised me as no kind of Casanova.

But so many of you have asked for an encore of the love column that I thought I'd risk bringing it out for a bow. It's been tucked away for four years but, as far as I know, nothing much has changed the dynamics of love in the meantime.

A definition of love is a handy thing to have. A lot of people go through life looking for one and never find it. A lot of people don't even know they are supposed to look.

Millions of songs have been written on the subject. But love songs are a bad place to look for a definition of love. Most so-called love songs aren't about love at all. They are about lust or ego.

The lust songs fall into the "I-gotta-have-you-because-you-make-me-feel-good" category. If you think about them a little, you'll see that they really aren't very romantic. They could be written, for example, about a car. As in "Toyota . . . Oh What You Do For Me!"

But lust is not love. And picking a person to love isn't the same as picking a car to love. In a way, that's too bad. Most lovers learn a lot more about the car they choose than the mate they choose. That's why the divorce rate is so high. That's why couples who agree to split up argue about who gets to keep the Honda.

Eventually, we all get rid of our cars. Usually long before they are worn out. We just get tired of them. Another car comes rolling off the assembly line and we like it better. That becomes the car we've gotta have. We lust anew. The law of lust is that new lust is always better than old lust. If you confuse love with lust, you're apt to trade in lovers or spouses as often as you trade in cars. And, secretly, you're going to wish there was some kind of leasing program.

Preachers preach more sermons about lust than they preach about ego. But, when it comes to counterfeit love, ego is probably more dangerous than lust. There are ego "love songs" too. They are written for collectors, not lovers. "You belong to me," they say. "Be mine. Whatever you do, wherever you go, you can't get away from me."

Jukeboxes are full of these sugar-coated threats. Misty-eyed lovers croon them to each other on the dance floor. But they are the most frightening kind of so-called love songs. They are love songs for stalkers.

Maybe the strangest thing you hear about love is that it is possible to fall in love. As if love were an open manhole.

"I fell in love with him. I just couldn't help it. It just happened." You hear that stuff all the time. It's pretty revolting, really. It makes love seem like a rash.

"I suddenly broke out in love, Doctor. Down here in this embarrassing spot. I can't explain it. I don't know how I got it, really. Maybe it will just clear up."

You're smart to stay away from somebody who claims that love is something he caught from you like stomach flu. Next week, if his resistance is low, he may catch it from somebody else.

So much for what love isn't. But what is it? I've got an answer to that question. And the answer is my tardy valentine to you.

It's a borrowed answer. Only the very lucky among us are smart enough to discover what love is without help. There was a time in my life when I needed such help. When it was very important for me to know what love is. And even more important to know what love isn't.

I found the answer in M. Scott Peck's wonderful book *The Road Less Traveled.* I read a lot and I recommend a lot of books to people. But Peck's book is just about the only book I recommend to everybody.

Peck says this: "Love is the will to extend one's self for the purpose of nurturing one's own or another's spiritual growth."

Love, in other words, is not a feeling. It's a decision. An act of will. It has a goal. Feelings don't have goals. But love's goal is to become better and make the loved one better. It has a price tag. Feelings don't have price tags. The price is work. The work of giving. Not giving a dozen roses or a pebble of polished carbon glued to a gold circle. Giving the best you've got to make somebody else better. And, in the giving, becoming better yourself.

If the relationship you're in doesn't make you a better person, then it isn't love. And a lot of people are in relationships that actually make them worse. If you've ever said or thought, "I don't like myself as much when I'm around him," you're not in love. You're in trouble.

Whatever else you heard on Valentine's Day, that's what love is. Don't expect to see it on the soaps. Or go shopping for it at Victoria's Secret.

Since I borrowed the definition, I can peddle it without conceit. So draw a heart around this column and send it to your special someone. You missed Valentine's Day, but, when it comes to love, the rule is better late than never.

—February 17, 1997

Godspeed, John Glenn

Once, John Glenn and I flew a mission high above the Earth. The sinking sun had set fire to the western horizon, showing us the kind of sunset you only see from an airplane. Below, the world was already dressed in the soft blue shadows of evening.

Glenn was at the controls of a four-seat plane. I was supposed to be there covering him. But I wasn't covering him. Life is short and pays us a minimum wage of magic moments. I wasn't going to dilute this one with journalism.

So as we flew, I thought about an Army day room in New Mexico in February 1962. Army day rooms back then all sounded the same—a steady syncopation of Ping-Pong mixed with the soft, random click of billiard balls. Maybe now they sound like video arcades and *Oprah*.

The Ping-Pong stopped. The pool cues were racked. We gathered around the black-and-white TV, where a gray rocket was leaving a launching pad, trailing a streamer of light gray flame. A voice came out of the television set and it was the voice of the planet. "Godspeed, John Glenn," it said.

He is the last old-fashioned hero from an era that is dust. What he did, he did alone, like Lindbergh. At the end of that decade, another Ohioan would step on the moon. But, by that time, it wasn't the same America any more. Our soul was bullet-riddled with assassinations, a bad war had ripped us in two, and our pure, childlike sense of wonder had been replaced by a jaded feeling of dread. We were pessimists. Cynics, looking for distraction in the galaxy the way a drunk seeks solace in a bar.

The old-time heroes stop with Glenn. He is the last of the line. He strapped himself inside a fancy bullet and became the shot heard 'round the world. He risked incineration on the way down. Smart men had chalked equations on a blackboard, but nobody knew for sure. He went up to find out. Like Columbus or Lewis and Clark or Earhart, he would come back with answers or not come back at all.

Who dares such dares any more? It is all computers now.

Death is a laboratory miscalculation. We are stuck with the heroes we get from the Frankenstein surgeries of campaign consultants. Celebrities are manufactured through press releases and agents. Larry King does wonders for them. Media hype launches them and they blaze, then burn to a cinder after $3 million and a book contract.

But once, I flew with John Glenn as the world got ready for night, turning its face slowly away from the sun like a tired child turning her head on a pillow. And I (a Metzenbaum man then) was busy storing a memory to share with future grandchildren. Then, Glenn, the legendary airman, spoke:

"Where are we?" he said.

Quite a kidder.

He dipped a wing and we circled down until we could read the big words painted on an airport hangar. "LANCASTER, O."

"Must be Lancaster," Glenn observed.

Everybody in town was waiting for an autograph. A week before, I had been with Howard Metzenbaum on the main street of Ashland, Ohio. Metzenbaum wore a button the size of a dinner plate on his lapel. It said, "HI! I'm Howard Metzenbaum, running for U.S. Senate."

But Ashland didn't care that year. John Glenn was already an Ashland resident, living in the history books at the public library and in the science curriculum at the public schools. Glenn won the election. Metzenbaum thought he was robbed, and it took years for the frost between Ohio's two senators to melt. But it finally did.

Glenn's mission in the Senate is almost over. Yesterday, he said goodbye in a moving, gracious speech from his alma mater, Muskingum College in New Concord. And I watched him on television again. On cable this time, and in color.

Because he is a good man, he has been a good man to know. His love affair with his wife, Annie, is a sonnet to gentle romance. In interviews and covering other campaigns, I've picked up more Glenn memories. Once in New York, I stood outside his hotel room door with a note pad while he was inside learning he wasn't going to get a shot at the vice presidency. He would have made a good one. He tried for the presidency and lost, perhaps because he never learned to speak in sound bites. The country's loss was bigger.

"There is no cure for the common birthday," he told the kids at Muskingum yesterday, explaining why he won't run again. They stood and applauded him, and now they will have their memories of him too.

But watching him, I thought of a man charting a course through the twilight above a canvas of soft blue shadows and lingering orange sunset. His flight, he said, is not yet over. And I looked at my TV and told it Godspeed.

—February 21, 1997

Throwing things away

Everybody knows the Law of Finally Throwing Things Away.

Let's say you've got an old lamp that just doesn't look right anywhere in the house. But you paid good money for it and you hate to throw it away. Then, finally, one week you do.

"You know that lamp that's been kicking around for 10 years?" you tell your wife. "Well, I finally threw it away. I put it out with the trash."

And then, the very next week, you rearrange the furniture in the living room. You move the couch over there and the chair and table over here. But the room seems a little out of balance. It needs something.

"Guess what would be perfect over there on that end table?" your wife says.

You don't have to guess. The answer is obvious. The late and unlamented lamp is exactly what you need. But it's gone. Garbage-picked by a man and a boy in a Dodge truck. And you are a victim of the Law of Finally Throwing Things Away, which states: "A perfect use will be found for any item in your house approximately one week after you finally get around to throwing it away."

This law, which is immutable, lurks grinning behind a spate of recent news stories. Politicians and city planners, the stories tell us, are yearning for a form of public transportation to move Greater Clevelanders to and fro between the city and the frontier stockades they have carved from the wilderness with their own two incomes. But what form of transportation should it be?

"If only," a politician says dreamily, "there was something that ran on rails. Something that didn't have to wait at every traffic light and stop sign. Something that would pull people around in a string of cars all attached together. Of course, I'm just brainstorming here."

"No, no, I think you're on to something," another politician says. "You mean something that went 'clickety-clack, clickety-clack' and gave people nice, big seats to sit in and never got bogged down in a thicket of orange barrels?"

"That's it! That's it!" the first politician says. "It would be like the rapid transit only bigger, and it might even go to other cities like Columbus and Youngstown and Toledo!"

"Maybe it could even come right into the Terminal Tower!" the other politician says. "There could be a grouchy old gray-haired guy sitting up on a big marble platform, rasping things into a microphone."

"What kind of things?" the first politician says.

"Things like: 'Neeeeyyooooow leaving on Track greeb! No. 13 for Mczksville, Rzamp, Krammmmmton, ZakkkKKKburg and Sandusky. All passengers for Mczksville, Rzamp, Krammmmmm-ton, ZakkkKKKburg and Sandusky . . . Alla-BoooOOORD!'"

"Didn't we used to have things like that?" the first politician says.

And the answer is yes. We did. We called them trains. Our town used to be full of them. But we finally threw them away. And naturally, according to the Law of Finally Throwing Things Away, now we want them back.

For years, the worst traffic jam in Cleveland has been on I-77, where it is possible to spend longer in rush hour than Shannon Lucid spent in space. And Shannon Lucid had things to do in space. She wasn't just stuck up there doing her nails and listening to Howard Stern.

About a half mile east of I-77 and parallel to it, a railroad line runs south to Akron. In summer, people take excursion trips on it to show their kids what life was like in the grim old days when, instead of saying the rosary on tense takeoffs in cramped airplanes, travelers were forced to snooze or read or look out of a window beyond which there was something to see.

Take a walk through the Cleveland Metroparks' Huntington Reservation and you'll find the crumbling trestles of an Inter-Urban line that once ran west to Toledo. Why should anybody but a starling have to fly to Toledo? But that's what you have to do. Unless you want to drive, or board Amtrak's lone insomniac special that departs once daily from the Amshack somewhere near the Shoreway, which has the casual elegance of the powder room at a freeway rest stop.

We threw our trains away and now we're sorry. One of the toughest decisions a society has to make is what to keep and what to throw away. Throw away the wrong stuff, like lamps and trains and morals and ethics, and pretty soon you'll wish you hadn't. It hurts to admit it, though. You always feel like such a dope.

—April 23, 1997

....

Royko's last call

"Well," said the bartender, "he's gone. Can you believe it?"

"Yeah," said Fats Grobnik. "Because if he wasn't gone, he would've been here by now."

"Do you think he went to heaven?" the bartender said.

"Depends on whether they let you smoke there. He wouldn't go to no place that didn't have a smoking section."

"If he went to heaven, I wonder what he's doing right now," said the bartender.

"He's probably trying to find a manual typewriter," said Fats Grobnik. "An Underwood or a Remington. If they make him use a word processor in heaven, he'll raise holy hell."

"What does he need a typewriter for?" asked the bartender. "You don't think they got journalism in heaven, do you?"

"Naw, of course not," said Fats Grobnik. "That's blasphemy."

"Well then . . . ?"

"He wasn't no journalist," said Fats Grobnik. "He was a newspaperman."

"What's the difference?"

"A journalist thinks he's in Holy Orders because he goes to college and they give him a science degree and tell him he's in charge of humanity. A newspaperman is a human being who works for a newspaper. He can be a woman, too. Some of the greatest newspapermen are women."

"Well, he sure could write."

"He was the best," said Fats Grobnik. "When you read the stuff he wrote, it seemed like he was saying everything you wanted to say, like he took the words right outta yer mouth. Except you couldn't of said it that good in a million years. And you knew that. But it was you talking anyway. Does that make sense?"

"It does," said the bartender. "They said he was the voice of the little guy."

"Where do they get this 'little guy' crap?' Fats Grobnik said. "Every time somebody remembers where he came from and writes nice short sentences in plain English and uses some common sense, they say he's the 'voice of the little guy.' If you work your butt off and support your family and pay your taxes and send your kid off to war, you're a 'little guy.' Little compared to what?"

"Take it easy," said the bartender. "Have one on the house."

"Make it a ginger ale."

The bartender squirted some ginger ale out of a rubber hose into a little glass. It sat there weakly percolating tiny bubbles of anemic joy.

"You'd have to say he was no saint," the bartender said. "He had his troubles with the drink."

"A lot of them did," said Fats Grobnik.

"Why is that, I wonder?"

"Who knows? His old man was a saloon keeper. But a lot of them don't touch it. In the old days, a lot of newspapermen

drank because they thought they were supposed to. But if you
gave me one guess in his case, I'd say maybe it was fear."

"Fear! Him? You gotta be nuts! Better have a Kessler's."

"He was on top," Fats Grobnik said. "Everybody thinks the
struggle is getting to the top. But that's nothing compared to the
struggle of stayin' on top. All them deadlines and no place to go
but down. Everybody standing there with a stopwatch, lickin'
their chops and clockin' your fastball. Compared to stayin' on
top, gettin' on top is a picnic. Ask any elderly baseball pitcher."

"Fear my eye!" said the bartender. "What are you, some kind
of armchair podiatrist? Leave his brain alone when he ain't here
to defend himself."

"You ast me and I told you, that's all."

"OK, OK," said the bartender. "Have you seen the papers?
He got some pretty good write-ups."

"He prob'ly woulda got even more space if he didn't pick the
same day to die that Ellen came out on," said Fats Grobnik.
"There's some whaddaya call it, irony, in that."

"A lot of them wrote that the times had passed him by," the
bartender said. "They said he had stayed the same but the times
had changed."

"That was supposed to be a kind of a put-down," Fats Grobnik said. "But considering what the times are changing into, it's
a great thing to say about anybody. A lot of people hung on to his
column by their fingernails while the times was trying to sweep
them away."

"Speakin' of hangin' on to things, where's your cousin Slats?"
said the bartender. "He oughta be hanging on to a barstool by
now. I haven't seen him since it happened."

Fats Grobnik looked at the bartender carefully to make sure
he wasn't kidding. Then he said softly:

"Slats went with Mike."

"Oh," said the bartender. And for a moment he looked
stricken. But then he said:

"Well, I don't blame him. So did a little bit of me."

—May 2, 1997

Blowing hot air

Big Brother is turning into Big Mother. There is a new gadget that checks up on restaurant employees to make sure they wash their hands properly. The National Restaurant Association previewed it at a trade show the other day.

Employees wear a badge that triggers an infrared sensing device that times them to make sure they stay at the sink for more than 15 seconds. If they don't, the badge blinks.

"Did you wash your hands, Billy?" the boss can ask.

"Yeah," Billy can say, sullenly.

"No, you didn't," the boss can say. "Your badge is blinking. Now march right back in there and do it again!"

The whole gizmo is based on the notion that nobody is going to stand in front of a lavatory sink for 15 seconds without washing his hands. But this is a flawed idea. Some people might. Present company excluded, of course.

I used to be a fastidious hand-washer of the type to make any mother proud. But then, back a good number of years ago, a squad of hot-air blower salesmen swept across America, changing the drying habits of American restrooms. They took the towels away and installed hot-air blowers in their place.

You turned from the sink, your hands dripping wet, and, instead of finding a nice dispenser of paper towels, you found a little chrome cannon on the wall with a sign beneath it that read: Rub hands briskly together under nozzle.

Now everybody knows that these things do not dry hands. You can stand there rubbing hands briskly together under nozzle until you are rubbing bones, and the bones will be damp. The only answer is to rub hands briskly on pants, behavior that neither Mom nor Big Mother could possibly condone.

But it is better than the alternative, which is to emerge from the restroom with wet hands. In certain circumstances, that can be very humiliating. Let me give you an example:

There was a period in my life when I made a good number of speeches. For reasons never clear to me, program chairmen would invite me to drive an hour or two from Cleveland to places such as Mansfield and Ashland to prattle banalities at captive audiences. It was easy money, so I kept it up until I got sick of the sound of my own voice. Making speeches is a nice racket until you make the mistake of listening to yourself. After that, it's an enterprise no principled person can continue.

Often I would arrive a little late, and the program chair-woman would be anxiously awaiting me. "Oh, I'm so glad you're here," she would say. "The first thing I want you to do is meet some people."

But I am over 50, and when I make a two-hour drive, the first thing I want to do upon arrival is not meet some people. The first thing I want to do is visit the men's room. And my wish pre-vails. Because my motivation is the stronger.

So I go to the men's room. And, while I'm in there, people approach the program chairwoman to ask if I've arrived. "Yes," she chirps. "He's here. He's . . . (she discreetly lowers her voice) in the men's room."

I wash my hands. I turn around. No towels. Just a blower on the wall. Outside, some of the best people in Ashland are wait-ing to shake my hand. They have all been told where I am. Can I walk out and look them in the eye and offer them a damp hand to shake? What do you think?

The temptation is great not to wash your hands at all. But suppose there's somebody else in the men's room with you? Then you will hear the little voice of your mother or the National Restaurant Association whispering in your ear.

"What will that guy over there think of you if you don't wash your hands?" the little voice accuses.

And one answer is to fake it. To stand in front of the sink for a couple of minutes with the water running, then let the blower wheeze on you, then walk out nonchalantly like a pickpocket escaping into a crowd.

Now, I know nobody reading this has ever done anything like that. Of course not. And, needless to say, I haven't either. But if anybody did do something like that, it would fool the National Restaurant Association's clever little machine. Just because machines are smart enough to play chess doesn't mean they know everything.

AS I WAS SAYING...

So if Big Mother is going to follow us into the men's room, maybe it's time to throw in the towel.

—May 21, 1997

....

Shephardson's folly wasn't one, after all

Ray Shephardson is not nuts. He was right. I was the one who was wrong. And after 25 years, it is high time I said so.

I have an excuse, but to buy it you have to remember what things were like in our town 25 years ago. The city was beginning to fade and grow shabby. The jokes had started on the late-night talk shows. Pessimism was a sign of mental health. Civic spirit was comatose, kept barely alive on fantasy.

On the front pages of the papers, pipe dreams were printed as truth. Maybe there was going to be a jet port in the lake. Maybe there was going to be a bridge to Canada—wouldn't that be swell? Maybe pedestrians would be propelled around the decaying downtown on moving sidewalks to see the dwindling sights. Little drawings appeared of all these wonders. We were trying to rebuild a city with doodles the way a drunk sketches his future on a bar napkin.

I would run into Ray, in those days, in the old Hanna Pub on what was left of Playhouse Square. There weren't any playhouses there anymore except the Hanna. The great old movie theaters had finally closed and their threadbare splendor was decaying behind locked doors as they patiently waited to become parking lots.

"We can bring it all back," Ray used to say. "We can turn it around." And then he would begin to talk, animatedly, about how it could all be done. We would sip intoxicants, and he would enthuse, and I would listen. His enthusiasm was fun, but noncontagious. "He's smart," I thought. "He's gifted. But he's nuts. What's gone is gone."

Ray wasn't even a theater guy. He was an anthropology major

from some college in his home state of Washington. Inspired by the election of Carl Stokes as mayor, he came here to take a job in the Cleveland school system.

His destiny overtook him one day when he was getting a haircut. The *Life* magazine on his lap carried a story titled "Goodbye to the Glory Days," about the decline of the movie palaces. There was a color photo of a mural Ray had seen in the lobby of the old State Theatre.

Something occurred. Some brain chemistry ignited a cause. He got the backing of Lainie Hadden, then president of the Junior League. He prowled dark theaters like the Phantom of the Opera, looking for a way to coax magic from their ruins.

And things began to happen. He turned the lobby of the State Theatre into a cabaret. *Jacques Brel* played there. He developed the instincts of an impresario and the hunches of a crap shooter. He booked the Budapest Symphony Orchestra, and Cleveland's Hungarian population—the largest outside Hungary—made it a sellout occasion.

Where the theaters were too decrepit for big shows, he scooped out enough room for revues such as the *All-Night Strut*. When he had refurbished enough seats, he booked lounge acts into larger venues, offering such artists as Sarah Vaughan and Duke Ellington at ticket prices less than a club cover charge.

In 1979, he left town. He had turned the lights back on again in the theater district, where they have since burned brighter and brighter.

By then he was in demand all over the country. In cities throughout America, people were sorry they had let great old theaters expire. Ray was the man to see about reincarnation. He restored houses in Columbus, Louisville, Seattle, St. Louis, Los Angeles, Chicago, Pittsburgh, Portland, Minneapolis and San Antonio.

In Detroit, somebody handed him an old porno theater and asked him to make a lady out of it. On opening day, he woke up to newspaper headlines that said:

"Fifteen Die as Area Digs Out of Worst Snowstorm in Decade."

Driven by desperation, he tried a stunt. He double-booked

the theater, staging two different shows each day to lure customers through the drifts. It worked. And now he's sold on it.

This fall, having refurbished it, Ray will reopen the Hanna Theatre. With the help of Lainie Hadden and some encouragement from the Hanna's great, retired impresario, Milton Krantz, he has turned the theater into a cabaret. It will stage two-a-day shows at bargain prices. Everything from magic to new vaudeville to his talisman, *All-Night Strut*, which will open it. He has already sold four of his eight available company boxes.

He has returned to a different city from the one he left. The other day, we sat in a restaurant, just like in the old days, and I listened to his enthusiasm again. But this time I took notes.

"I'm sorry I thought you were crazy," I said.

"It's not your fault," he said, charitably. "Back in the old days, I didn't know enough to know what I wanted to do couldn't be done."

And maybe that's the definition of genius. Don't ask me.

—July 11, 1997

Buried treasures

An unfortunate Akron woman got into the news the other day because she can't throw anything away. She filled three houses to bursting with stuff she accumulated and couldn't bear to part with. Housing inspectors intervened. She is now seeking therapy.

It's not nice to rejoice in the misfortunes of others. But the Akron woman's story gave my day a little lift. She has three houses crammed with stuff she can't throw away. I only have one. Therefore, I'm not as bad as she is. And neither are you. But that doesn't mean we're good, does it?

For reasons odd but perfectly legal, I have moved three times in the last six years. Each time, I paid moving men to move cartons of stuff I never use but can't throw away. Before each move, I gave myself a little lecture.

"Listen here," I said sternly to myself. "No more of this paying good money to move junk around the countryside. This time, throw out the stuff you don't want before the movers come."

But this never seems to happen. It all goes into boxes anyway. The best I've been able to do is label the boxes.

"Hey, Mac," the movers say at each new residence. "Where do you want all these boxes marked 'Stuff I'll never use'?"

"Put 'em someplace I'll never go," I say. Which they cheerfully and expensively do.

The trouble is, they are all things I wanted when I got them. So what if they've been in the attic for 10 years? Seeing them again brings back a little of that old attachment. Meeting an old vase you used to prize is like running into an old girl you used to date. A little chord throbs on the dusty strings of past connection. Especially at my age, when the vase is apt to be in better shape than the girl.

And then there is the intoxicant of nostalgia that clouds reason and impairs judgment. Sit me down, cross-legged on the floor, in front of a box of utterly useless things, and suddenly the rubble serenades me with sentiment.

Here is an old receipt from a Paris hotel, dated 1987. I certainly can't throw that away! What fun it will be to find it again in about nine years and pause to reminisce for two or three seconds about that quaint McDonald's on the Right Bank.

And how about these seven keys that seem to unlock nothing? Let's not be hasty. Somewhere, there is a lock they fit. Someday, I may find it. If so, it will be nice to know I have the key. Or had it. It's somewhere. Wherever I put it. It's just waiting for me to find it. Which I'll do. Someday.

There's certainly no mystery about these two boxes of skinny neckties. Fifteen years ago, wide neckties went out of fashion and skinny neckties came in. In a fit of misguided generosity, I gave my wide ones to the Salvation Army. Then, a scant six years later, skinny ties were out and wide ones were back. Once burned, twice shy. This time I'm hanging on to the skinny ones as an investment. The laws of fashion will not catch me napping twice in the same century.

That's why I still have my Nehru jacket. The 50th anniversary of India's independence may well rekindle its popularity. If so, I am ready. Who wants to buy a Nehru jacket twice in one lifetime?

It is, alas, a little snug. That's why I keep it in a big box along with six suits that will fit me again once I shed that temporary and annoying extra 20 pounds I put on during the Johnson administration. My plan is to lose it by Christmas—a plan as fresh today as it was when I made it, the year the mood ring was a hot Christmas item. What rash fool would throw out suits with watch pockets in the trousers. Why, I don't think they even make them anymore.

Naturally, I wouldn't dream of getting rid of my boxes of old magazines that might be fun to look through again one day. Then there are all those perfectly good lamps without shades. I probably could part with my T-shirt collection. It's a carry-over from the days where, at every function I attended, somebody handed me a T-shirt with a boring and often incomprehensible logo on it.

But those things make good rags. Except for the polyester ones that repel water. And if you save those, then you have two sets of rags—good rags and not-so-good rags.

Until recently, I would have told you there was no cure for the pack-rat syndrome. But now I have reason to hope. My new street has an annual neighborhood garage sale. A neighbor coaxed me into lugging over several of the most valueless and lowly prized things I never use from my collection. And when I came back home, I had a fist full of money.

It was a kind of spiritual breakthrough. I can't describe my feeling of accomplishment. I was like a junkie who had kicked a decades-old habit and had made a fresh start.

And you ought to see the neat new junk I bought!

—August 20, 1997

....

Religions have rules

A national newspaper took a poll and asked Americans how many considered themselves religious. A sizable number said they did. Well, how many considered themselves spiritual? A much larger number said they did.

The results aren't surprising. It is more pleasant to be spiritual than to be religious. Being spiritual means you don't have to follow any rules.

Religions have rules. At some point, the god of every major faith got a couple of his followers together and said, "Here's what you gotta do." Sometimes the followers beat their god to the punch. "Tell us what to do," they asked him. And he did. Or she.

But the trouble with rules is that, once you hear them, you are stuck with them. After you've learned what the rules are, you can't pretend you don't know. To retain membership in the religion, you have to follow the wise guy motto: You gotta do what you gotta do.

The convenient thing about spirituality is, it isn't about doing. It's about feeling. If you feel spiritual, you can claim you are spiritual. Who's going to call you a liar? Who's going to ask you to prove it?

For most of my life, when people asked me if I was religious, I would say "not exactly." Then I would explain, smoothly, that, while I followed no organized religion, I certainly considered myself a spiritual person. Just saying that made me feel a little special, which, of course, is the way a spiritual person wants to feel.

If somebody asked me the difference between being religious and being spiritual, I had the standard answer ready.

"I don't think you have to follow any religious propaganda to feel the presence of God," I would say. "I think you can get just as close to God by walking in a forest or watching a sunset."

Very few people will argue with you when you say that. I got a lot of mileage out of it for years — even in Cleveland, where the weather makes the sunset as rare as an Elvis sighting and the trees are being evicted for housing developments with names like "Hunters Hollow."

A spiritual person is reluctant to admit he can feel pretty good about himself even when alone in a fruit cellar. He doesn't want to be accused of thinking himself the center of his universe. He doesn't want his spiritual journey confused with mere ego gratification or self-esteem. Photos of his pilgrimage, he feels, should be more than self-portraits. There should be a little of God's scenery in the background. A tree or a sunset. Just to prove he was there.

On the Christian calendar, Christmas is the great feel-good holiday. That's why it's the most popular holiday of the year. It's the easiest holiday to like. It brings good tidings of great joy. It urges us to be happy. It won't take no for an answer.

The joy of Easter seems to come with strings attached. Its message implies a certain debt outstanding, a responsibility to be shouldered. "Christ died for your sins." (Uh-oh.) "He died so that you might have everlasting life." (Uh, is there a charge for that?)

But Christmas appears to arrive duty-free, except for the matter of the January VISA bill. It is all "Hark, hark, hark" and "Ho-ho-ho." And its supporting cast features those feel-good, lifesaving friends-in-need at the top of everybody's spiritual hit parade: Angels.

Never have angels been more popular. They adorn birthday cards, cuff links and wall plaques. Television specials have been made about them, and music written for them is available on CD. They are the perfect poster holies for the age of religion without rules. For they show up, we are told, in the nick of time to help us out of a jam whether we deserve help or not. No cover, no minimum, no dues required.

I love Christmas. I love the memories and the lights and the tree. I love the fact that, for 24 hours at least, you can get some decent music on the radio. I love the sentiments and the ideals, the image of the beckoning star, the wary shepherds, the three wise men making their long journey because you gotta do what you gotta do. I like the mother and the baby and the astonished father, standing a little apart thinking, "I must calm down . . . I must not lose my head."

It all makes me feel good—about myself and everybody else for a little while.

But I know, though I would rather I didn't, that the story goes on. The baby grows up. He wanders for a while in the wilderness. He attracts a band of followers. He makes them feel very good and very special. Not to mention quite spiritual. And then one day, he calls them together and he gives them the sobering news:

"Now listen carefully," he says. "Here are the rules . . ."

—December 22, 1997

Two gifts

We needed what Reinhold Erickson and Moriah Davis gave us last week.

It was a raw week, full of February weather and wintry news. Rumors of war. Scandal in the White House. Execution in the big house. Stuff that makes the spirit shrivel.

But, in the middle of it all, we learned about Reinhold Erickson's legacy of light and Moriah Davis' gift of gold. And some of the edge went off the chill of other events.

Reinhold Erickson was an East Cleveland dentist. He made a lot of money, just like my dentist does. But he didn't spend much and he had nobody to leave it to.

His wife, as *Plain Dealer* reporter Karen Long tells us, abandoned him decades ago, bewitched by the charms of an Army sergeant. He did not remarry. He had no children. He liked to fish—a quiet, reflective pastime in which the arrival of a fish is sometimes an unwelcome breach of the peace.

When he died at 87, he left $370,000 to the Cleveland Foundation. And he left a letter of instruction for its use. At first, some officials at the foundation thought his request seemed "off the wall" and "oddball." But then they thought again.

"One of the rewarding parts of this job," said Steven Minter, executive director and president of the foundation, "is that sometimes donors think of wonderful things that we wouldn't ordinarily think about."

Erickson's money will pay to light the classic old steeples of 21 Cleveland churches so they can be seen from the freeways at night. He had a lot of years to think about how to spend his life's savings. And the steeple plan is what he came up with.

He wasn't a particularly religious man, Erickson's lawyer told this newspaper. But the sight of a church steeple gave him comfort, and he thought it would be especially comforting for people journeying home through the darkness.

That was an old man's legacy of light.

The young girl's gift of gold, reporter Patrick O'Donnell tells us, is resting in a vault in Florida today.

Moriah Davis, 10 years old, had waist-length blond hair. It had taken six years for it to grow that long, and Moriah was proud of it.

Last week, her aunt snipped it off with a pair of scissors. Moriah held the braided golden rope in her hands for a while and mourned a little. Then it was put into a box and sent to the Locks of Love Foundation in Florida.

There, it will be used to fashion hairpieces for children whose illnesses have robbed them of their hair.

Moriah had heard that sick children who cannot afford hairpieces are often scorned by other children. And Moriah, a child herself, knows that children can be cruel.

She has been spared, so far, a knowledge of the special cruelty of adults, in all its myriad and fantastic forms.

Such cruelty is regularly examined in this space. In this rectangle of the newspaper, outrages are usually welcomed. They are dismantled, analyzed and commented upon, often with sarcasm.

But a steady diet of sour news leaves a sour taste in the mouth. And, over the years, it becomes obvious that almost all outrages are committed by people who are said to be in the prime of their lives.

It is the middle, productive years that produce the world's

supply of envy, lust, greed, hunger for power, lies, cheating, theft, ego, ruthlessness, impatience, murder and deceit.

Ten-year-old girls and 87-year-old men are seldom capable of such things. So their adventures are rarely deemed newsworthy. That will never change.

But somehow, in a week full of gloom, confrontation and Sam Donaldson, an old man's quiet gift and a young girl's simple sacrifice captured a few brief headlines. And reminded us that there is so much more to life than the tiny, misshapen, oddball, off-the-wall phenomena we call the news.

So here's to Moriah, whose classmates will tease her today. And to Reinhold, who gently lighted 21 candles and left them for us, hoping we would find our bearings in their glow.

—February 9, 1998

I miss Ma Bell

The phone rang. I picked it up. And the guy on the other end said something so interesting that I wrote it down for you:

"May I please speak to the person in charge of making household telephone decisions?" he said.

It was an unusual question. I figured it deserved an unusual answer.

"The election's next week," I said.

"Pardon me?" he said.

"Right now, the post of household telephone decision-maker is vacant," I said. "Naturally, that has led to a certain amount of anarchy. So we're going to have an election and elect one next Tuesday."

"Excuse me?" he said.

"She's campaigning on a platform of being nice and polite to everybody who calls, no matter what they're selling. That's her great weakness. She's soft on nuisances."

"Sir, if you would just . . ." he said.

"I, on the other hand, am running on a program of zero tolerance. None of this mushy 'Three strikes and you're out' stuff for me. Call me in the middle of my cup of coffee and you're out before you can even finish your windup. Watch."

And I hung up. But I was clearly in the wrong. Because, as usual, I was living in the past.

Let your fingers do the walking back through the yellowing pages of time. Back to 1984, when Ma Bell was the mother of all telephone decision-making.

Most of us thought she was a pretty good mother. Telephoning was calm and uncomplicated. In my book, it was just what telephoning ought to be.

Then the government moved in to solve a problem not many of us thought we had. Beneath her motherly image, Ma Bell was really a repressive monopoly, the government revealed.

The right thing to do was to break her up into smaller, competitive companies. We would all go to live in little foster homes, where life would get telephonically better in some unspecified way.

But life didn't get telephonically better. It just got telephonically different.

Salesmen started calling us at mealtime trying to peddle long-distance service. Ma Bell never interrupted our dinner. She didn't try to get us to change long-distance carriers more often than we changed our socks, either.

Suddenly we were expected to keep abreast of the long-distance market with the alertness Donald Trump uses to keep up with the stock market. Who's got time for that kind of alertness? I don't. And if I did, I would alert myself to something more satisfying.

My last long-distance bill showed a charge for 14 bucks for calls to a number in California that nobody answered. Ma Bell didn't charge me for stuff like that. She was no cheap chiseler, Ma Bell wasn't. She didn't pick your pocket with the fine print.

Since she has been gone, the telephone has abandoned its basic function. It is no longer a device to let one human being communicate with another human being. It has become a device to allow one frustrated human being to be tortured by a smug machine.

"Welcome to the Acme Dynamite Co.'s electronic switch-board," the machine drones in your ear. "If you have a touch-tone phone, press 2. If you are calling from a rotary phone, please remain on the line . . ."

What we've all learned is: Never press 2! Once you've pressed 2, you can't get back out of 2. And all 2 will do is lure you deeper and deeper into a maze of irrelevant choices and then dump you in line with the rotary people.

After 14 years without Ma, all we have is the empty satisfaction of knowing that we got out from under the thumb of her benign empire. That's why it was startling to learn the other day of a planned merger between Ameritech and another big phone company.

The news accounts said this would create a new phone empire. So what's gone around is mysteriously coming back around. Except it's coming back in worse shape than it left, like a ball team coming home from a bad road trip.

These telephone decisions are made someplace. But not in my household. I should have been nicer to the guy who called. I should have just told him he had the wrong number.

But maybe he figured that out.

—May 27, 1998

....

Taps

"I didn't give my life for my country. I gave my life for a guy named Bill, who was a friend of mine. He got shot and couldn't get back to the lines.

"He was hollering, 'Help me, help me.' We all kind of froze for a minute and then I was the one who made a lunge.

"To be honest with you, I couldn't tell you why I did it. I guess

I just figured I could make it if I did it fast. It was only about 50 feet to where he was. I got about 45 feet. Then they opened up and Bill and I died looking at each other. He's here too, someplace.

"The president was here this morning. Well, somebody was. Heard somebody gabbing through a loudspeaker. Too far down the hill for me to tell who it was. Laying a wreath at the Tomb of the Unknowns.

"One of them's missing, of course. They say that pretty soon, they'll figure out who he is and he'll be a known. Naturally, we already know who he is. Everybody knows everybody here.

"To us, you are the unknowns.

"You are the ones we can't figure out.

"You come once, maybe twice a year to thank us for all we did for the country. You say we died to preserve your freedoms and to save a very special way of life.

"You seem to be sincere. Sometimes you even cry. So we don't like to insult you or hurt your feelings.

"But, to be honest about it, you are a puzzle to us. Just like the guys down the hill under the big monument are a puzzle to you.

"I already told you I died trying to save a guy named Bill. I'd just as soon you'd leave it that way. Because if you're telling me I shed my blood to buy your way of life, then I'm telling you I got cheated.

"You got an interesting idea of freedom. To you it means freedom from responsibility. Freedom to get something for nothing. Freedom to stay in the club without paying your dues.

"You took freedom of speech and made it freedom of spin. You lie to each other all the time. You wrap screwy ideas in slick paper and sell them to each other. You fall for each other's con games. I'm not even sure you'd know the truth anymore if it hit you in the . . .

"I'm sorry. I'm forgetting my manners. You're a guest here.

"Listen . . . hear that?

"That's a bird. Isn't that pretty?"

"We hear them here when you're not around making speeches. But we can't see them, obviously.

"You'd know a little more about freedom if you were stuck down here in this box for a while.

"If I had the freedom to get out of this box, you know what I'd do with it?

"I'd feed those birds. I'd watch them for a while. I'd drink a glass of cold water. I'd eat some fresh-baked bread. I'd look at the sky. I'd love to see the sky again. I'd listen to music. I mean good music. They only play one song here. Over and over. On a bugle.

"I'd meet the girl I never met and have the kid I never had. I'd take care of that kid and teach him about birds and bread and music and love. I wouldn't let his brain get polluted with all the garbage you've made out of that freedom you claim I died for.

"Your kids sing songs about murdering people. You teach them much about sex and little about love. You make them too old while they are still young. They don't know how to handle that and neither do you because you are afraid of them or lazy or something . . .

"I don't know. I told you, we can't figure you out. To us, you are the unknowns. Are you beginning to see why?

"I died on a battlefield with the sound of gunfire in my ears. You've made battlefields out of schoolyards. Your kids are lying in schoolyards saying, 'Help me, help me.' And nobody's making a move.

"Do you think for one minute any of these guys here would act that way? Do you know what it's like to lie here and not be able to do anything about it while you're up there walking around with all that fancy freedom you've got?

"Awww, forget it. I always did have a big mouth. When I had a mouth . . .

"It's getting dark, isn't it? The birds are telling me. They sing differently when it starts to get dark. Pretty soon they'll stop and that will be the end of another Memorial Day.

"When we can't hear the birds, we know it's dark where you are, too. But you've got the moon. We've got nothing. Pitch black. So how come it seems that you're more in the dark than we are?

"In a minute the bugler will start playing that song again. Listen to it. Listen hard. He's playing it for you. I had mine."

—May 25, 1998

"Why too Kay?"

There was a meeting of movers and shakers the other day and I was invited as the token inert.

The subject was the state of the economy. During the question period, a mover or shaker raised his hand and addressed the speaker.

"What about the why too kay problem?" he said.

("Huh?" I thought.)

"Well, it's a bad problem, all right," the speaker said. "It's being worked on, but not fast enough."

Murmurs of concern followed this revelation. I politely murmured some concern too, though I didn't know why. Then the dawn broke.

It wasn't the "why too kay" problem they were murmuring about at all. It was the "Y2K" problem. A monogram that stands for "Year 2000."

These guys were speaking business-hip. Nobody in business utters the word "thousand" anymore. "Thousand" is a word that belongs in a lexicon for lightweights. "My commission on that order was 150K," you say if you want to be taken for a high-roller. Say "thousand" and you stand revealed as a nerd, even if you're wearing an Armani suit.

Being of nerdish origin myself, I am always most at ease in the company of nerds—not that nerds are particularly at ease in any company. In my high school, there were two kinds of nerds: book nerds and slide-rule nerds. I was a book nerd.

The only thing we two tribes shared was our nerdishness. And the disdain of our student council president-prom king-starting halfback-firm handshake-Pepsodent smile classmates who were, even then, obviously destined for moverdom and shakerdom.

We book nerds were dreamy, vague types. After graduation, we dissipated like a fog, drifting off in various unplanned directions. Some of us teach English; some of us cruise the aisles at Border's on Friday night. Some of us write for newspapers, and some of us even read them.

But the slide-rule nerds marched off into legend. They went

on to conquer the Earth.

Unlike book nerds, the slide-rule nerds had the ability to con-centrate. When they walked down the hall, eyes glazed, bump-ing into locker doors, you could tell they were dreaming in formulas and solving equations in their heads. Behind the eye-glasses with the taped frames.

They threw away their slide rules and invented computers the size of a condo. They kept thinking, thinking, thinking. And the computers got smaller and smaller. But the smaller they got, the more powerful they became. Pretty soon, everything in the world was in their grasp.

The slide-rule nerds had become the most important people in America. They reinvented the American economy. The hip movers and shakers who had previously scorned them now worked for them—couldn't function without them. It was truly the Revenge of the Nerds. And even though I was a lesser nerd, I basked in their reflected glory.

The slide-rule nerds drew a line and commanded everybody to stand on it, and soon the whole world was online. They spun a Web and there was a land rush for Web sites. They replaced the reality of Genesis with the virtual reality of genius. The planet owed all its tomorrows to nerd planning, nerd brilliance, nerd logic.

And then, somebody noticed something.

"Hey," somebody said, "there's something weird here. When it gets to be the year 2000, all the computers are going to think it's 1900. They'll all shut down. The world will turn off like a faucet."

Naturally, nobody believed this at first.

"The nerds are too smart to let that happen," somebody said. "They must have something up their sleeves."

"Yeah," somebody else said. "If the nerds were smart enough to reinvent the whole world in the '80s and '90s, they couldn't possibly be dumb enough to have overlooked the fact that the year 2000 was right around the corner."

"That's right," said somebody else. "Why, the dumbest kid in class would have figured that out."

"Send for a nerd!" everybody cried. "Let's straighten this out right now."

So a slide-rule nerd was sent for. And I, a book nerd, was rooting for him. Surely he would have an answer. Surely all his scientific brilliance wouldn't be shipwrecked by a tiny problem that needed little more than a book nerd's prudence or a book nerd's common sense.

"What about the why too kay problem?" the nerd was asked.

"Huh?" he said.

—June 10, 1998

....

Baby boomer Clinton short on apologies

Naturally, the first baby boomer president didn't know how to apologize. So he gave an excuse, invented by his generation.

"The dog ate my homework," he said. Or carefully crafted words to that effect.

But he didn't say it wouldn't happen again.

The dog that ate the homework was Kenneth Starr. The first half of the president's apology was mechanical *mea culpa*. The last half was angry Starr culpa. That's where we saw the sincere emotion. The president was sincerely emotional about getting caught.

"The independent counsel investigation moved on to my staff and friends," he said sternly, "then into my private life. And now, the investigation itself is under investigation.

"Even presidents have private lives. It is time to stop the pursuit of personal destruction and the prying into private lives and get on with our national life."

This is not the kind of apology I would accept from one of my kids. If a kid of mine said, "Kenny's as bad as I am," I would assume a lack of genuine remorse. I would suspect an evasion of personal responsibility.

It is bizarre to think of the president of the United States as one of your kids. Or at least it was until this president came along.

But his generation is probably the most immature generation of the century.

Overeducated and underprincipled. Shallow as a cookie sheet. Pampered and petted and raised to believe that the ultimate virtues are a good haircut and a talent for being cute, which may be developed by practice in front of a mirror.

Much has been made of the age difference between the president and Monica Lewinsky. Chronologically, they are many years apart. Emotionally, they seem to be peers. Each of them had a sexual agenda, and both of them are products of a culture that teaches that sexual dalliance is no big deal. Just a game without rules.

"Our country has been distracted by this matter for too long and I take my responsibility for my part in all this," Bill the Boomer said firmly.

The prolonged distraction, of course, stemmed from the fact that he wouldn't tell the truth until cornered. For seven months, he allowed his supporters—some of whom might have actually believed him—to squander their credibility on the Sunday talk shows insisting he was being framed.

He should have apologized to them the other night. They, after all, bore some real injury because of his lies. Any sincere apology would have included the troops he had double-crossed.

But not a word of contrition was aimed at the supporters he duped. I find that telling, don't you? If I had done what the president has done, my most painful regrets would probably have been reserved for the loyalties I had betrayed. Yet the president did not favor his supporters with a single mournful phrase.

"I misled people, including even my wife," he said. Who in America with any sense believes that? Does Hillary Clinton seem an easy woman to mislead? Are we really supposed to buy the fantasy that she only smelled a rat last weekend? It's an insult to our intelligence. But maybe the denizens of the Clinton White House assume we haven't got any. It's an assumption which, until now, has brought them prosperity.

It was not a sincere act of contrition that shaped the president's remarks.

Honesty did not inspire the cute, vague, hair-splitting phrases crafted by lawyers from legal la-la land. What we heard was contrition-by-committee with one eye on the polls. The president knows the public is sick of this story. It embarrasses us. It is bad for our children. We want it to go away.

Monday night, after allowing the country he leads to suffer for half a year, the president exploited the nation's revulsion. He did the minimum he thought he had to do and said the minimum he thought he had to say.

They handed him a script and he read it. But he was an actor who didn't quite understand the part. Honor and ethics are foreign concepts to his culture. He is a man of spin and hair spray. His generation can create shame without feeling it.

—August 19, 1998

McGwire's tribute a vindication for Maris

Through the TV screen Monday, you could feel Roger's ghost rounding the bases with Mark McGwire. Then McGwire and the ghost crossed the plate, matching stride for peerless stride.

It was a haunted moment and McGwire knew it. He pointed to Roger Maris' son, sitting in the grandstand. Then he tapped his chest at the spot over his heart. The message was clear. "Your dad's in here," he was saying.

Much is written about what Mark McGwire has done for baseball this season. Less is said about what McGwire has done for Roger Maris. He has rehabilitated Maris' memory and made some of us who wronged him feel ashamed.

I was one of many who rooted against Maris back in 1961. When he broke in, here with the Indians in 1957, he seemed like just another journeyman outfielder passing through on his way to oblivion. He hit .235 that year and managed 14 home runs. Nobody wanted his bubble gum card, and the next year he was gone.

When he arrived in New York, he revealed an unsuspected

ability to hit the ball out of the park. This was regarded as a quirk. Mickey Mantle was the darling of the New York media and their anointed successor to DiMaggio and Ruth. Maris lacked both charisma and a friendly press corps willing to invent it for him. Legends need one or the other.

So when Maris began to close in on Babe Ruth's record, his effrontery was considered an act of vandalism. The common sentiment was, "Who does this guy think he is?"

He was regarded as a freak of nature. An accidental and unworthy nominee of destiny. It was as if fate had become a steroid and some random force had carelessly injected Maris with undeserved prowess.

It should have been a golden summer. But the ghost of Ruth was not a generous ghost. Each time Maris began his home run trot, the ghost of Ruth tugged at his belt and hampered his stride. In his book, *Baseball*, Ken Burns writes:

"He wasn't Babe Ruth and Ruth's fans never let him forget it. Under the relentless strain, Maris' hair began to fall out in clumps. Always taciturn, he now kept virtually silent, drinking black coffee and smoking Camel after Camel before every game, refusing most interviews, keeping to himself."

On Sept. 26, he tied Ruth's season record of 60 home runs. The tie held for the next three games. Somebody asked Ruth's widow how she felt. "I hope he doesn't do it," she said.

I shared her hope. Babe Ruth was an icon. They had even made a bad movie of his life, starring William Bendix. Ruth, we learned, visited hospitals and promised dying kids he would hit home runs for them . . . and did, instantly restoring them to apple-cheeked health. I didn't hear about Maris raising the dead in any hospitals. By the end of September, he looked like he belonged in one.

He broke Ruth's record on the last day of the season. But the ghost of Ruth refused to surrender. Once, Ford Frick had been a ghost writer for Ruth, spinning out fanciful "first-person" stories.

Now Frick was the baseball commissioner. Since Maris' season was longer than Ruth's, Frick branded Maris' record with an asterisk that stayed in the books for years. The message of the asterisk was clear. "He did it, but he didn't really do it." All die-hards said amen. I was one of them.

Maris had beaten my prediction for him. He had escaped oblivion. He had won, instead, flawed and second-rate fame — fame with a disclaimer attached.

He never made it to the Hall of Fame. He died young. He never really had a chance to bask in glory.

Before he died, he told a friend, "It would have been a helluva lot more fun if I had never hit those 61 homes runs. All it brought me was headaches."

It took 37 years for somebody else to do what Roger Maris had done. And when Mark McGwire did it the other day, Roger's ghost rounded the bases with him. Then, in his moment of triumph, McGwire took time, as he has all year, to pay tribute to Maris' lonely and derided achievement.

And I was sorry that, all those years ago, I was one of the many whose narrow-mindedness helped tarnish a man's solid accomplishment. Deeds should speak louder than hype. In a martyr's way, Maris helped smooth McGwire's road.

Now, McGwire will go beyond him, and he can rest in peace.

At his news conference after the game, McGwire said that, when he gets to heaven, the first person he wants to see, after God, is Roger Maris.

He shouldn't have to go that far. We ought to see him in Cooperstown.

—September 9, 1998